Legible Bodies

Race, Criminality and Colonialism in South Asia

Clare Anderson

Oxford • New York

First published in 2004 by

Berg

Editorial offices:

1st Floor, Angel Court, 81 St Clements Street, Oxford, OX4 1AW, UK

175 Fifth Avenue, New York, NY 10010, USA

Berg is the imprint of Oxford International Publishers Ltd.

Library of Congress Cataloging-in-Publication Data

Anderson, Clare, 1969–

Legible bodies : race, criminality, and colonialism in South Asia /
Clare Anderson.

p. cm.

Includes bibliographical references and index.

ISBN 1-85973-855-9 (cloth) — ISBN 1-85973-860-5 (pbk.)

1. Criminals—India—Identification—History—19th century.
2. India—History—British occupation, 1765–1947. 3. India—Ethnic
relations. 4. Criminal justice, Administration of—India—History—19th
century. 5. Criminal anthropology—History—19th century. I. Title.

HV7092.A15 2004

365'.954'09034—dc22

2004003083

British Library Cataloguing-in-Publication Data

A catalogue record for this book is available from the British Library.

ISBN 1 85973 855 9 (Cloth)

1 85973 860 5 (Paper)

Typeset by JS Typesetting Ltd, Wellingborough, Northants.

Printed in the United Kingdom by Biddles Ltd, King's Lynn.

www.bergpublishers.com

For Sam

Contents

Figures

Acknowledgements

I carried out research for this book in a number of libraries and archives, primarily the National Archives of India, the India Office Library, Edinburgh University Library and the Tamil Nadu State Archives. Inadvertently, I picked up further references in the Archives Office of Tasmania and Mauritius Archives. I would like to thank the staff in these libraries and archives for their guidance and continued support. In addition, Anne Barrett eased my passage through the Imperial College Archives; Rupert Cox and Chris Wright aided my work in the Royal Anthropological Institute's photographic collection; and Kevin Greenbank assisted me in the Centre of South Asian Studies Archives, University of Cambridge. The inter-library loans section of the University of Leicester Library also dealt with my requirements with great efficiency. The research could not have been carried out without the generous support of several funding bodies – the British Academy, British Academy South East Asia Committee, Carnegie Trust for the Universities of Scotland, and Faculty of Social Sciences, University of Leicester – to whom I am grateful. The manuscript was completed with the support of an Economic and Social Research Council Research Fellowship, which I am also thankful for.

Over the last few years, the ideas in this book have taken shape through extended discussions with colleagues, particularly at conferences and seminars where I have had the opportunity to present my research. These have included: the Social History Society conference, University of York, January 1999; 'The Colonial Eye' conference, University of Tasmania, Febuary 1999; Department of History seminar, Jawaharlal Nehru University (JNU), New Delhi, April 1999; 'Foucault, Governmentality and the Colonial Order' workshop, School of Oriental and African Studies (SOAS), University of London, October 1999; 'Colonial Places, Convict Spaces' conference, University of Leicester, December 1999; American Association of Asian Studies annual meeting, San Diego, CA, March 2000; European Association for South Asian Studies conference, University of Edinburgh, September 2000; and the University of Leicester interdisciplinary postcolonial research seminar group. My first musings on tattooing in South Asia appeared in *Written on the Body: The Tattoo in*

European and American History (Reaktion, 2000). I am particularly grateful to the book's editor, Jane Caplan, for her incisive comments. Additionally, an earlier version of Chapter 4 appeared in *History Workshop Journal*, 52 (2001). I am grateful to its editor, Laura Gowing, and the journal's anonymous referees, for suggesting further avenues to explore.

I would also like to thank the following people for discussing ideas, suggesting further references, or reading earlier drafts of the material that forms this book: Richard Allen, David Arnold, Jordanna Bailkin, Imre Bangha, Andrew Bank, Crispin Bates, James Bradley, Mark Brown, Rob Colls, Frank Conlon, Neil Davie, Clive Dewey, Ian Duffield, Elizabeth Edwards, Michael Fisher, Lucy Frost, Durba Ghosh, Riho Isaka, Roger Jeffery, Patricia Jeffery, Shruti Kapila, Hamish Maxwell-Stewart, Preetha Nair, Anoma Pieris, Arnaud Sauli, Satadru Sen, Radhika Singha, Deborah Sutton, George Weber, Chris Williams and Anand Yang. Berg's reader made further insightful suggestions. James H. Mills and Harald Fischer-Tiné kindly lent me the proofs of their forthcoming collections (edited with Satadru Sen and Michael Mann respectively) *Confronting the Body* and *Colonialism as Civilizing Mission*. Additionally, Mark Summers translated a substantial quantity of the German literature for me. Simon Barnard drew the map. At the University of Leicester, my heads of department (and school) – Huw Bowen and Peter Musgrave – made possible extended research trips in Britain and overseas. Mark Maynard, Sandy Pearson and Jamie Knox supported my IT needs. Finally, it has been a pleasure to work with the team at Berg – Kathryn Earle, Ian Critchley and Christine Firth. I would like to thank Kathleen May in particular for her ongoing support of this project and her patience as it reached an end. Needless to say, any errors and omissions remain my own.

It is to my family, though, that I am most grateful. Hugh Rowell Duffield was a constant reminder of other important things. But this book is dedicated to Sam, my intellectual companion and soulmate, who made me tea and brought me cake, and still doesn't mind when I 'shout about convicts'.

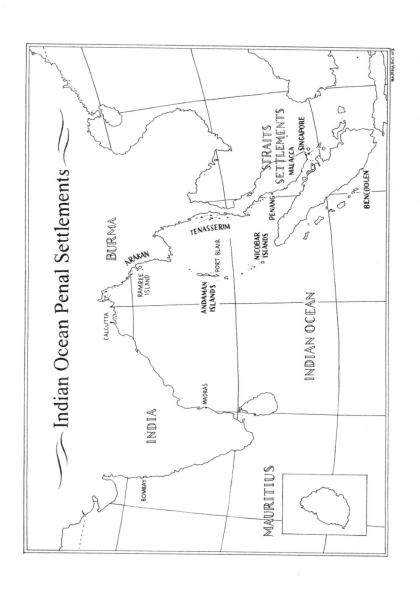

~ Indian Ocean Penal Settlements ~

BURMA

ARAKAN

RAMREE ISLAND

CALCUTTA

INDIA

MADRAS

BOMBAY

TENASSERIM

ANDAMAN ISLANDS

PORT BLAIR

NICOBAR ISLANDS

STRAITS SETTLEMENTS

PENANG

MALACCA

SINGAPORE

BENCOOLEN

INDIAN OCEAN

MAURITIUS

BARNARD 03

Introduction: Textualizing the Indian Criminal Body

This book began when four photographs fell out of a file I was reading in the National Archives of India, New Delhi. At the time, I was engaged in research on nineteenth-century penal settlements in South East Asia and the Indian Ocean, and I was working my way through the archive's holdings on the Andaman Islands, the largest and best known penal colony in the region. The British had settled the Andamans as a destination for convicts in the wake of the 1857 Uprising, an earlier attempt at turning the Islands into a penal colony having failed (1793–6).[1] The photographs were unlike any I had seen before. They were taken in 1875, and depicted three male convicts, scantily clothed, seated and photographed from the waist up. The men were unnamed and had no claims to special status or notoriety. There were no textual pointers beneath the prints and, but for the way one of the men wore his hair and beard, there were no indicators of their convict status. Though it was clear that they were not typical ethnographic shots, at least at first glance they could have been photographs of South Asian labourers. The pictures illustrated very little, but the accompanying files revealed a fascinating narrative of their production, circulation and consumption. As I followed the paper trail it became clear that convict photography – like the photographing of habitual offenders (those convicted at least twice) and prisoners incarcerated on the mainland – was a short-lived experiment. Taking photographs was relatively simple; indexing and reading them was not so easy.

At the time of my encounter with the Andaman convict photographs, I had long been interested in penal tattooing (*godna*). I first came across this permanent mark of criminality in convict descriptive rolls, detailed records of physical appearances that accompanied Indian convicts into transportation to penal settlements in South East Asia and the Indian Ocean during the first half of the nineteenth century. The settlements were all in recent colonial acquisitions, and thousands of convicts were shipped there to work on infrastructural labour projects. They were at Bencoolen (1787–1825), Penang, otherwise known as Prince of Wales Island (1790–1860),

Mauritius (1815–53), Malacca and Singapore (1825–60) and the Burmese provinces of Arakan and Tenasserim (1828–62).[2] Like transportation convicts, life prisoners incarcerated in mainland jails were also subject to *godna*. The prison system expanded greatly under British rule and, during the nineteenth century, tens of thousands of prisoners passed through the jail gates.[3] Until the middle of the century, thousands more were put to work on outdoor road gangs.[4] Late-eighteenth- and early-nineteenth-century regulations on *godna*, ordering the marking of the name, crime and date of sentence on the forehead of convicted offenders, seemed to describe the inscription of colonial power on the body. A close reading of convict descriptive rolls, however, hinted at a practice that was incredibly diverse and uneven. This impression was confirmed by correspondence from the penal settlements complaining about the receipt of convicts without the requisite *godna* marks, difficulties in reading the inscriptions, and a pattern of escapes that in some places could be correlated directly with the presence or absence of penal tattoos. I was struck by the parallels between the experiment in convict photography and penal tattooing. Though separated by time (*godna* was abolished in 1849) and employing different technologies (the needle against the camera), both attempted to make a permanent record of individual criminality. In reflecting the ambiguities rather than the relentlessness of colonial power, neither quite delivered it. They were part of what Antoinette Burton refers to as the 'unfinished business' of colonial regimes.[5]

Behind these efforts at fixing individual identities lay the conviction that because bodies were stable entities, they could be linked to themselves across time and space. As Simon A. Cole argues in a fine study of nineteenth-century criminal identification in Europe and North America, new identificatory techniques aimed to mark the body in some way, and to render it visible. This was necessary because the massive social and economic changes of the nineteenth century – notably industrialization and migration – disrupted the community networks and personal connections on which identification had formerly relied.[6] The project of individual legibility (or as one paper on naming practices puts it, 'the conquest of illegibility') was thus central to the process of centralized state building.[7] In South Asia too, new modes of identification were invoked to record and describe similarly anomic criminal bodies, particularly unknown persons picked up in the growing cities on the suspicion of being habitual offenders, and itinerant social groups who could not be anchored to particular localities.[8] Yet beyond broader patterns of social and economic change, Indian prisons and penal settlements tried (though often failed) to *create* spaces of social disjuncture, for imprisonment, banishment and transportation were all conceived as punishments with the disruption of kin networks in mind. Subsequently, from the 1790s penal administrators cajoled jail clerks into carefully noting the minutiae of each prisoner's physical appearance, together with details of their offence, date and place of conviction and caste, beginning the process of what we might term the textualization of the Indian criminal body. As Jane Caplan and John Torpey put it in their analysis of the development of identificatory techniques in Europe, 'writing on the body gave way to reading off it.'[9]

The thousands of descriptive rolls that survive (mostly for transportation convicts during the period to 1857) provide a fascinating insight into colonial crime and resistance during the early colonial period, as well as the prevalence of cultural practices like therapeutic branding and patterns of disease (smallpox scars were recorded). Their purpose was, however, the verification of identity. When convict identities were in question – for instance if an individual was suspected of being an escaped prisoner or an absconder from one of the penal settlements, but had no *godna* mark – they could be physically inspected and their appearance compared to their supposed descriptive roll. Height and stature, together with marks, scars and other physical peculiarities, were viewed as the key to unlocking details of their crime, date of conviction and sentence. Given the subjectivity of clerks' descriptions, coupled with the instability of bodily appearance, however, inevitably the rolls did not always provide the unwavering proof of identity that the colonial authorities were searching for. There were problems in the identification of habitual offenders too, where there was no effective or uniform system of indexing prisoners' rolls. If a newly arrested individual used an alias, it was almost impossible to access their prior record. As Cole notes, even when photographs were added, 'the most acute problem facing the nineteenth-century police and penal bureaucracies was not *recording* information, but *ordering* it.'[10]

Towards the end of the nineteenth century, some Indian authorities thought they had found the answer to the problem of ordering information in 'Bertillonage', a system devised in Paris for the identification of offenders. Bertillonage was a tripartite system, combining descriptions and photographs with sets of anthropometric measurements, each recorded on systematically indexed cards. It was said to provide a less ambiguous means of identification than descriptions or photographs alone. However, in its reliance on human agency in the recording of bodily signs and its failure to solve the problem of the mutability of the body, it shared the problems of both and turned out to be more inaccurate than was at first assumed. It was not until the adjunct of the fingerprints of offenders on the rolls at the beginning of the twentieth century that criminal records could be more precisely connected to individual bodies. These were unique, unchangeable marks, and eventually fingerprinting (dactyloscopy) replaced the whole Bertillon system. Colonial efforts to render the bodies of prisoners, convicts and habitual offenders legible – their use of visible signs to connect individuals to their written record – and their frequent failure to do so, form the first broad theme of this book.

Second, I want to consider the ways in which the colonial authorities attempted to use the Indian body to construct broader social groupings, both in relation to penal hierarchies and in the making of sociological categories of criminal 'types'. The themes of individualization and categorization are inextricably intertwined, for the paradox of identificatory techniques is that the individual is always made part of a collective group. To put it another way, there were complex slippages between individual and social legibility, for whilst the bodies of Indian prisoners and convicts were sites of inscription and agency they also embodied local colonial practices.[11] *Godna* for instance ideally marked both the general and the particular, representing a criminal conviction of some sort as well as detailing the specific offence of an individual. Clothing and other penal props were later used to classify groups of individual prisoners and convicts, and the introduction of uniforms, the shaving of hair and the use of different types of fetters all became visual representations of penal status. Their variable application came to define and divide offenders according to the increasingly complex hierarchies introduced into jails and penal settlements during the nineteenth century.

From the 1830s administrators used particular forms of *godna* in what was perhaps the earliest physical demarcation of a criminal typology per se: the colonial construction of thuggee. During the early nineteenth century, the British 'discovered' thuggee, describing it as a secret cult of hereditary killers who carried out ritual murder, robbery and burial in worship of the Hindu goddess Kali, otherwise called Devi or Bhawani. Thugs were said to share a common language and perform the same mysterious rituals in the commission of their crimes. Notable amongst these was the consumption of *gur* (unrefined sugar) before each expedition, and the use of a silk scarf to strangle their victims; thug rituals that were said to have taken place for centuries. Colonial discourses thus narrativized thugs as members of quasi-religious criminal collectivities, quite different from ordinary individual offenders.[12] Having created the problem, the British then stepped in with a civilizing mission that aimed to rescue India from its barbarity. The officer in charge of the campaign against thuggee, Colonel William Sleeman, wrote in 1843 that his men had been employed 'in the execution of one of the truest measures of utility, wisdom and benevolence which the British government has ever displayed to the people of India'.[13] The invention of thuggee was part of the orientalization of India, and a source of seemingly endless fascination to Europeans. As late as 1891, a handbook for travellers advised a visit to Jabalpur Jail to see 'the last of that terrible tribe of murderous devotees'.[14]

Yet colonial representations of thuggee were always paradoxical. Though colonial images of thuggee seemed certain, the offence remained remarkably vague because the authorities never really defined it. Rather, it encompassed all sorts of criminal acts, notably those committed by itinerant communities. These even included poisoning and the kidnapping of children. Neither was there ever a clear distinction between thuggee, murder and gang robbery (dacoity);[15] when I refer to 'thugs' or 'thuggee' in the pages that follow I mean only to refer to offenders convicted of that offence. Despite the ambiguity of the offence, the British administration treated those convicted of thuggee quite differently from other offenders. The mode of securing thug convictions was extraordinary. Legislation passed in 1836 decreed that any person found guilty of having belonged to a gang of thugs would be imprisoned for life, even retrospectively. They did not have to be convicted of a specific crime. Convictions could be secured on the testimony of approvers alone, who were often convicted thugs who had their sentence remitted or were pardoned on the condition that they name their accomplices and testify against them.[16]

The courts in Central and Upper India convicted several thousand thugs during the first half of the nineteenth century. Transportation was by far the most common punishment. Of 3,849 prisoners committed for trial on a charge of thuggee between 1826 and 1841, 460 were sentenced to death, 933 to life imprisonment, 81 to a term of imprisonment, and 1,504 to transportation overseas.[17] In 1843, Sleeman noted that most of the life prisoners were approvers. He explained that a relatively low number of thugs were executed because 'the prospect of a foreign and unknown land, or perpetual hard labour only to cease with death, is dreadful to them; their imaginations suggest horrors, the truth of which can never be known, all the transportations being for life.'[18] There is a great deal of evidence to suggest that by the 1840s convicts had a relatively sophisticated spatial understanding of the penal settlements, and the differences between them. Convicts sometimes preferred transportation to known spaces of punishment over life imprisonment in India. This was widely acknowledged by penal administrators on the ground.[19] Yet senior officials continued to argue that Indians feared transportation more than the death penalty, as when the 1838 *Report of the Committee on Prison Discipline* described it as a sentence regarded with 'indescribable horror'.[20]

Sleeman's campaign against the thugs centred on Sagar and Narbada, territory which had been annexed from the Marathas between 1817 and 1818. That it was a 'non-regulation' area led one contemporary to describe it as a theatre for legislative experiments.[21] With a handful of exceptions, thugs sentenced to transportation were shipped to the Tenasserim Provinces in Burma, which had first received Indian convicts a couple of years after their annexation in 1826. Underscoring their special criminal status, the Indian authorities always noted the presence of thugs on board convict ships, where they were lodged in specially constructed quarters below deck.[22] One Bengal official warned the Commissioner of the Tenasserim Provinces of the embarkation of part of a 'desperate gang of thugs' in 1831: 'the atrocious nature of their crimes renders their safe custody an object of paramount importance.'[23]

In 1839, the Calcutta superior criminal court (*Nizamat Adalat*) ceased sentencing thugs to transportation for a time, over fears that the Burmese authorities were unable to cope with them.[24] The authorities in the North West Provinces expressed the same concerns. It was not until 1844 that thugs convicted there were even sentenced to transportation. The Register of the *Nizamat Adalat* feared that 'those who have once been habituated to the murderous pursuits of the tribe and initiated in their secrets never voluntarily abandon their practices'. He explained that although their conduct in prison had been exemplary, this was evidence of their secrecy and cunning, and anticipated that thugs would introduce their criminal activities as soon as they arrived in the settlements.[25] When it was eventually agreed that it was safe to transport thugs overseas, it was only on the condition that special notice of their character be given.[26]

From the middle of the nineteenth century, surveillance measures were taken against other social groups considered criminal, usually itinerant or displaced tribal communities. After 1871, many of these were classified under a set of repressive colonial legislation known as the Criminal Tribes Acts. The first 1871 Act emerged out of earlier colonial discourses on the Indian criminal, particularly orientalized accounts of thuggee that referred to its secretive, timeless nature. The 1871 and later Acts propagated the view that criminality was hereditary, and that particular castes and tribes consisted exclusively of born criminals. They were initially applied to the North West Provinces, Awadh and the Panjab, and were gradually extended across India. By Independence in 1947, the Acts classified 13 million people as criminal types, and imposed disciplinary measures to control them. Criminal tribes were made subject to registration and a pass system, and forced into reformatory and agricultural settlements, which like prisons and penal settlements tried to restrict their mobility. This was an attempt to transform marginalized groups into settled communities and reclaim them as what Sanjay Nigam refers to as 'the moral subjects of the Raj'.[27] The problem for the colonial state was, of course, how to identify individuals registered as criminal. With penal tattooing having fallen from favour, it turned from marking the body to interpreting its physiognomic and cultural signs. Drawing on ethnographic literature on caste types, well into the twentieth century most police handbooks and manuals described what we might term a 'generalized look' – and noted the style of decorative tattoos, clothing and jewellery – in their representations of the typical appearance of particular criminal communities. Together with descriptions of their habits and manners, these readings became what Rachel J. Tolen describes as 'tokens' of a criminality resistant to wage labour and changing modes of production.[28]

As David Arnold has established in his groundbreaking study of nineteenth-century Indian prisons, jails were metaphors for broader social practices in the construction of colonial knowledge.[29] I shall take this up in the book's third theme, which will explore how during the latter part of the nineteenth and the early twentieth centuries incarcerated communities comprised a convenient sample for colonial explorations of the nature and significance of race and caste in the subcontinent. I do not propose to enter fully the historiographical debate on the politics of race and caste here; readers unfamiliar with the literature can turn to other more detailed studies.[30] However, in the pages that follow I want to examine some of the ways in which prisoners and convicts were drawn upon in producing colonial understandings of social difference in India, whether these were based on an emphasis on cultural or biological distinctions. I have already hinted at some of these cultural readings in noting colonial discourses on supposedly criminal types. Further, and in relation to biological ones, I shall note the ways in which the bodies of prisoners and convicts were used in nineteenth-century anthropometric projects. They were also appropriated in broader global studies of the supposed physical manifestations of racial difference. Some were made subject to phrenological analysis; others to anthropometric photography. During an experiment in the Andamans, the eyes of deceased convicts were even used in the construction of race hierarchies based on apparent retinal difference.

Finally, I want to make some tentative suggestions about the gendered nature of colonial discourses and practices of criminal identification. Female prisoners and convicts were also made subject to colonial efforts to fix identities and penal hierarchies, though as was typical in the nineteenth century, male bodies predominated in colonial articulations of race.[31] Satadru Sen has argued persuasively that in the later nineteenth-century

Andamans, convict women's bodies were marked out primarily as a means of rehabilitating men through marriage. In contrast, mainland jails, saturated with discourses of rescue as well as reform, sought to insulate them from all sexual activity. The punishment of women there was useful precisely because it constituted a measurement of the effectiveness of a Victorian colonial regime.[32] In the first half of the nineteenth century too, the colonial administration in Indian prisons and penal settlements gendered the criminal body in its organization of convict labour and the penal hierarchy. Women and men were assigned to seemingly appropriate work tasks and punished in ways that reflected colonial ideas about their visibility in productive social spaces. In this sense, gendered colonial categories were infused – or in Anne McClintock's words articulated with – class, racial difference and criminality.[33] The roots of the Andaman system of reform-through-marriage can also be found in the South East Asian penal settlements, where women were generally released much earlier than men on the condition that they get married.

The nineteenth century saw the creation of gender-specific penal discourses and practices in the marking and reading of female bodies, as well as in the organization of penal space. I want to elucidate the seeming enigma of why women were made subject to penal tattooing and head shaving, for instance, yet were exempted from flogging and hard labour. I would also like to touch on the process of emasculation implied by the quest for legibility. If it is true that, as Burton has argued, gender and sexuality were foundational to projects of colonial modernity, there is however a considerable amount of space for more research on both women and gender difference and the relationship between colonial discourses of masculinity and the 'native criminal'.[34] To be sure it was the case that technological innovations in identificatory practices were complicated by discourses of gender, and by the second half of the nineteenth century were restricted by colonial notions of appropriate contact with women. As Radhika Singha puts it, the visibility and seclusion of Indian women was always a 'site of contest between the colonial state and its subjects'.[35] As we shall see, there was considerable anxiety about posing the body for the taking of photographs or anthropometric measurements. In effect, this limited the ambit of colonial knowledge over female prisoners and convicts. One of the main advantages of fingerprinting was that women's prints could be taken easily, and without the removal of clothes. In this sense, the desire to bring female prisoners and convicts into the purview of the colonial state shaped strategies and procedures of identification in important ways. Moreover, their metaphorical unveiling might be seen as an allegory for the conquering of a feminized colonial landscape.[36]

No book about the history of punishment and the body would be complete without acknowledging the enormous impact that Michel Foucault has had on historians. Foucault has famously conceptualized the relationship between scientific disciplines and social practices in the modern age which, he argued, are important 'technologies', or strategies of power implicated in the ordering, classification and control of individual bodies. Knowledge of the body constitutes power relations, and those power relations also constitute a field of knowledge.[37] In its focus on the Indian criminal body as a site for the exercise of colonial power and the construction of colonial knowledge, this book is full of Foucault's insights. In particular, I want to draw out some of the ambiguities of the circulation of power-knowledge, especially in relation to the elusive figure of the 'criminal woman', and also to push Foucault's concept of the relationship between power and resistance, so tantalizingly hinted at but relatively unexplored in his work, further. After all, what made the textualization of the criminal body necessary was the potential fragility of penal discipline and the permeability of nineteenth-century jails and penal and reformatory settlements. On occasion it was the very ambivalence of colonial power that provided spaces for prisoner and convict resistance against it. Moreover, resistance and human agency were decisive factors in the development of identificatory practices.[38]

Two broader questions will be dealt with, but only briefly. First, was the Indian subcontinent a laboratory for developments in Britain? Second, is the relationship between colonial power, knowledge, resistance and the body described in these pages peculiarly South Asian? In relation to the first point, the nature of the relationship between what have traditionally been termed metropole and periphery is only tentatively explored in the pages that follow. However, it is clear that there were very many parallels between developments in Britain and its colonies both in the conceptualization of the 'criminal classes' and in the treatment of prisoners, convicts and habitual offenders.[39] When one slots Europe and North America into the equation, there are still more.[40] Indeed, one might contend that the interchange of ideas between metropole(s) and periphery(ies), and the interface between the colonies themselves, was so great that the boundaries between them can be substantively blurred.

Yet despite this, and in relation to the second point, I would contend that there was something peculiarly South Asian about colonial efforts to mark and read the criminal, or what Arnold has termed the colonization of the body.[41] This was bound up with three things. First, British ideas about punishment were merged with supposedly local practices, to produce (and sanction) penal interventions like *godna* that were politically impossible in both the metropole and other colonies. Second, both biological and cultural colonial readings of Indian society attached great significance to race and caste as social determinants. This greatly influenced the making of penal space and notions of the hereditary offender. Third, and in relation to this, Indian criminal bodies were used in the making of broader racial hierarchies – based on their physical attributes – with little or no reference to their status as convicted offenders. In contrast to Europe and despite ideas about hereditary crime South Asian convict bodies were primarily viewed as social, as opposed to biological, criminals. The unique textualization of the South Asian criminal body is exemplified in the way that the practice of penal tattooing was played out in the subcontinent. So it is to a discussion of *godna* that we shall first turn.

Notes

1. On nineteenth-century transportation to the Andamans, see Satadru Sen, *Disciplining Punishment: Colonialism and Convict Society in the Andaman Islands* (Oxford University Press, 2000). Accounts focusing on the transportation of political offenders to the Islands include S.N. Aggarwal, *The Heroes of Cellular Jail* (Publication Bureau, Punjabi University, 1995); L.P. Mathur, *Kala Pani: History of Andaman and Nicobar Islands with a Study of India's Freedom Struggle* (Eastern Book Company, 1992); R.C. Majumdar, *Penal Settlement in Andamans* (Gazetteers Unit, Department of Culture, Ministry of Education and Social Welfare, 1975).

2. The histories of these penal settlements have yet to be written, especially those in Burma. Geographically limited studies include my own *Convicts in the Indian Ocean: Transportation from South Asia to Mauritius, 1815–53* (Macmillan, 2000); Anoma Pieris, 'Hidden Hands and Divided Landscapes: Penal Labor and Colonial Citizenship in Singapore and the Straits Settlements, 1825–1873', PhD in Architecture, UC Berkeley (2003); K.S. Sandu, 'Tamil and Other Indian Convicts in the Straits Settlements, A.D. 1790–1873', *Proceedings of the First International Tamil Conference Seminar of Tamil Studies, vol. I* (International Association of Tamil Research, 1968), 197–208; C.M. Turnbull, 'Convicts in the Straits Settlements, 1826–67', *Journal of the Malay Branch of the Royal Asiatic Society*, 43, 1 (1970), 87–103.

3. David Arnold, 'The Colonial Prison: Power, Knowledge and Penology in Nineteenth-Century India', in David Arnold and David Hardiman (eds), *Subaltern Studies VIII* (Oxford University Press, 1994), 148–87.
4. IOR P/141/9 (14 Mar. 1837): Second and Concluding Report of the Committee of Convict Labour, 28 Jan. 1837.
5. Antoinette Burton, 'Introduction: The Unfinished Business of Colonial Modernities', in Antoinette Burton (ed.), *Gender, Sexuality and Colonial Modernities* (Routledge, 1999), 1.
6. Jane Caplan, '"Speaking Scars": The Tattoo in Popular Practice and Medico-Legal Debate in Nineteenth-Century Europe', *History Workshop Journal*, 44 (1997), 126–7; Simon A. Cole, *Suspect Identities: A History of Fingerprinting and Criminal Identification* (Harvard University Press, 2001), 2–3. For a broader survey of the relationship between sedentarization, statecraft and social legibility, see the magisterial James C. Scott, *Seeing Like a State: How Certain Schemes to Improve the Human Condition Have Failed* (Yale University Press, 1998).
7. James C. Scott, John Tehranian and Jeremy Mathias, 'The Production of Legal Identities Proper to States: The Case of the Permanent Family Surname', *Comparative Studies in Society and History*, 44, 1 (2002), 4–44 (quote 7). See also Scott, *Seeing Like a State*, 64–71.
8. Radhika Singha, 'Settle, Mobilize, Verify: Identification Practices in Colonial India', *Studies in History*, 16, 2 (2000), 154–61.
9. Jane Caplan and John Torpey, 'Introduction', in Jane Caplan and John Torpey (eds), *Documenting Individual Identity: The Development of State Practices in the Modern World* (Princeton University Press, 2001), 8.
10. Cole, *Suspect Identities*, 29.
11. On embodiment, see Kathleen Canning, 'The Body as Method? Reflections on the Place of the Body in Gender History', in Leonore Davidoff, Keith McClelland and Eleni Varikas (eds), *Gender and History: Retrospect and Prospect* (Blackwell, 1999), 87–8.
12. On colonial discourses of thuggee, see Sandria Freitag, 'Crime in the Social Order of Colonial North India', *Modern Asian Studies*, 25, 2 (1991), 227–61; Stewart Gordon, 'Scarf and Sword: Thugs, Marauders, and State-formation in 18th Century Malwa', *Indian Economic and Social History Review*, 4, 4 (1969), 403–29; Parama Roy, 'Discovering India, Imagining *Thuggee*', *Yale Journal of Criticism*, 9, 1 (1996), 121–45; Radhika Singha, '"Providential" Circumstances: The Thuggee Campaign of the 1830s and Legal Innovation', *Modern*

Asian Studies, 27, 1 (1993), 83–146; Radhika Singha, *A Despotism of Law: Crime and Justice in Early Colonial India* (Oxford University Press, 1998), ch. 5; Martine Van Woerkens, *The Strangled Traveler: Colonial Imaginings and the Thugs of India* (tr. Catherine Tihanyi) (University of Chicago Press, 2002).

13. William Sleeman, 'Report on the Depredations Committed by the Thug Gangs of Upper and Central India, from the Cold Season of 1826–27, down to their Gradual Suppression under the Measures Adopted Against Them by the Supreme Government in the Year 1839', *British and Foreign Review*, 15, 29 (1843), 291. Sleeman compared the significance of the thuggee campaign to the abolition of widow self-immolation (*sati*) in 1829.

14. W.S. Caine, *Picturesque India: A Handbook for European Travellers* (Routledge, 1891), 380–1.

15. Roy, 'Discovering India', 126; Singha, '"Providential" Circumstances', 84.

16. Singha, *A Despotism of Law*, 168–9, 174.

17. W. Sleeman, 'Report on the Depredations': 'Tabular Statement of the Result of the Trials which have Taken Place at Different Places since the Operations for the Suppression of the System of Thuggee Commenced' (n.p.).

18. *Ibid.*, 286.

19. Clare Anderson, 'The Politics of Convict Space: Indian Penal Settlements and the Andamans', in Alison Bashford and Carolyn Strange (eds), *Isolation: Places and Practices of Exclusion* (Routledge, 2003), 41–4.

20. *Report of the Committee on Prison Discipline, 8 Jan. 1838* (Baptist Mission Press, 1838), 86.

21. Singha, *Despotism of Law*, 173–4.

22. IOR P/143/1 (12 May 1847): J. Sutherland, Secretary Marine Board, to R.H. Mytton, Superintendent Alipur Jail, 23 Apr. 1847.

23. IOR P/139/72 (20 Sept. 1831): J. Thomason, Deputy Secretary to Government Bengal, to A.D. Maingy, Commissioner Tenasserim Provinces, 20 Sept. 1831.

24. IOR P/141/39 (12 Sept. 1839): J. Hawkins, Register *Nizamat Adalat* to F.J. Halliday, Secretary to Government Bengal, 23 Aug. 1839.

25. IOR P/142/24 (20 Nov. 1844): G.F. Edmonstone, Register *Nizamat Adalat* (North West Provinces), to J. Thornton, Secretary to Government North West Provinces, 14 Sept. 1844.

26. *Ibid.*: T.R. Davidson, Officiating Secretary to Government of India, to Halliday, 2 Nov. 1844.

27. Sanjay Nigam, 'Disciplining and Policing the "Criminals by Birth"', Part 2: The Development of a Disciplinary System, 1871–1900', *Indian Economic and Social History Review*, 27, 3 (1990), 287. On the criminal tribes see also David Arnold, *Police Power and Colonial Rule, Madras 1859–1947* (Oxford University Press, 1986), 138–47; Crispin Bates, 'Race, Caste and Tribe in Central India: The Early Origins of Indian Anthropometry', in Peter Robb (ed.), *The Concept of Race in South Asia* (Oxford University Press, 1997), 219–57; Mark Brown, 'Race, Science and the Construction of Native Criminality in Colonial India', *Theoretical Criminology*, 5, 3 (2001), 345–68; Stewart Gordon, 'Bhils and the Idea of a Criminal Tribe in Nineteenth-Century India', in Anand A. Yang (ed.), *Crime and Criminality in British India* (University of Arizona Press, 1985), 128–39; Andrew Major, 'State and Criminal Tribes in Colonial Punjab: Surveillance, Control and Reclamation of the "Dangerous Classes"', *Modern Asian Studies*, 33 (1999), 657–88; Sanjay Nigam, 'Disciplining and Policing the "Criminals by Birth"', Part 1: The Making of a Colonial Stereotype – The Criminal Tribes and Castes of North India', *Indian Economic and Social History Review*, 27, 2 (1990), 131–64; Meena Radhakrishna, 'The Criminal Tribes Act in the Madras Presidency: Implications for Itinerant Trading Communities', *Indian Economic and Social History Review*, 26, 3 (1989), 271–95; Meena Radhakrishna, 'Surveillance and Settlements under the Criminal Tribes Act in Madras', *Indian Economic and Social History Review*, 29, 2 (1992), 171–98; Meena Radhakrishna, 'Colonial Construction of a "Criminal Tribe": The Itinerant Trading Communities of Madras Presidency', in Neera Chandhoke (ed.), *Mapping Histories: Essays Presented to Ravinder Kumar* (Tulika, 2000), 128–60; Rachel J. Tolen, 'Colonizing and Transforming the Criminal Tribesmen: The Salvation Army in British India', *American Ethnologist*, 18, 1 (1991), 106–25; Anand A. Yang, 'Dangerous Castes and Tribes: The Criminal Tribes Act and the Magahiya Doms of Northeast India', in Yang (ed.), *Crime and Criminality*, 108–27.
28. Tolen, 'Colonizing and Transforming', 112.
29. Arnold, 'Colonial Prison', 158–9. James H. Mills takes the same approach in his consideration of another institution of confinement, the asylum: *Madness, Cannabis and Colonialism: The 'Native-Only' Lunatic Asylums of British India, 1857–1900* (Macmillan, 2000).
30. Susan Bayly, *Caste, Society and Politics in India from the Eighteenth Century to the Modern Age* (Cambridge University Press, 1999); Susan Bayly, 'Caste and "Race" in the Colonial Ethnography of

India', in Robb (ed.), *Concept of Race*, 165–218; Nicholas B. Dirks, *Castes of Mind: Colonialism and the Making of Modern India* (Princeton University Press, 2001); Peter Robb, 'Introduction: South Asia and the Concept of Race', in Robb (ed.), *Concept of Race*, 1–76.

31. Ruth Roach Pierson, 'Introduction', in Ruth Roach Pierson and Nupur Chaudhuri (eds), *Nation, Empire, Colony: Historicizing Gender and Race* (Indiana University Press, 1998), 12.

32. Satadru Sen, 'The Female Jails of Colonial India', *Indian Economic and Social History Review*, 39, 4 (2002), 417–38.

33. Anne McClintock, *Imperial Leather: Race, Gender and Sexuality in the Colonial Contest* (Routledge, 1995).

34. For an overview of the historiography of masculinity in colonial India, see Mrinalini Sinha, 'Giving Masculinity a History: Some Contributions from the Historiography of Colonial India', in Davidoff, McClelland and Varikas (eds), *Gender and History*, 27–42. On the relationship of gender and sexuality to colonial modernity, see Burton, 'Introduction', 2.

35. Singha, 'Settle, Mobilize, Verify', 185.

36. On gender and colonial mapping, see Alison Blunt and Gillian Rose, 'Introduction: Women's Colonial and Postcolonial Geographies', in Alison Blunt and Gillian Rose (eds), *Writing Women and Space: Colonial and Postcolonial Geographies* (Guilford Press, 1994), 1–25.

37. Michel Foucault, *Discipline and Punish: The Birth of the Prison* (Allen Lane, 1977).

38. As argued for Europe by Caplan and Torpey: 'Introduction', 7.

39. Seán McConville, *English Local Prisons 1860–1900: Next Only to Death* (Routledge, 1995); Martin J. Wiener, *Reconstructing the Criminal: Culture, Law and Policy in England, 1830–1914* (Cambridge University Press, 1990).

40. Daniel Pick, *Faces of Degeneration: A European Disorder, c. 1848–1918* (Cambridge University Press, 1989); Nicole Hahn Rafter, *Creating Born Criminals* (University of Illinois Press, 1997).

41. David Arnold, *Colonizing the Body: State Medicine and Epidemic Disease in Nineteenth-Century India* (University of California Press, 1993).

2

Inscribing the Criminal Body:
The Penal Tattoo

Introduction: the Recapture of Wodoo and Lutchma

At the end of 1837, two men were arrested in Arakan (northern Burma) on suspicion of being escaped convicts. They called themselves Wodoo and Lutchma. The men claimed that they had been transported from the Bellary district of Madras to Prince of Wales Island (Penang), a penal settlement from 1790 to 1860. They said that they had escaped from the island shortly after their arrival, and had made their way north. In order to establish their identity, the authorities at Arakan shipped the men across the Bay of Bengal to Calcutta, from where they were transferred to Alipur Jail, the most important penal institution in India at the time.[1]

Wodoo and Lutchma had attracted the attention of the Arakanese authorities because they were tattooed with marks known as *godna* (*godena*). These were penal tattoos inscribed on the foreheads of convicts convicted in the Bengal and Madras presidencies from the late eighteenth to mid-nineteenth centuries. Including written details such as name, crime for which convicted and place of conviction, *godna* was designed to identify offenders as prisoners or convicts and to pin that general identity to an individual body. It was both a penal sign and a surveillance strategy. The Bengal authorities' next step was, then, to write to their counterparts in Madras, who in turn requested details of the men's *godna* inscriptions so that they could identify them.[2] The Superintendent of Alipur Jail, J.H. Patton, replied that he could not read the tattoos. They were written in a vernacular with which he was unfamiliar, and the characters had been almost completely effaced, certainly by the convicts themselves.[3] As the Bellary district court had records of convicting three 'Lutchmas' to transportation since 1820, but no 'Wodoos', it was at a loss to recognize the men from their tattoos alone.[4]

The narrative of Wodoo and Lutchma's escape, recapture and identification raises a number of interesting issues surrounding the practice of *godna*. Discussing identification practices in colonial India, Singha suggests that *godna* bore testimony to 'the inexorable process of colonial justice'.[5] In fact, it was far more equivocal than she suggests. *Godna* is part of a larger argument about the unevenness of colonial rule, for whilst it was developed in Bengal and adopted in Madras, the authorities in Bombay refused to use it, choosing to rework pre-colonial forms of public exposure instead. It was their intransigence about the introduction of *godna* that led to its abolition in the other presidencies in 1849. Even in areas where the regulations were in force, there were considerable differences of opinion about when, where and how *godna* should be carried out, and further practical difficulties in its performance. This meant that though penal tattoos could be read as general marks of criminality, often they could not be anchored to individuals, creating considerable tension between intentions of permanence and individuation and the effects of transience and illegibility. The breach between regulations on and practices of *godna* also opened up spaces in which convicts could exercise their own forms of power. Notwithstanding failures of individual identification, there is evidence to suggest that convicts removed or faded their marks. Also, the tattoos sometimes served as reminders of pre-existing social hierarchies, rather than as expressions of undifferentiated convict status. In addition, whilst *godna* fed into the making of criminal typologies, in this case the discourse of thuggee, it sometimes had unintended consequences and unsettled the seemingly stable categories of colonial rule.

Penal tattooing might also be perceived as a gendered colonial practice, for it was women who usually wore the decorative tattoos also known as *godna*.[6] It is interesting that the colonial authorities adopted the same terminology for penal tattoos, though given that *godna* can also mean to wound (or lacerate) a person's feelings, it was perhaps an apt choice.[7] The connection between decorative and penal tattooing was made explicit in the first regulations on *godna*, passed at the turn of the century. *Godna* was then described as the means through which Hindu women 'ornament their faces, and which leaves a blue mark which cannot be effaced without tearing off the skin'.[8] I would like to conceptualize the significance of this as a means of emasculating the 'native criminal'. Further, though women were exempted from some corporal punishments they were made subject to *godna*. I shall unravel this seeming paradox through a broader examination of the place of *godna* in gendered notions of penal space.

The Equivocality of *Godna*

Pre-colonial Indian law prescribed a variety of punishments that were employed with considerable discretion and latitude in a bid to reform the offender (*tazir*). Offenders could be sentenced to pay a fine; less common were sentences of imprisonment or execution. Mutilation, such as the amputation of the nose, ears or hands, was a further kind of punishment, leaving a permanent reminder that the person had once committed a crime. *Tashir*, or public shaming, was another. Convicted offenders could have their hair shaved off or their face blackened, be seated backwards on an ass and paraded around their community. It was also a discretionary punishment, and its form was decided after consideration of the offender's status and other potentially mitigating factors.[9]

There is some evidence that pre-colonial lawmakers used penal marking as a punishment in the subcontinent, though it is not conclusive. It has been said that high-caste Hindu Brahmins were marked on the forehead with a representation of their crime,[10] though it is not clear that these marks were permanent. N. Majumdar has indicated that in murder cases this depended on the status of the victim;[11] Singha suggests that the drawings may have been temporary, due to sanctions against wounding the flesh of Brahmins.[12] In 1794, for instance, the British Resident of Banaras, Jonathan Duncan, reported that a recently tried prisoner named Moolwa had previously been punished with mutilation (his nose and ear had been cut off) and had been branded on the forehead. The fact that there was no longer any trace of the brand suggests that either it was some sort of impermanent mark, or that it had not been properly done, a theme to which we shall return.[13]

There is more evidence that tattooing and branding were used for similar purposes in Europe, serving to both stigmatize and identify marginalized groups. In late antiquity, delinquent slaves, criminals, soldiers and prisoners of war were all tattooed.[14] The branding of galley and other public slaves was the norm until the nineteenth century; galley slaves in France for instance had the letters 'GAL' marked on their shoulders. The sixteenth-century *Carolina* penal code in Germany – in force until the eighteenth century – also provided for convict branding.[15] A century later, French convicts sentenced to forced labour still had the letters 'TP' (*travaux perpétuels*) branded onto their bodies.[16] During the same period, British army deserters had a small 'D' burnt into their left side.[17] It seems that tattooing and branding had not altogether disappeared from the European penal repertoire even by the second half of the nineteenth century. Public slaves (*katorshniki*) in Siberia had 'KAT' pricked onto their cheeks and forehead and gunpowder rubbed into the wounds, a practice not abolished until 1863.[18]

As European empires expanded, so did the use of tattooing and branding for the marking and controlling of slaves. At one level, indelible marks designated ownership and, like naming practices designed to strip slaves of extra-European identity, were powerful symbols of unfreedom.[19] Slaves were also branded for resistance to authority. The Barbados Code of 1688 – copied by settlers in the Windward Islands (St Lucia, St Vincent, Tobago and Dominica) – directed the branding of slaves with a hot iron as punishment.[20] The repressive 1723 Code Noir in the French Indian Ocean colony Ile de France (Mauritius) also legislated for the branding of maroon slaves on the shoulder.[21] A 1733 slave ordinance in the Danish Virgin Islands ordered leaders of slave desertions to be 'pinched thrice with a hot iron' before being hanged.[22]

The British did not commonly brand or tattoo criminal offenders in these colonies, however. It would seem that they seized upon limited evidence of penal marking in pre-colonial India as a justification for creating a unique form of punishment. The colonial authorities first introduced *godna* in Banaras in 1789, using tattooing rather than branding or drawing. Anxious about the erosion of British prestige and the possibility of inflaming anti-colonial feelings there, and mindful of pre-colonial practice mitigating the punishment of high-caste offenders, the British Resident, Jonathan Duncan, directed that a Brahmin offender convicted of murder, Bhowanny Buksh, be tattooed on the forehead and banished rather than executed.[23] The first colonial regulation on *godna* was passed a few years later in 1797. It directed that all Bengal Presidency life prisoners have their name, crime, date of sentence and the division of the court by which convicted tattooed on the forehead. The regulation stated that the purpose of such immediately visible marks was the easy recapture of escaped convicts.[24] As Singha notes, *godna* was chosen above branding or mutilation because it allowed individuals to be precisely connected to their offence.[25] The regulation invoked the marking of *all* life prisoners and was not, in practice, discretionary. This was a uniform treatment of offenders that drew on Enlightenment ideals of the social contract, where only the certainty of punishment was an effective deterrent against crime. *Godna* was later extended to further territories in Bengal, as they were ceded to East India Company control.[26]

The 1797 regulation also made perjurers subject to *godna*. This time, the inscription would consist of the Persian *duroghgo* (liar) or a similar word. Here, the aim was not identification in case of escape, but public shaming, where district courts considered *tashir* 'insufficient' – in other words, impermanent.[27] The authorities counselled caution, though, 'so that none but the proper objects of a perpetual stigma may in any instance be made liable to it.'[28] In 1803, forgers were also brought under the regulations. The use of the inscription *duroghgo* was once again sanctioned, together with the Persian term *jal saz* (cheat).[29] As Singha has established, these regulations stemmed from colonial mistrust of native testimonies. East India Company officials believed that Indians did not see perjury or forgery as a social disgrace, but rather as a means through which they could manipulate the colonial courts to their own ends. *Godna* was an attempt on the part of the Company to provide the deterrent against perjury and forgery that public opinion did not.[30] It also had an important practical purpose. The third judge of the Dacca division, for example, wrote that *godna* marks would be a useful means of preventing perjurers from appearing in court a second time.[31] According to Singha, problems in proving perjury and forgery meant that the regulations were rarely used though.[32]

Nevertheless, the motivating thrust behind the regulations on inscribing perjurers and forgers with *godna* marks was quite different from that relating to other offenders. Perjurers and forgers were almost always sentenced to a term rather than imprisonment for life. After serving their sentence they would return to their kin networks displaying the stigma of a penal tattoo – designed as the deterrent that community values did not provide. This perhaps explains why only a simple inscription ('liar' or 'cheat') was necessary. Life convicts, on the other hand, were sentenced to perpetual imprisonment or transportation. Their tattoos had a different purpose. *Godna* was supposed to mark individual identity and represent prisoner status. The details that should have been inscribed on lifers – name, date of sentence, court by which convicted – not only connected individuals to their offence, but also facilitated their penal management. In this sense, their inscriptions can be conceptualized as permanent embodiments of the potential fragility of convict discipline.

The use of *godna* on perjurers and forgers was relatively short-lived. It came to an end in 1817 when a regulation prohibiting the marking of term prisoners was passed. The reason for this related to the initial enthusiasm for the practice, the immediate visibility of penal tattoos. Far from being a useful check of a past conviction that was otherwise covered, penal tattoos rendered it almost impossible for ex-convicts to find gainful employment. This obviated their successful return to the labour market and greatly increased the likelihood that they would reoffend. So, in 1817, a regulation directed once again that only life convicts would be tattooed. The *Nizamat Adalat* was also given the power to exempt prisoners from it 'where there may appear to be special reason', of what kind it did not elaborate.[33] The 1817 regulation formed the basis of the *godna* regulations that remained in force for Bengal life prisoners until 1849. The Bengal Code was extended to the Madras Presidency in 1802. Initially, it directed that only lifers would be marked. Its stated aim was the same as in Bengal: to facilitate the recapture of escaped prisoners. Where a sentence of *tashir* was passed on life prisoners, the inscription of the tattoo *duroghgo*, or a similar word, on the forehead was also sanctioned.[34] In 1811, the regulations were applied to offenders convicted of perjury and forgery. Once again, the punishment of *tashir* was replaced with the tattooing of *duroghgo* or *jal saz* on the forehead.[35]

From their very inception, the *godna* regulations were riddled with difficulties. The colonial authorities in Bengal often found it difficult to find Indian tattooists (*godnawali*) who they considered appropriate for the task of marking prisoners.[36] Like the tattooists of a group of thugs in 1835, many *godnawali* were women from low-caste itinerant communities.[37] Tattooing the face was an intimate process; worries about the propriety of using women to tattoo male prisoners were compounded by fears that they might be open to convict bribes. In the absence of any direct evidence, to what extent the women themselves were unwilling or fearful of the social consequences of carrying out the operation is difficult to say. What we do know is that although the correct procedure was for prisoners to be tattooed in the district where they were convicted, many convicts sentenced to life imprisonment or transportation overseas arrived at the holding jail at Alipur with no *godna* marks at all. A *Nizamat Adalat* Circular of 1836 made the first of several complaints on this issue.[38] Ten years later, unmarked convicts were still being sent there.[39]

Similar problems arose in Madras, where transportation convicts were frequently tattooed at the holding jail at Chengalpattu – rather than in the district in which convicted – just a few days before their shipment to the South East Asian penal settlements. In 1823, the criminal court (*Faujdari Adalat*) there reminded the district judges that it was their responsibility to ensure that *godna* was performed after sentence was passed.[40] There were further difficulties when convicts were convicted outside the regulation provinces. In 1840, for instance, convict Bukra was sent to Alipur from the South West Frontier (Chota Nagpur), without a mark of *godna*. The Agent there claimed that *godna* was never performed on prisoners in the district.[41]

If convicts were destined for transportation, their descriptive rolls (sometimes called ship indents) were compiled in the district in which they had been convicted, before they were sent to the presidency jails. These rolls were designed to link the vernacular *godna* inscriptions to English records, for the benefit of British penal administrators. They reveal that during the 1820s and 1830s hundreds of other transportation convicts were dispatched without the requisite *godna* marks. Some districts performed worse than others in this respect, though this varied during the period the regulations were in force. By the 1840s, however, the application of the regulations had become much more systematic, and it was relatively unusual to find unmarked convicts in the records.

There are no surviving accounts of the performance of *godna* in Indian prisons, and nothing in the archives that suggests violent resistance or support from the wider community against it, as there was over the performance of labour, common messing and the withdrawal of the brass drinking vessels known as *lotahs*.[42] We shall return to other forms of convict resistance to *godna* later. Yet the infliction of *godna* must have been an extraordinary piece of colonial theatre. What did prisoners know about the operation before it was performed on them? Was it necessary to restrain them? How intense was the pain? How long did it take? As we shall see in the next chapter, decorative tattooing was mostly performed by and associated with the low caste. Many convicts – especially men of high caste or social standing – would have experienced penal tattooing as a complete subversion of social hierarchies. Indeed, as Singha has established, this was an important innovation in colonial penal practice.[43] In other areas of convict management, the prison authorities were sympathetic to pre-existing social hierarchies, particularly those that related to caste, and exploited them in their organization of prisoners.[44] The 1817 regulation was no exception to such latitude, giving the authorities the right to exempt prisoners from *godna* 'where there may appear to be special reason'.[45] Interestingly, however, there is no evidence at all to suggest that this discretion was ever used. Brahmins for instance were not exempt from *godna*, a considerable departure from pre-colonial forms of discretionary punishment. Neither did queries about individual prisoners ever result in mitigation of the sentence.

In 1816, for example, the Criminal Judge of Cuddapah (Madras Presidency) enquired whether the fact that convicts transported to penal settlements like Penang were employed in outdoor labour, by implication exposing their tattoos to the public gaze rather than to the scrutiny of their jail overseers, exempted them from *godna*. The *Faujdari Adalat* replied that the regulations were not affected 'by any variation which circum-stances may occasion in the mode of their confinement'. It reminded the judge that the purpose of *godna* was to facilitate the recapture of escaped convicts, which applied as much to prisoners shipped to the penal settlements as imprisoned in local jails.[46] In 1837 the question arose once again, this time in relation to three high status men convicted of political offences. The Criminal Judge of Kannur (also in the Madras Presidency) asked whether it was proper to tattoo Chokasoor Chenniah, Soobraya and

Pleedambady Ammal, who had been convicted of treason and rebellion and sentenced to transportation to the Tenasserim Provinces (Amherst, Tavoy and Mergui) in south-east Burma, penal settlements between 1828 and 1862. In the eyes of the Governor of Madras, that they were political prisoners made the need for the social subversion implied by the penal tattoo all the more pressing. His answer was an immediate and resounding 'yes'.[47]

Despite this seeming lack of discretion in the enforcement of *godna* regulations, convict ship indents reveal that there was considerable regional diversity in what the tattoo marks actually consisted of. The district jail clerks who compiled the rolls usually made a simple note of the fact that convicts had been marked or inscribed with *godna* on the forehead and occasionally also between the eyebrows and/or on the nose. From time to time, they added further details. We know that in the 1820s, in Shahjahanpur *godna* consisted of a blue cross (+) on the forehead alone, for instance.[48] Bengal Presidency records also reveal the different scripts used – Devanagari, Bengali or Persian, according to the district in which convicts were tried.[49] The authorities believed that invariably escaped convicts would attempt to return home, which explains why *godna* marks were inscribed in the local vernacular. Thus convicts sentenced to transportation in Burma and shipped to jails on the Indian mainland were given equivalent inscriptions in Burmese.[50]

The records also show that it was not unusual for Bengal convicts to be tattooed with only part of the required description, and it is possible to trace regional patterns. Most frequently, descriptive rolls describe *godna* marks as a simple record of a convict's crime.[51] In other cases the sentence alone appears to have been noted.[52] These smaller marks were undoubtedly preferable to convicts, but a potential cause of difficulty to the prison authorities who could not use the tattoos to identify them as individuals. In other places, inscriptions were more detailed and more useful in this respect, as they included each convict's name, crime and date of sentence.[53] Officials in the penal settlements were all too aware of the huge diversity in the type and size of inscriptions made. As J.W. Salmond, Resident Councillor at Penang, noted in his response to questioning by the 1838 Prison Discipline Committee:

> It would be of advantage to the convict office here in keeping the books if there were one form throughout the presidencies. Convicts when sentenced to transportation for life are by some courts marked with their names, crimes and date of sentence on their foreheads; by other courts they are only so marked when convicted of murder; and by others not at all for any crime. They are at present marked in different native characters.[54]

By 1838, the authorities in Bengal and Madras knew of these differences in *godna* practices and they had made attempts to regularize them, but to little avail. In Madras, a Circular Order of 1815 noted that regulations were not being enforced, and ordered that courts of circuit should direct the infliction of *godna* inscriptions when passing sentence.[55] An 1836 Bengal Circular drew attention to the 1817 regulations, reminding district magistrates that all life convicts should be properly marked.[56] In 1847, it was ordered that every convict convicted in the Bengal Presidency should be sent to Alipur Jail with a 'Certificate of Godna', certifying that the operation had been performed, the marks were still legible and they had not been effaced.[57] The reference to the legibility and removal of the marks in part hints at the lengths convicts went to to remove their inscriptions, a theme we shall discuss later. However, it also raises the question of how effective the marks actually were. A full *godna* inscription contained a lot of detail on a relatively small area of skin. Presumably, it required prisoners to keep perfectly still for a not inconsiderable period of time. If low-caste *godnawali* were employed, the tattooist was probably illiterate. This may have impacted on the quality of the inscription, though according to Edgar Thurston, who was appointed Superintendent of Ethnography in the Madras Presidency at the end of the nineteenth century and wrote about decorative tattooing there, once names or letters were drawn out for them first, they were able to tattoo them with considerable skill.[58] Nevertheless, there was clearly some practical rift between *godna* as a penal sign, and as an individuating penal strategy.

The writings of some European contemporaries who came into contact with life convicts are suggestive of some of these limitations. One nineteenth-century visitor to the penal settlement at Singapore (1825–60), Frank S. Marryat, wrote that *godna* consisted of the simple inscriptions *doomga* or murder (Figure 2.1).[59] Marryat also described the marks as brands, rather than tattoos, raising further questions about the process. The 1797 and 1803 regulations on *godna* both directed the use of permanent blue tattoo marks.[60] On the rare occasions that jail clerks elaborated, this is usually how the descriptive rolls described it.[61] There are few records that describe the branding of offenders, unless they were convicted of thuggee.[62] Yet many contemporary commentators described *godna* as branding, even when referring specifically to a blue mark.[63] The Superintendent of Alipur Jail, J.H. Patton, who would have been familiar with the practice, for instance, referred to *godna* as branding.[64] So did S.G. Bonham, Governor of the Straits Settlements (as Singapore, Penang and Malacca were known after 1825),[65] and J.F.A. McNair, Comptroller-General of Convicts there between 1857 and 1877. McNair elaborated that the operation was performed using a hot copper iron.[66]

Figure 2.1 'Convict'. Frank S. Marryat, *Borneo and the Indian Archipelago, with Drawings of Costume and Scenery* (Longman, Brown, Green and Longmans, 1848), p. 215

Why were there such discrepancies in accounts of *godna*? It may be that tattooing and branding were both used, or that branding became more common during the period that *godna* regulations were in force. It would have been much quicker to brand prisoners, and therefore deflect any resistance on their part. Invariably, though, brands could not contain the individual details required by early *godna* regulations. They would have marked prisoner status, or perhaps designated membership of particular colonial categories like 'thug', rather than individual identity. It is also possible that 'brand' – a word more strongly associated with infamy and stigma than 'tattoo' – was a linguistic device that signalled a penal inscription of whatever kind. However, it is perhaps significant that an 1842 Bengal Circular on *godna* referred for the first time rather ambiguously to 'marking', which covered both options.[67] The 1849 Act outlawing *godna* similarly referred to the abolition of branding *and* inflicting 'indelible marks' on offenders.[68] Of course the process may also have developed to incorporate aspects of both. Convicts might be first branded and then the exposed skin coloured with blue dye. This was practised elsewhere – in imperial Russia, for instance, where prisoners were branded and gunpowder rubbed into the wounds.[69]

The Tattooed Thug

As well as signifying prisoner/convict status in a general sense, penal tattoos were also used in the making of the criminal typology 'thug' and became a means of distinguishing them from other convicted offenders. In the Sagar and Narbada Territories, where William Sleeman's campaign against thuggee was concentrated, penal tattooing was introduced for thugs in 1830. Its purpose was to provide for the easy recognition of old offenders, who the British believed were sure to return to their 'hereditary calling'. As such, it was directed that all thugs sentenced to seven years' imprisonment or more would be tattooed on a part of the body not normally exposed to view, such as the back or shoulders. The inscription would include their name and the words 'convicted thug'. It would not be an immediately visible mark, but would allow the authorities to verify their supposed occupation should they be rearrested.[70] In 1833, the Political Agent of Sagar and Narbada elaborated further. He wrote that thugs sentenced to life should have 'thug' (in English) marked on the forehead, and those sentenced to a term of imprisonment the word *phansigar* (strangler) instead.[71] In practice, g*odna* took a rather different form, combining inscriptions on the forehead with marks on the cheeks, nose, shoulders, hands and/or forearms.[72]

Again it is not clear how *godna* was performed. Branding may have been a quicker mode of inflicting these more standard inscriptions, and thugs' marks were not infrequently described in the ship indents as brands rather than tattoos.[73] However inscribed, the marks of life prisoner thugs signified something different from those of ordinary offenders. It was not simply what they said, but where they were positioned that marked thugs out. Other convicts would have known that they had been convicted of thuggee even if they could not read the inscriptions, for ordinary transportation convicts never had *godna* marks on the nose, cheeks, shoulders, arms or hands. During sentence they were also a means of identification. After six thug convicts escaped from Moulmein Jail (Tenasserim Provinces) in 1846, for instance, the 'wanted' notice faithfully recorded their *godna* marks on the forehead and arms.[74] Equally, after term prisoners were released the vernacular inscriptions were supposed to provide a warning of their hereditary profession.

There are several surviving representations of the facial marks of convict thugs, and I would argue that they constituted part of the orientalization of the offence. Figure 2.2 shows the *godna* marks of convict Multhoo Byragee Jogee as sketched by Colesworthy Grant on board the ship *Phlegethon*, which transported thug convicts to the Tenasserim Provinces in April 1844.[75] Grant wrote about convict 'brand' marks in a Burmese travelogue published shortly after the illustrations.[76] That only some of the convicts Grant drew have penal tattoos is curious, as the descriptive roll that accompanied the ship reveals that all the convict dacoits and thugs on board had been marked with *godna* – the dacoits on the forehead and the thugs on the cheeks. Multhoo Byragee Jogee is presumably the convict named as Rumzanee *alias* Mullthoo (no. 6).[77]

It is not clear why Grant did not draw the tattoos. Had the convicts effaced them? Or did Grant choose not to show them in what were essentially orientalist representations? Certainly, the convicts are pictured

Figure 2.2 'Multhoo Byragee Jogee: A Thug Convict'. Lithograph by Colesworthy Grant, from *Sketches of Oriental Heads* (Calcutta, 1839–46). (Courtesy of British Library, P2572/3)

draped in white cloth as though roused from Mediterranean antiquity. I am reminded here of Charles Darwin's description of Indian convicts in Mauritius as 'noble looking men', and another's representation of them as reminiscent of 'the pictures of Abraham by the old masters'. Mauritian Governor Lowry Cole's wife also wrote that when she first saw Indian convicts, it was like an image from *The Arabian Nights*. These were picturesque representations that transformed convicts into exotic others.[78]

The other surviving representation of tattooed thugs shows the inscription 'thug' on the cheeks. Held in the papers of J.S. Paton, an assistant to Sleeman's anti-thug operations, this drawing is a more accurate reflection of the practice (Figure 2.3). Another visitor to the subcontinent, Leopold Von Orlich, wrote that he had visited a thug prison in Lucknow where he had seen thugs thus branded.[79]

By far the most famous representation of penal tattooing is that written by Philip Meadows Taylor in the best-selling *Confessions of a Thug*. First published in 1839, the book was enormously popular, going through two editions in four months. Meadows Taylor had been the Assistant

Figure 2.3 'Tattooed Thugs'. J.S. Paton Papers: Collections on Thuggee and Dacoitee, by Captain James Paton (1798–1847), First Assistant to the Resident at Lucknow and Extra Assistant to the Superintendent for the Suppression of Thuggee and Dacoitee. (Courtesy of British Library, ADD 41300)

Superintendent of Police in the South-western District (Hyderabad) between 1826 and 1829. In his autobiography, he claimed that he was involved in efforts to suppress thuggee during this period, interrogating a number of men denounced as thugs by approvers arrested by William Sleeman.[80] In *Confessions of a Thug*, Meadows Taylor writes as the central thug character, Ameer Ali, who is branded on the forehead for his crimes:[81]

> They threw me down . . . I struggled, yet it was unavailing; they held my arms, and my legs, and head, and a red-hot pice [*paise*; Company coin] was pressed upon my forehead; it was held there as it burnt down to the bone, ay my very brain seemed to be scorched and withered by the burning copper. They took it off, and raised me up. Allah! Allah! The agony that I endured – the agony of pain, and, more than that, of shame – to be branded publicly that the world might think me a thief – to have a mark set on my forehead that I must carry to my grave – a mark only set on the vile and on the outcasts from society . . . I bound my turban over my still burning and aching brow, so that man might not see my shame.[82]

Meadows Taylor was alluding to the marking of Cain, a reference that would have been obvious to his readers. After Cain kills Abel, he is 'marked' by God before being sent into exile.[83] There are of course obvious parallels between this Old Testament story and the tattooing (marking) and transportation (exile) of Indian criminal offenders. Meadows Taylor's description was undoubtedly a sensationalist account (in another account of thuggee meant for the consumption of his Victorian readers, he wrote of 'the fangs of the blood-thirsty demons')[84] rather than an accurate portrayal of the practice of marking thugs. Yet his is the only narrative to bring out the pain of the operation, and to hint at the public shame associated with Ameer Ali's experience of it. Of particular concern to Ameer Ali was the fact that he might be mistaken for a common thief. In practice, of course, this would not have been the case, as the nature and position of thug tattoos were different from those given to ordinary offenders. Yet this reflected Meadows Taylor's firm opinion that thugs considered theft a disgrace, and resisted being described as thieves.[85] Neither is there any evidence that prisoners were ever branded with Company coins in the way Meadows Taylor describes.[86] Rather, the marking of the names of William and Mary on Ameer Ali's forehead might be seen as a neat metaphor for the literal embodiment of colonial rule that *godna* ideally represented.

The Company view of thugs was unequivocal: they were the scourges of India. Penal administrators in Burma regarded them with rather more ambivalence. To some degree mainland discourses on thuggee were echoed there. When three thug convicts murdered their peon in Moulmein Jail in 1835, for instance, Commissioner E.A. Blundell claimed that they 'gloried in the act and vied with each other in assuming the guilt'.[87] In 1836 the Governor of Penang wrote of their 'peculiar habits'.[88] Ten years later the new Commissioner of the Tenasserim Provinces, H.M. Durand, wrote of the necessity of separating thugs from ordinary offenders as they would invariably seek to instruct them in their trade.[89] In 1851 an elderly thug convict hanged himself in Sandoway Jail (Arakan). The Principal Assistant to the Commissioner wrote of the deliberation with which he had twisted the knot in his rope. This, he added, was an indication of the man's skill in his former profession.[90] As late as 1879, when the Straits Settlements penal colonies were broken up (transportation had ceased in 1860), it was agreed that convicted thugs would be treated differently from other convicts. All convicts who had completed twenty-five years of imprisonment would be pardoned, except those convicted of professional poisoning, dacoity, belonging to a gang of dacoits, mutiny or rebellion accompanied with murder; or the crimes of thuggee or belonging to a gang of thugs.[91] That the Straits proviso was issued with little comment perhaps reflects the fact that there were no surviving thugs there. Indeed, the authorities usually regarded all convicts primarily in relation to the needs of the penal settlements, rather than the crime for which they had been transported. Thugs were no exception. On the arrival of one batch of thug convicts at Moulmein in 1837, Blundell complained that they were 'infirm and paralytic men who can be put to no work and who must remain a useless incumbrance to the jail til death carries them off'.[92]

Yet running parallel to these discourses were convict administrators' descriptions of thugs as the most orderly men in their charge. This sentiment was first expressed in Assistant Commissioner (Tenasserim Provinces) T. De La Condamine's report to the Prison Discipline Committee in 1838.[93] A year later, Commissioner A. Bogle wrote that he agreed to receive thug convicts in Arakan only after Blundell told him that the thugs in Moulmein were amongst the quietest and best behaved convicts in the Tenasserim Provinces. Bogle continued: 'Although they prove to do murder on the large scale, they are above petty violence and that altogether they are a very orderly set of prisoners.'[94] It is interesting to note that officials expressed similar concerns in the management of Bengal jails and the Andaman Islands later on, where prisoners and convicts convicted of serious offences like murder were seen as easier to manage than petty thieves, on the grounds that they were unlikely to reoffend.[95] After 1847, thugs in the Tenasserim Provinces were promoted to positions of authority, convict management incentives offered only to the trustworthiest men.[96]

By the following year, there were 133 thugs in the Convict Police there, employed as overseers, orderlies and hospital attendants.[97] Despite the occasional breach of convict discipline, the Magistrate of Moulmein Jail described thugs as 'the most orderly men in prison'. Their conduct was exemplary, and their response to convict resistance 'marked by resolute determination and good faith'.[98] The new Commissioner of the Provinces, J.R. Colvin, agreed, adding that he regarded them with complete confidence and did not subject them to special restrictions.[99] It was not long before the East India Company agreed to grant the thugs' request to live at large after serving sixteen years, like other convicts in Burma.[100]

Thugs' special *godna* marks were supposed to draw administrators' attention to them as a potentially troublesome, not to mention dangerous, convict population. However, in the Burmese penal settlements they were transformed into marks of a quite different sort. Thug tattoos were an easy means of identifying convicts who could be relied on and incorporated into a colonial management strategy that offered rewards for good conduct as well as punishments for breaches of discipline. Literally embodied on the offender, the very meaning of the word 'thug' underwent a fundamental shift. To what extent this was the result of the way in which ordinary convicts regarded them is difficult to say. Was the appeal of thugs as overseers grounded in the fear that they engendered in other convicts? This was certainly a potentially effective convict management technique, and may explain the choice of Indian convict overseers elsewhere in South East Asia and the Indian Ocean during the same period. It was certainly the case later on elsewhere. Peter Zinoman shows that in the prisons and penal settlements of colonial Vietnam, violent criminals were most likely to be selected as overseers (*caplans*).[101] Or, as Meadows Taylor suggested in 1833, was it that men convicted of the serious offences often categorized as thuggee distanced themselves from other offenders and considered themselves honest and trustworthy? Whatever the case, convict thugs embodied some of the complex slippages of colonial categories of rule.

'I was a Runaway Convict, He Knew from the Mark on my Forehead'

As we have seen, colonial regulations defined *godna* as a deterrent to convict escape. Absconding was a particular risk when prisoners were worked on road gangs or were transported to penal settlements, where they were usually employed on public works. In a general sense, marked convicts were unable to pass themselves off as free, because their identity as convicts was immediately visible. The penal authorities, at least in theory, could then use *godna* markings to fix individual identities. The authorities frequently picked up men with *godna*, on the (correct) assumption that they were escaped convicts. It was then up to the penal authorities to identify them.

Local populations were openly incorporated into the operation and regulation of colonial punishment. They could not claim ignorance about an individual's status when they had *godna* marks. In 1843, for instance, Rugbur Sing, a Native Commissioned Officer in the Madras Artillery was charged with helping Dhurmoo Tewarry to escape from Penang. It seems that Dhurmoo Tewarry had asked Rugbur Sing to employ him as his servant. Initially, Rugbur Sing refused, his deposition translated thus: 'I told him that he appeared to be one of the convicts of the Island from his being branded with marks on his forehead and that I could not under those circumstances take him with me.' Dhurmoo Tewarry then produced a piece of paper, which he claimed was a certificate of freedom. Rugbur Sing took the man with him, protesting after his arrest: 'if I have been betrayed to error, it was inadvertintly [*sic*] and not wilfully'. Rugur Sing was reprimanded; Dhurmoo Tewarry rapidly returned to the Straits Settlements.[102]

Local communities were also actively encouraged to participate in the recapture of escaped convicts. Rewards were routinely awarded if they brought in 'wanted men' whose *godna* marks made their convict status obvious. Indeed, when convicts escaped their descriptive rolls were copied to the authorities in India for distribution to the police and circulation in their home districts, to which it was thought they would return. These notices always alluded to convicts' *godna* marks, if the process had been performed.[103] As Subrattee, who escaped from a road gang in the Tenasserim Provinces in 1848 put it in his deposition: 'I met a Patan [*pathan*] who spoke to me and said I was a runaway convict, he knew from the mark on my forehead I told him I was not – he said he knew I was and gave me in charge of the head man of the Town'.[104] A not insubstantial twenty-five rupee reward was issued to the authorities there.[105]

The administrators of the penal settlements were unequivocal about the importance of *godna*. When the penal settlement at Mauritius began to receive Bombay convicts after 1830, there was an explosion in convict desertion on the island, for the Bombay Presidency never adopted the practice of *godna*. William Staveley, head of the Convict Department, wrote that the fact that these convicts were not marked with *godna* on the forehead meant that convict absconders (*maroons*) were able to elude capture by blending in with the free population.[106] Difficulties in identifying them were compounded by the fact that no descriptive rolls had accompanied the Bombay convicts sent to the island before 1831.[107] As indentured labour migration to the island accelerated during the 1830s and 1840s, convict absconders found it easier to pass themselves off as free. One notorious *maroon* called Sheik Adam was found living on a sugar plantation, where a M. Béchard employed him as a servant. The Mauritian Chief of Police, J. Finniss, lamented: 'planters ought to ascertain who persons really are before they take them into their service.'[108] Another Bombay convict (Antonio) was discovered by chance ten years after his escape in the Immigration Depot using the name Ramasamy on his indentured immigrant ticket.[109] A third absconder was employed as a free labourer for nine years. His employer – M. Ravallon – maintained that he did not know the man was a convict.[110]

In 1837, the Acting Resident Councillor of Singapore requested that only marked convicts be transported to the penal settlement there, as they found it much more difficult to escape.[111] The lack of indelible markings on Bombay convicts made it impossible to distinguish them from free Indian settlers, which had real implications for the maintenance of penal discipline. In 1843, Governor S.G. Bonham tried to encourage the government to adopt *godna*, writing that brands on the forehead – 'however slight' – were both a deterrent against escape and a useful means of recapturing convicts. A mark on the forehead was the only way in which local Malays could distinguish convicts from free Indians or other settlers.[112] Nevertheless, the Bombay government consistently refused to inflict *godna* on life prisoners convicted in the presidency.[113] We shall return to the reasons why in a moment. First, I would like to discuss convicts' experiences of *godna*, and the ways in which they resisted the infliction or display of their penal tattoos.

Resisting *Godna*

As we have seen, Regulation XVII of 1817 prohibited the infliction of *godna* on term prisoners, directing that in future only life prisoners should be marked with a penal tattoo. It also made a parallel observation about convicts' efforts to remove penal tattoos. It counselled: 'The operation is to be carried out early in the day and the magistrate will adopt precautions to prevent the convicts defacing the inscription in the course of the day. If the inscription becomes defaced, the magistrate shall direct it to be re-done.'[114] The *Nizamat Adalat* drew further attention to the issue of illegibility later on in 1836, suggesting that district jails did not always carry the regulations into effect and that convicts continued to remove their inscriptions.[115] An 1842 Circular attempting to tighten up practices raised the same concerns.[116] It was much easier for prison guards to keep watch over newly tattooed convicts during the day, and prevent them from altering the marks. It was more difficult to take such preventative measures after dark. Nevertheless, some prisoners succeeded in persuading tattooists not to perform *godna* in whole or in part. Others altered or lightened the marks once the process had been carried out. Such resistance to the ordering of the convict body impacted on colonial surveillance practices in the jails and penal settlements. Not only did convicts render their bodies individually illegible, but also they prevented their recognition as part of a criminalized social body.

Several convict rolls record the presence of only 'slight marks of godna'. This was the case for Urjaon, sentenced to transportation in Bundelkhand, and shipped to Mauritius in 1815.[117] The rolls describe the marks of four men transported from Midnapur to Penang in 1821 in the same way – Bheem Lodha, Seertram Foujdar, Gobind Muktee and Koocheel Mundul.[118] Either the operation had not been performed according to colonial regulations, or the convicts had successfully faded their marks. Convict Bhoruttee, transported from Midnapur to Mauritius at the end of 1816 was also described as having 'light marks of small godna'.[119] As we have seen, the size of *godna* markings varied from convict to convict, due to regional diversity in the types of inscriptions made – and during this period Midnapur convicts were often marked with 'life imprisonment' alone. However, it is significant that no other Midnapur convicts had their marks described as small. This description possibly signifies convict participation in the production of his penal tattoo. The authorities certainly recognized convicts' capabilities in this respect.

The 1842 Bengal Circular noted that *godna* was often performed 'in a very imperfect manner'. This was a particular problem when tattooists were confronted with 'influential prisoners', producing marks so light that they were either difficult to see or easy to efface. It underlined the need to inscribe *godna* 'upon the forehead of the convict <u>immediately above the eye-brows</u> in a straight line', and made local magistrates personally responsible for it.[120] The circular did not elaborate on who the 'influential' inmates it referred to were, but in all probability they were prisoners of rank or high caste, violent or dangerous offenders, or those in possession of material resources. Tattooists might have been concerned about the consequences of marking particular prisoners. They necessarily had extremely close physical contact with them and were potentially open to violent resistance against the procedure. Indeed, it is perhaps this that made branding – a much quicker alternative– an attractive option to tattooing to jail administrators. Tattooists could also have been unwilling to participate in the inversion of social hierarchies that the *godna* procedure frequently implied. Of course prisoners with money could offer to pay tattooists to produce especially feint or small marks. Is this what convict Beng, transported to Penang in 1817 with a 'different crime marked on the forehead in the Bengallee character', had done, or had there been a genuine mistake?[121] Jail manager overseers (*darogahs*) were complicit in reproducing social hierarchies within prisons. As the 1838 Prison Discipline Committee reported, in putting prisoners to work they looked to their caste, rank or ability to pay for favours.[122] The secretary of the Bengal Medical Board at the time, James Hutchinson, despaired of the possibility of reform until they were replaced.[123]

It is hardly surprising that some convicts made efforts either to prevent the infliction of these dramatically visible penal marks or to remove or conceal them once the operation had been performed. *Godna* delineated and fixed individual identities only in relation to criminal convictions. There is no evidence that *godna* marks became an 'honoury restraint', as was the case with fetters, neck chains and handcuffs. According to the Superintendent of Alipur Jail, John Eliot, writing in 1815, convicts proudly displayed them as proof of resistance to authority – and resistance to hard labour, which heavily chained prisoners were unable to perform.[124] In contrast, convicts appear to have made every effort to deface or hide their *godna* inscriptions. They were permanent marks, and did not signify involvement in anti-colonial resistance, except in the very broadest sense.[125] Unlike chains, which performed a dual role in both sustaining and confounding the goals of prison management, penal tattoos were not desirable as a means to evade labour. Convict officials like J.F.A. McNair (Comptroller-General of Convicts Straits Settlements) were in no doubt about how convicts viewed *godna* – as a stigma.[126] At the end of the nineteenth century, the writer on crime in India, H.L. Adam, constructed it in the same way: 'It constituted a very grave disability to the culprit, who became a social outcast for all time, shunned by all but his own criminal class.'[127] Though subalterns do not speak to this point, official descriptions of their marks (or their erasure) do.

It is difficult to say precisely how convicts spoiled their tattoos, but we know that they did. The jail clerk describing Nubba, who was transported to Mauritius in 1815, for instance, wrote 'the Bengally characters written with the Godena on his forehead is nearly effaced'.[128] The absence of penal marks assisted convicts in escape bids, though of course it did not completely preclude their recapture. Convict Rampershaud Nye *alias* Greedhur Manna was sentenced for returning from transportation in 1816, and reshipped to Mauritius. Rampershaud Nye's descriptive roll records:

'the Godena marks were removed by him'. The marks do not appear to have been reinscribed before Rampershaud Nye's retransportation.[129] Caustic preparations were used to remove tattoos as long ago as imperial Roman times.[130] In the 1830s, officials claimed that prisoners working in road gangs used roots, leaves and fruits to induce ulcers, swelling and inflammation;[131] it is not unlikely they used similar preparations on their tattoos. Lyon's 1889 *Medical Jurisprudence for India* later noted that tattoos faded if a non-carbonaceous pigment was used, or they could be removed by escharotics, though this left a scar.[132]

It is interesting that so few nineteenth-century narrative accounts of Indian convicts mention their penal tattoos. It is possible that observers did not wish to draw attention to what, as we shall see, even some officials in India referred to as a 'barbarous' practice. Even transportation itself was often considered distasteful; most contemporaries writing of visits to or residence in South East Asia and Mauritius did not mention the convicts amongst their otherwise picturesque descriptions at all. However, it may be that when they did note their presence, they did not write about *godna* marks because they could not see them. McNair wrote that convicts often wore turbans low over the forehead to conceal their marks.[133] Women might have covered their faces too. Contemporary writers most commonly noted the convicts' fetters; the one exception to this was a Mrs Bartrum, who lived in Mauritius between 1820 and 1827. She wrote of their 'dirty white, or dusky red' turbans.[134] As we shall see in our discussion of convict dress (Chapter 4), surviving pictorial and written evidence suggests that most transportation convicts wore turbans during the second half of the nineteenth century. Was this also the case during the period that *godna* regulations were in force? Several contemporary drawings of convicts suggest that it was. Marryat's picture of a tattooed convict is a case in point (Figure 2.1), as are Colesworthy Grant's sketch (Figure 2.2) and J.S. Paton's representation (Figure 2.3). However, one should bear in mind that inclusion of turbans in the pictures served a second purpose: the orientalization of the images. A fourth picture, a watercolour of convicts on Ramree Island in Kyaukpyu (Arakan), also shows convicts wearing turbans, though the figures are too distant to draw any conclusions about whether they concealed *godna* marks (Figure 2.4).

Besides avoiding, removing or concealing *godna* marks, transported convicts sometimes used different names to those recorded in the descriptive rolls and, by implication, often inscribed on their foreheads. There is considerable space for more research into the development of (and resistance to) colonial naming practices in nineteenth-century India. A useful starting point would be Scott, Teharanian and Mathias' theorization

Figure 2.4 'Arracan [Arakan] 14th Febry [1849] Kyook Phoo [Kyaukpyu] Ghat & Prisoners Carrying Water in Buckets, Isle of Ramree'. Watercolour by Clementina Benthall. (Courtesy of Centre of South Asian Studies, University of Cambridge, Benthall Papers)

of the development of permanent patronyms (surnames) as a mode of determining identity, cultural affiliation and history. According to them, surnames were part of knowledge-power systems that help create or destroy communities, and were thus integral to the development of modern nation-states.[135] It is clear that the textualization of the Indian criminal was at least partly necessitated by the instability and transience of individual names. Problems of transliteration and prisoners' common use of multiple names (or *aliases*) continued to confound colonial penal practice. Despite his tattoo, the hapless 'Wodoo', for instance, was unidentifiable. Many other tattooed convicts could be only tenuously linked to their criminal records, as when a few years after its establishment the first Andaman Islands settlement was abandoned. The surviving convicts were transferred to Penang, where they immediately petitioned for release. The authorities were at a loss to identify them; the convicts claimed that the list of names that had accompanied them was full of mistakes. The Penang authorities thus forwarded a second list to their counterparts in Calcutta, as pronounced by the convicts themselves.[136]

Gendering the Penal Tattoo

I would now like to turn to a discussion of the penal tattooing of women under colonial *godna* regulations. In general terms, the East India Company punished female offenders both like and unlike pre-colonial regimes. Women faced some punishments previously accorded only to men. For example, women could be executed for wilful murder, a departure from pre-colonial practice in parts of India.[137] Yet the Company also inflicted gendered modes of punishment for female offenders. It prohibited the flogging of women in 1825 on the grounds of 'delicacy and humanity'.[138] After 1839 female prisoners in Bengal were not fettered; the circular issued by the *Faujdari Adalat* on the matter noted that it was, 'for obvious reasons, improper'.[139] It seems curious, then, that women sentenced to transportation for life did not escape the punishment of *godna*. In this section, I would like to untangle some of the complexities of *godna* as a gendered mark.

Women made up a small proportion of prisoners. Relatively few women were jailed or transported overseas. Between 1815 and 1837, just six women were shipped to Mauritius, making up half of 1 per cent of the total number of convicts.[140] In 1824, there were just 24 women out of 1,469 convicts in Prince of Wales Island.[141] The transportation of women seems to have accelerated during the 1840s, for reasons that are not absolutely clear. It may have been related to colonial efforts to monitor and control the incidence of infanticide.[142] It was also possibly a solution to dividing female term from female life prisoners, one of the principal recommendations of the 1838 Prison Discipline Report. By the early 1840s, to the chagrin of the *Faujdari Adalat*, not a single jail in Bengal separated them.[143] Yet the number of female transportees never rose above 10 per cent of the total, probably because women did not commonly commit the types of crimes that were given a life sentence (notably dacoity or murder), and therefore avoided transportation in large numbers. Towards the end of the period of transportation to South East Asia, there were 191 women out of a total of 2,077 convicts (9 per cent) in the Straits Settlements.[144] Women made up a similar proportion of the total in the Andaman Islands during the second half of the century.[145]

In the years leading up to the middle of the nineteenth century, jails were increasingly transformed into productive spaces. Female prisoners were put to work on indoor labour (notably the hand-mill to grind wheat, but also stone-breaking, spinning and weaving),[146] as an alternative to those forms of hard labour (outdoor work such as road-building or land clearance) considered suitable for men. By the time the Prison Discipline Committee published its findings, this was the case in most mainland jails.[147] In the penal settlements too, convict women were usually put to labour 'suited to their sex'. Like in mainland jails they worked indoors, their tasks including the grinding of paddy and domestic chores like sweeping and cleaning the convict lines.[148] I would argue that this division of penal servitude engendered a sharp distinction between 'public' and 'private' productive space. This reflected bourgeois aspirations about the appropriate sexual division of labour, and the visibility of women in work, rather than *necessarily* replicating pre-existing productive spheres.

Postcolonial analyses have argued that one of the ways that the colonial state sought to legitimize itself was through a civilizing mission that prevented what it saw as cultural barbarities like thuggee or *sati* (widow self-immolation).[149] As Sen shows, during the late nineteenth century its assumption of the role of protector of apparent Indian victims extended to the female jail.[150] Yet during the first half of the century there is no evidence that the authorities used the discretion accorded to them in the regulations to avoid tattooing women. Convict indents show that female convicts were inscribed with identical *godna* marks to men, and the language, content and positioning of their inscriptions followed the patterns noted above.[151] The sole exception to this was a handful of women convicted of thuggee in Agra and shipped to Penang. They were inscribed on the forehead only, and not the cheeks, hands, arms or shoulders as well.[152]

Abby M. Schrader writes that in eighteenth-century Russia, the authorities refused to brand women. This was partly because they believed (erroneously) that they rarely escaped. Their main concern was, however, that men would refuse to marry them, compromising the goal of family formation amongst exiles.[153] In contrast, Indian women barely ever absconded. In one rare instance the escape involved a woman who had been released on security for seven years.[154] British officials too promoted marriage amongst convicts in the penal settlements. Fears about the sexual desirability of Indian convict women did not emerge though, and women were made subject to *godna*. Why was this? I think the answer partly lies in the fact that convict women were twice removed from the public gaze – transported to overseas penal settlements and then kept at indoor labour. This gendering of penal space explains their exemption from public displays of flogging and hard labour, but their subjection to *godna*, which must have been seen only rarely, especially if women veiled the inscriptions. Women were usually released early if they got married; finding a partner was not difficult in the grossly gender imbalanced penal colonies. At this point too the covering of the face was socially sanctioned, but *godna* marks were undoubtedly a useful means of verifying the identity of ex-convicts who had served only limited terms.

It is also worth noting that in marked contrast to the circulating discourses of abolitionists outraged by the corporal punishment of slave women in the West Indies,[155] convict women did not elicit sympathy. Undoubtedly, this was related to the fact of their conviction and suspicions about their promiscuity. As Philippa Levine has argued, 'orientalist sociology' created and consolidated colonized sexualities distinguishable from middle-class British 'norms'.[156] I would argue that discourses about hereditary crime fused with these colonized sexualities in representing convict women primarily in relation to their reproductive capacity. On a visit to Arakan in 1847, Clementina Benthall (wife of district judge Edward) wrote of female convicts as 'horrid creatures'.[157] The Earl of Elgin (later Viceroy of India) noted his encounter with convict women in 1857 Singapore: 'I cannot say that their appearance made me envy the [male] convicts much'.[158] In 1846 the Commissioner of the Tenasserim Provinces requested that six thug women be sent back to India. He wrote: 'If no other evil occurs, it seems likely that a brood of thugs may 'ere long be hatched, who may hereafter do incalculable harm in this Province, where thuggee is wholly unknown.'[159] This was part of the transformation of female prisoners into what Sen calls 'the agents of moral corruption'.[160] Indian elites too were indifferent about female convicts. As Mary Carpenter noted in 1869, there were no philanthropic efforts on behalf of female prisoners at all.[161]

Given that decorative tattooing was most strongly associated with women, I would also contend that *godna* did not simply subvert social hierarchies, but might also be seen as part of a more general emasculation of Indian society.[162] Indeed, as Mrinalini Sinha has argued, histories of masculinity and effeminacy in the subcontinent were intertwined with colonial power relations. The gendering of India was mutually constituted by other colonial categories – notably race, caste and class – in which the emergent Indian middle class also had a stake.[163] In its inscription of convict men and women, penal tattooing was part of the making of new lines of attachment between colonial ideologies of gender, punishment and the public/private spheres. Chain gangs and public flogging too were theatrical performances in which convicts were demeaned and emasculated during the consolidation of colonial power relations.[164] It is interesting that most early-nineteenth-century travel writing constructs male convicts in a similar way to the 'effeminate Bengali' during the later period. The human agency that characterized prisoners' experiences of incarceration and transportation (and to a large degree drove penal reform) was rarely mentioned. Male convicts were instead most commonly described as orderly, well behaved, contented and nonchalant.[165]

'A Practice so Barbarous': the Abolition of *Godna*

Though *godna* was practised in the Bengal and Madras presidencies, the Bombay authorities never adopted it. It was not included in the 1827

Bombay Code, and no offenders in the Bombay Presidency were ever tattooed or branded. Though local governments in penal settlements like Mauritius complained bitterly about the implications of this for convict management, the Bombay authorities considered the issue seriously in 1842 only after the Governor of the Straits Settlements, S.G. Bonham, asked the presidency to consider introducing it. Bonham was in broad agreement with the Mauritian authorities, writing that however slight the marks on the forehead were, they prevented escapes and eased the recapture of convicts.[166] The Bombay government stood firm on the issue, however, and refused to adopt *godna* regulations. Despite the sentiments expressed in the penal settlements, the Governor of Bombay wrote that he did not believe that it was a useful means of recognizing escaped convicts.[167]

By 1844, Bonham's request came to the attention of the Government of India. It agreed that *godna* should not be extended to the Bombay Presidency. Handwritten judicial proceedings records reveal the rationale: 'we do not recommend the extension of this practice so barbarous even in the case of transportation for life'. It urged the adoption of 'less objectionable measures', of what kind it did not say, to prevent convict escapes.[168] 'So barbarous' was left out of the version of the document of proceedings eventually sent to the Bombay government, probably to avoid direct criticisms of penal practices elsewhere in India.[169] Predictably, the Governor of Bombay agreed with its recommendation.[170]

Within the Bombay Presidency, however, there was more disagreement on the issue than this correspondence suggests. The debate on *godna* re-emerged in 1847 after a man calling himself Bappoo bin Gunnoo was arrested on suspicion of being the escaped convict Shrawun Sokacha. He had been one of sixty-two Bombay convicts who had risen against their guards whilst under sentence of transportation to Aden. The man was brought to trial on the charge of escaping from transportation, a capital offence, but his physical appearance did not seem to match that recorded in the original ship indent. As he was a Bombay convict, he had no *godna* mark. His identity could not, therefore, be established and he was acquitted.[171] After the trial, the Session Judge recommended that in future all convicts should be indelibly marked, so that convicts could be more easily recognized. This would avoid cases of mistaken identity. He wrote: 'an escaped convict would have neither home nor safety.'[172] Two other judges agreed.[173] The Bombay superior criminal court (*Sadar Faujdari Adalat*) subsequently recommended that convicts should be 'stamped' with a letter on the shoulder or back, rather than tattooed on the forehead. This would allow the *verification* of criminal identity, but would not constitute a permanent *display* of it, and convicts would be able to return to society. If marked on the forehead, any good conduct on their part would in contrast be 'of comparatively little value'.[174] The Governor of Bombay, however, did not agree and, given the Government of India's earlier recommendations, refused to forward the draft act to them.[175]

The Government of India then decided that if the measure was not extended to Bombay it ought to be abolished in Bengal – but that the two presidencies had to agree on the matter.[176] In practice, the Bengal presidency had little choice in its course of action, and a year later, *godna* was abolished across East India Company territories. Public exposure (*tashir*) was also banned.[177] Ironically, the Bombay authorities were trenchant in their resistance to the abolition of *tashir*, a pre-colonial form of punishment that they had reworked. They defended it on the grounds that it constituted the disgrace that community values did not. The Register of the *Sadar Faujdari Adalat*, M. Larkin, wrote that public disgrace was 'well suited to the character of the natives of India'. Though it was rarely used, it stigmatized particular criminal acts without resorting to corporal punishment or imprisonment.[178] One of the judges of the court added that it was a deterrent that produced a 'salutary effect'.[179] The Bombay government much regretted its abolition.[180] Some officials in Bengal were equally disconcerted by the abolition of *godna*. The Superintendent of Alipur Jail, R.H. Mytton, responded to the publication of the draft Act to abolish *godna* with the suggestion that it should exclude life convicts: 'it undoubtedly affords a very great security against escape and assistance in reapprehension'.[181]

The reason for the abolition of *godna* was changing colonial sensibilities about marking prisoners with indelible inscriptions. It is worth noting that a parallel debate was taking place over the merits of the punishment of flogging, which left permanent welt marks on the offender's back – what Singha describes as 'a visible mark of the criminal process'.[182] He thus became a marked man (*daghi*), which prevented his return to honest labour.[183] In the same way, if tattooed or branded on the forehead, pardoned and/or released convicts could still be recognized as criminals, with the stigma that implied. *Godna* clashed with broader claims about colonialism as a 'civilizing' process. An 1851 letter to *The Times* talked about the branding of military deserters on the following terms, though it has broader relevance to the *godna* debate in seeking to redraw the lines of attachment between 'enlightened' and 'barbaric' penal practices: 'I ask whether we have any moral right to brand a fellow creature, and whether this same branding does not place us English on a par with the Asiatic who resorts to chopping off a hand, slicing off a nose, or shaving off an ear.'[184]

H.L. Adam, who wrote about crime and punishment in India in the early twentieth century, mentioned *godna*, but carefully avoided any reference to it as a colonial practice: 'At one time, many years ago, *they* used to brand criminals in India on the forehead, so that, when once convicted, they carried the evidence of their crime with them to the grave . . . Eventually the mischievous and wholly unjust custom *was* abolished, and should never have been instituted.'[185]

Once *godna* was off the statute books, penal administrators looked to the development of different penal signs. They continued to record the peculiarities *of* the individual body and developed what we might term 'visual tags' to be worn *on* it. We shall consider those penal displays in our analysis of prison dress (Chapter 4). In the mean time, I want to examine the ways in which colonial ethnographers and administrators tried to use decorative tattoos as a means of fixing individual and collective identities. At one level, tattoos were permanent marks and so useful as a means of identification. At another, they fed into ideas about the nature and significance of broader Indian social categories like 'race' and 'caste'. Colonial administrators used the body – particularly the female body – to anchor individuals to these categories, especially those that implied supposedly hereditary criminal tendencies.

Notes

1. IOR P/141/20 (9 Jan. 1838): J.H. Patton, Superintendent Alipur Jail, to Halliday, 26 Dec. 1837.
2. IOR P/141/23 (10 Apr. 1838): H. Chamier, Chief Secretary to Government Madras, to Halliday, 23 Mar. 1838, enclosing H. Bushby, Criminal Judge Bellary, to W. Douglas, Register *Faujdari Adalat* [criminal court], 26 Feb. 1838.
3. IOR P/141/25 (19 June 1838): Patton to Halliday, 29 May 1838.
4. IOR P/141/23 (10 Apr. 1838): Bushby to Douglas, 26 Feb. 1838.
5. Singha, 'Settle, Mobilize, Verify', 167.
6. *Godna*: to prick, to puncture, to dot, to mark the skin with dots or to tattoo. See Duncan Forbes, *A Smaller Hindustani and English Dictionary* (W.H. Allen, 1862); R.C. Pathak, *Bhargava's Standard Illustrated Dictionary of the Hindi Language* (Chowk, 1962), 300; John T. Platts, *A Dictionary of Urdu, Classical Hindi, and English, vol. II* (W.H. Allen, 1889), 923. In Bengal, decorative tattooing was also

known as *ulki:* IOR MSS Eur E295/14A: 'Tattooing in Bengal', compiled from notes of E.G. Gait, ICS, at the time of the last census (henceforth Tattooing in Bengal).

7. Pathak, *Bhargava's Standard Illustrated Dictionary*, 300; Platts, *Dictionary*, 923.

8. Regulation IV, Section xi (1797): A regulation for making sundry alterations in and additions to Regulation IX 1793, 13 Mar. 1797, cited in IOR V/8/17: *Regulations Passed by the Governor-General in Council, 1796–1803, vol. II* (Court of Directors, 1828), 35; Regulation VII, Section xxxv (1803): A regulation for the establishment of a Court of Circuit for the trial of persons charged with crimes, in the Provinces ceded by the Nawab Vizier to the Honourable the East India Company, 24 Mar. 1803, cited in *Regulations Passed by the Governor-General in Council, vol. II*, 387.

9. On discretionary punishment, see Tapas Kumar Banerjee, *Background to Indian Criminal Law* (R. Cambray and Co., 1990), 58–62; Singha, *Despotism of Law*, 60–6.

10. Sukla Das, *Crime and Punishment in Ancient India (c. A.D. 300 to A.D. 1100)* (Abhinav, 1977), 64, 75.

11. N. Majumdar, *Justice and Police in Bengal, 1765–1793: A Study of the Nizamat in Decline* (Firma K.L. Mukhopadhyay, 1960), 333. On pre-colonial and early colonial law, see also Jorg Fisch, *Cheap Lives and Dear Limbs: The British Transformation of the Bengal Criminal Law, 1769–1817* (Franz Steiner Verlag, 1983); Sumit Guha, 'An Indian Penal Régime: Maharashtra in the Eighteenth Century', *Past and Present*, 147 (1995), 100–26.

12. Radhika Singha, 'The Privilege of Taking Life: Some "Anomalies" in the Law of Homicide in the Bengal Presidency', *Indian Economic and Social History Review*, 30, 2 (1993), 200.

13. IOR P/128/15 (17 Oct. 1794): Jonathan Duncan, Resident Banaras, to G.H. Barlow, Sub-secretary to Government Bengal, 27 Sept. 1794.

14. C.P. Jones, '*Stigma:* Tattooing and Branding in Graeco-Roman Antiquity', *Journal of Roman Studies*, 77 (1987), 141.

15. Richard J. Evans, *Tales from the German Underworld: Crime and Punishment in the Nineteenth Century* (Yale University Press, 1998), 20, 98.

16. Caplan, '"Speaking Scars"', 115.

17. James Bradley and Hamish Maxwell-Stewart, '"Behold the Man": Power, Observation and the Tattooed Convict', *Australian Studies*, 12, 1 (1997), 81. Bradley has subsequently established that the 'D' was, in fact, *tattooed* on soldiers' bodies (personal communication).

18. For a detailed account of penal branding in Imperial Russia and the Soviet Union, see Abby M. Schrader, 'Branding the Other/Tattooing the Self: Bodily Inscription among Convicts in Russia and the Soviet Union', in Jane Caplan (ed.), *Written on the Body: The Tattoo in European and North American History* (Reaktion, 2000), 174–92; Abby M. Schrader, *Languages of the Lash: Corporal Punishment and Identity in Imperial Russia* (Northern Illinois University Press, 2002), ch. 4.

19. When the slaves 'Sam' and 'Tom' ran away from their master in Bengal in 1784, for instance, the advertisement calling for their capture noted that their right arms were marked just above the elbow – away from normal view, but visible enough for easy identification – with the initials of their master, J.H. Valentin Dubois. See W.S. Seton-Karr, *Selections from Calcutta Gazettes, vol. I* (Military Orphan Press, 1864), 66. Indrani Chatterjee also notes that in the 1840s an Indian slave owner branded her nurse maid (*ayah*) with the word 'liar' on her forehead in English, in what appears to be the private adoption of old public penal practice: 'Colouring Subalternity: Slaves, Concubines and Social Orphans in Early Colonial India', in Gautam Bhadra, Gyan Prakash and Susie Tharu (eds), *Subaltern Studies X: Writings on South Asian History and Society* (Oxford University Press, 1999), 50–1 (n. 5). See also Indrani Chatterjee, *Gender, Slavery and Law in Colonial India* (Oxford University Press, 1999), 3 (n. 11).

20. Hilary McD. Beckles, 'Social and Political Control in the Slave Society', in Franklin W. Knight (ed.), *General History of the Caribbean, vol. III: The Slave Societies of the Caribbean* (Macmillan, 1997), 201.

21. Maroon slave communities – perceived to pose a serious threat to 'life, limb and property' – emerged shortly after the French colonized the island that they named Ile de France. Marronage was thus countered with extreme violence. Richard B. Allen, *Slaves, Freedmen, and Indentured Laborers in Colonial Mauritius* (Cambridge University Press, 1999), 35–54, and 'Marronage and the Maintenance of Public Order in Mauritius, 1721–1835', *Slavery and Abolition*, 4, 3 (1993), 214–15.

22. Michael Craton, 'Forms of Resistance to Slavery', in Knight (ed.), *General History of the Caribbean, vol. III*, 239.

23. Singha, *Despotism of Law*, 101–2.

24. Regulation IV, Section xi (1797).

25. Singha, 'Settle, Mobilize, Verify', 167.

26. Regulation VII, Section xxxv (1803).

27. Regulation XVII, Section iii (1797): A regulation for authorizing the Courts of Circuit to inflict a perpetual Stigma, in certain cases, upon witnesses convicted of wilful and corrupt perjury, 1 Dec. 1797, cited in *Regulations passed by the Governor-General in Council, vol. II*, 72.

28. *Ibid.*

29. Regulation II, Section iii (1803): A regulation to provide more effectually for the punishment of perjury, subornation of perjury, and forgery, 29 Jan. 1803, cited in IOR V/8/17: *Regulations Passed by the Governor-General in Council, 1796–1803, vol. III* (Court of Directors, 1828), 72.

30. Singha, *Despotism of Law*, 245–6.

31. Singha, 'Settle, Mobilize, Verify', 168.

32. *Ibid.*, 168 (n. 99).

33. Parliamentary Papers, 1819 (583) XIII. 347: Regulation XVII, Section xii (1817): A regulation to provide for the more effectual administration of criminal justice in certain cases, 16 Sept. 1817.

34. Regulation VII, Sections xxxv and xl (1802), cited in *Regulations Passed by the Governor-General in Council, vol. III*, 228. 'Regulations for the establishment of the new Courts of Adawlut' are at IOR P/321/93 (1 Jan. 1802). See also IOR P/403/19 (21 June 1843): J.F. Thomas, Acting Chief Secretary to Government Madras, to F.J. Halliday, Assistant Secretary to the Government of India, 30 Mar. 1843.

35. IOR V/8/27: Fort St George Regulations, 1804–1814: Regulation VI, Section iii (1811).

36. See, for example, IOR P/142/47 (22 Apr. 1846): E.J. Pearson, Officiating Magistrate Sylhet, to A. Turnbull, Under-Secretary to Government Bengal, 26 Mar. 1846.

37. William Sleeman (officer in charge of the anti-thug campaign), cited in Woerkens, *Strangled Traveler*, 86.

38. IOR P/141/3 (13 Dec. 1836): Circular to the Magistrates and Joint Magistrates in the Lower Provinces, 13 Dec. 1836.

39. IOR P/142/47 (29 Apr. 1846): Mytton to Turnbull, 26 Apr. 1846.

40. IOR P/403/19 (21 June 1843): Circular Orders of the Court of *Faujdari Adalat* (Madras), 20 Feb. 1823.

41. IOR P/141/45 (5 May 1840): H. Hawkins, Register *Nizamat Adalat* [superior criminal court], to Halliday, 18 Apr. 1840, enclosing J.R. Ousley, Agent to the Governor-General and Commander South West Frontier (Chota Nagpur), to Hawkins, 2 Apr. 1840.

42. On Indian prisoner resistance, see Arnold, 'Colonial Prison', 148–87; Singha, *Despotism of Law*, 272–82; Anand A. Yang, 'Disciplining

"Natives": Prisons and Prisoners in Early Nineteenth Century India',
South Asia, 10, 2 (1987), 29–45; Anand A. Yang, 'The Lotah Emeutes
of 1855: Caste, Religion and Prisons in North India in the Early
Nineteenth Century', in James H. Mills and Satadru Sen (eds),
*Confronting the Body: The Politics of Physicality in Colonial and
Post-Colonial India* (Anthem, 2003), 102–17.

43. Singha, 'Settle, Mobilize, Verify', 166 (n. 90), 168.
44. Arnold, 'Colonial Prison', 169–75.
45. Regulation XVII (1817).
46. IOR P/403/19 (21 June 1843): Circular Orders of the Court of
Faujdari Adalat (Madras), 29 May 1816.
47. TNSA Judicial vol. 330B: G. Bird, Criminal Judge Kannur, to
Chamier, 5 Aug. 1837; Governor's Minute, n.d.
48. IOR P/140/54 (7 Mar. 1835): H. Rose, Officiating Magistrate
Shahjahanpur, to A. Campbell, Commission of Circuit Bareilly, 1 Dec.
1834; Circular to the Several Magistrates and Joint Magistrates of the
Lower Provinces, 6 Feb. 1835.
49. Some Bengali examples of Mauritian transportees can be found in the
ship indents at IOR P/132/8 (11 Sept. 1815): List of 115 convicts *per
Lady Barlow*, 10 Sept. 1815; IOR P/132/21 (22 Mar. 1816): List of
eleven convicts *per Union*, 19 Mar. 1816; IOR P/132/31 (20 Sept.
1816): List of forty convicts *per Union*, 15 Sept. 1816; IOR P/133/20
(27 Jan. 1818): List of thirty-one convicts *per Anna Robertson*, 27 Jan.
1818. For Devanagri in the Mauritian indents see IOR P/132/8 (13
Sept. 1815): Continuation of the list of convicts transferred from the
Lady Barlow to the *Helen*, 10 Sept. 1815; IOR P/132/65 (14 Oct.
1817): List of twenty-three convicts *per Magnet*, 14 Oct. 1817. For
similar patterns amongst Penang transportees see IOR P/133/26
(19 May 1818): List of thirty convicts *per Auspicious*, 10 May 1818;
P/134/33 (1 Dec. 1820): List of forty convicts *per Mary*, 26 Nov. 1820;
P/134/58 (31 Aug. 1821): List of forty convicts *per Minerva*, 24 Aug.
1821; P/135/37 (8 Nov. 1822): List of forty convicts *per Hero of
Malown*, 7 Nov. 1822.
50. See, for example, IOR P/142/62 (10 Mar. 1847): Statement of a
prisoner [Shiree-aung] transported from Akyab Jail [Arakan] to Alipur
Jail, 22 Oct. 1846.
51. See, for example, IOR P/132/31 (20 Sept. 1816): List of forty convicts
to Mauritius *per Union*, 15 Sept. 1816 (nos 26–40); IOR P/132/64
(25 Apr. 1817): List of thirty-two convicts to Mauritius *per Union*, 21
Apr. 1817 (nos 14–32).
52. See, for example, 'jeebanabhodee kyde' [*ji banna boddh qaid*] and
'daimal hubbus' [*damul habas*], (life imprisonment) at IOR 142/40

(10 Dec. 1845): List of ten convicts sentenced to imprisonment who have petitioned for transportation, now embarked on the *Enterprize* for Moulmein, 10 Dec. 1845; IOR P/142/35 (13 Aug. 1845): List of twenty-nine convicts to Arakan *per Enterprize*, 6 Aug. 1845; P/142/38 (22 Oct. 1845): List of thirty-four convicts to Moulmein *per Tenasserim*, 9 Oct. 1845.

53. See, for example, IOR P/142/39 (19 Nov. 1845): List of thirty-four convicts to Moulmein *per Enterprize*, 10 Nov. 1845; IOR P/133/31 (28 Aug. 1818): List of thirty convicts to Bencoolen *per Anna*, 17 Apr. 1818; IOR P/142/30 (2 Apr. 1845): List of fifty-six convicts to Arakan *per Irawaddy*, 28 Mar. 1845; IOR P/142/39 (12 Nov. 1845): List of thirty-four convicts to Moulmein *per Enterprize*, 10 Nov. 1845; IOR P/142/30 (2 Apr. 1845): List of fifty-six convicts to Arakan *per Irawaddy*, 28 Mar. 1845.

54. *Report of the Committee on Prison Discipline*, app. 4, 250.

55. IOR P/403/19 (21 June 1843): Circular Orders of the Court of *Faujdari Adalat* (Madras), 1 May 1815.

56. IOR P/141/3 (13 Dec. 1836): Circular to the Magistrates and Joint Magistrates in the Lower Provinces, 13 Dec. 1836.

57. For an example of the certificate, see IOR P/143/5 (4 Aug. 1847): A statement of convicts sentenced to transportation beyond seas for life despatched on 16 July 1847 to the Jail at Alipore from the Jail of Lohardugga [Lohardaga] Division, under Regulation XIII (1833) (convicts Duhroo and Beersa).

58. Edgar Thurston, *Ethnographic Notes in Southern India* (Government Press, 1906), 381.

59. Marryat, *Borneo and the Indian Archipelago*, 214–15.

60. Regulation IV, Section xi (1797); Regulation VII, Section xxxv (1803).

61. IOR P/133/56 (12 Mar. 1819): List of forty convicts to Bencoolen *per Auspicious*, 28 Feb. 1819; P/143/14 (19 Jan. 1848): List of forty-seven convicts to Akyab *per Enterprize*, 10 Jan. 1848.

62. IOR P/142/15 (15 Apr. 1844): List of thirteen convicts to Arakan *per Amherst*, 3 Apr. 1844.

63. IOR P/130/20 (7 Aug. 1813): G.J. Siddons, Acting Resident Fort Marlborough, to G. Dowdeswell, Secretary to Government Bengal, 17 June 1813; TNSA Judicial vol. 463: Humble Statement of Jemadar Rugbur Sing, n.d. (Sept. 1843).

64. IOR P/141/20 (9 Jan. 1838): Patton to Halliday, 26 Dec. 1837.

65. IOR P/403/15 (31 Jan. 1843): S.G. Bonham, Governor Straits Settlements, to J.P. Willoughby, Secretary to Government Bombay, 12 Nov. 1842.

66. J.F.A. McNair, *Prisoners their Own Warders: A Record of the Convict Prison at Singapore in the Straits Settlements Established 1825, Discontinued 1873, together with a Cursory History of the Convict Establishments at Bencoolen, Penang and Malacca from the Year 1797* (Archibald Constable and Co., 1899), 12.

67. IOR P/141/66 (9 July 1842): Circular to Session Judges and Joint Magistrates in the Lower Provinces, 10 June 1842.

68. IOR P/143/30 (28 Feb. 1840): Act II to abolish the practice of branding and exposing convicts, 27 Jan. 1849. See also IOR P/404/40 (27 Sept. 1848): Extract from Home Department proceedings, 12 Aug. 1848: 'After the passing of this act it shall not be lawful for any court or magistrate within the territories under the government of the East India Company to order that any brand or indelible mark of any kind be made, or renewed on any part of the person of any convicted offender'.

69. Schrader, 'Branding the Other/Tattooing the Self', 180.

70. G.W. Swinton, Chief Secretary to Government Bengal, to F.C. Smith, Agent to Governor-General, Sagar and Narbada Territories, 4 Aug. 1830, cited in *Selected Records from the Central Provinces and Berar Secretariat Relating to the Suppression of Thuggee, 1829–1832* (Government Printing, 1939), 2. I thank David Arnold for this reference.

71. IOR P/400/65. (13 June 1833): W. Borthwick, Political Agent Narbada and Sagar, to W.H. Wathen, Session Judge Thane, 6 May 1833.

72. IOR P/141/27 (21 Aug. 1838): List of two thug convicts (who were recaptured at Arakan) now embarked for Moulmein *per Snipe*, 12 Aug. 1838 (convicts Gunnooah and Goplah, convicted in Sagar and Narbada, 3 Dec. 1833); P/141/48 (6 Oct. 1840): List of seventy convicts under sentence of transportation for life beyond sea, 1 Sept. 1840; IOR P/142/15 (22 Apr. 1844): List of ninety-eight Lucknow dacoit and thug convicts, to Moulmein *per Phlegethon*, 12 Apr. 1844; P/142/29 (5 Mar. 1845): List of forty-two convicts to Arakan *per Amherst*, 22 Feb. 1845.

73. See, for example, IOR P/142/29 (5 Mar. 1845): List of forty-two convicts to Arakan *per Amherst*, 22 Feb. 1845.

74. IOR P/142/56 (2 Dec. 1846): H.M. Durand, Commissioner Tenasserim Provinces, to Halliday, 14 Nov. 1846.

75. This image is reproduced in Clare Anderson, '*Godna*: Inscribing Indian Convicts in the Nineteenth Century', in Caplan (ed.), *Written on the Body*, 111.

76. Colesworthy Grant, *Rough Pencillings of a Rough Trip to Rangoon in 1846* (Thacker, Spink and Co., 1853), 23.

77. IOR P/142/15 (22 Apr. 1844): List of ninety-eight Lucknow dacoit and thug convicts, to Moulmein *per Phlegethon*, 12 Apr. 1844 (no. 91).

78. N. Barlow (ed.), *Charles Darwin's Diary of the Voyage of the H.M.S. 'Beagle'* (Cambridge University Press, 1933), 401–2; Patrick Beaton, *Creoles and Coolies; Or, Five Years in Mauritius* (James Nisbet, 1859), 178; M. Lowry Cole and S. Gwynn (eds), *Memoirs of Sir Lowry Cole* (Macmillan, 1934), 206. On representations of convicts in Mauritius, see Anderson, *Convicts in the Indian Ocean*, 7–10.

79. Leopold Von Orlich, *Travels in India, including Sinde and the Punjab, vol. II* (tr. H. Evans-Lloyd) (Longman, Brown, Green and Longmans, 1845), 163.

80. Philip Meadows Taylor, *The Story of my Life* (W. Blackwood and Sons, 1878), 57, 72.

81. Meadows Taylor wrote elsewhere of a thug approver named Ameer Ali who claimed to have been present at the murder of 719 people – presumably the man on whom his fictional character was based. An Officer in the Service of Highness the Nizam [Philip Meadows Taylor], 'On the Thugs', *New Monthly Magazine*, 38 (1833), 286.

82. Captain Philip Meadows Taylor, *Confessions of a Thug, vol. III* (Richard Bentley, 1839), 333–4.

83. The Bible: Genesis, ch. 4, verse 15. I thank James Bradley for pointing this out.

84. Meadows Taylor, 'On the Thugs', 287.

85. Meadows Taylor wrote elsewhere: 'The denomination of *thief* is one that is particularly obnoxious to them, and they never refrain from soliciting the erasure of the term, and the substitution of that of Thug, whenever it may occur in a paper regarding them, declaring that, so far from following so disgraceful a practice as theft, they scorn the name, and can prove themselves to be as honest and trustworthy as any one else, when occasion requires it': 'On the Thugs', 286.

86. Meadows Taylor, *Confessions of a Thug, vol. III*, 333. In 1835 the Company issued coins for the first time in the name of William and Mary, rather than under the name of the Mughal Emperor. I thank Radhika Singha for this information.

87. IOR P/140/73 (29 Dec. 1835): E.A. Blundell, Commissioner Tenasserim Provinces, to R.D. Mangles, Secretary to Government Bengal, 4 Dec. 1835.

88. IOR P/140/82 (26 July 1836): H. Murchison, Governor Penang to Mangles, 11 June 1836.

89. IOR P/142/44 (25 Feb. 1846): Durand to Halliday, 19 Dec. 1845.

90. IOR P/144/9 (15 Oct. 1851): A. Fytche, Principal Assistant Commissioner's Office Sandoway, to A.P. Phayre, Commissioner Arakan, 11 Sept. 1851.
91. TNSA Judicial (3 Jan. 1880), 11–12: C. Bernard, Officiating Secretary to Government of India, to Cecil Smith, Colonial Secretary Straits Settlements, 12 Nov. 1879.
92. IOR P/141/12 (2 May 1837): Blundell to Mangles, 25 Mar. 1837.
93. *Report of the Committee on Prison Discipline*, app. 4.
94. IOR P/141/39 (12 Sept. 1839): A. Bogle, Commissioner Arakan, to Halliday, 26 July 1839.
95. Sen, *Disciplining Punishment*, 53.
96. IOR P/142/62 (10 Mar. 1847): J.R. Colvin, Commissioner Tenasserim Provinces, to Halliday, 22 Feb. 1847.
97. IOR P/143/17 (12 Apr. 1848): Nominal Roll of Thugs on the Establishment of Convict Police in the Provincial Jail of Moulmein, 10 Mar. 1848.
98. *Ibid.*: H. Bower, Magistrate Moulmein Jail, to Colvin, 11 Mar. 1848.
99. *Ibid.*: Colvin to Halliday, 13 Mar. 1848.
100. IOR P/143/29 (7 Feb. 1849): Colvin to J.P. Grant, Secretary to Government Bengal, 3 Jan. 1849.
101. Peter Zinoman, *The Colonial Bastille: A History of Imprisonment in Vietnam 1862–1940* (University of California Press, 2001), 112.
102. TNSA Judicial vol. 454: A. Freese, Magistrate Chengalpattu, to E.F. Elliot, Chief Magistrate and Superintendent of Police Madras, 23 Aug. 1843; TNSA Judicial vol. 463: Freese to H.D. Phillips, Acting Register *Faujdari Adalat*, 29 Aug. 1843; *Ibid.*: Thomas to W.J. Butterworth, Governor Straits Settlements, 30 Oct. 1843; *Ibid.*: Humble Statement of Jemadar Rugbur Sing, n.d. (Sept. 1843).
103. See, for example, IOR P/129/37 (2 July 1807): Descriptive roll of thirteen convicts absconded from Prince of Wales Island 28 Apr. 1807, 9 May 1807; IOR P/129/45 (13 May 1808): T. Raffles, Secretary to Government Fort Cornwallis, to Dowdeswell, 31 Mar. 1808.
104. IOR P/143/16 (15 Mar. 1848): Deposition of Life Convict Subrattee, 30 Jan. 1848.
105. *Ibid.*: Bower to Colvin, 1 Feb. 1848.
106. MA Z2A62: W. Staveley, Head of Convict Department, to J. Finniss, Chief of Police, 13 Apr. 1831.
107. IOR P/400/49 (19 Oct. 1831): Staveley to G.A. Barry, Colonial Secretary Mauritius, 25 July 1831.
108. MA Z2A108: Finniss to G.F. Dick, Colonial Secretary Mauritius, 30 May and 5 June 1838. For more on Sheik Adam's notorious

convict career in Mauritius, see Anderson, *Convicts in the Indian Ocean*, 75–9.

109. MA RA1118: W.A. Rawstone, Surveyor-General, to C.J. Bayley, Secretary to Government Bengal, 10 May 1851.

110. MA Z2A236: Civil Commissary of Plaines Wilhems to A. Wilson, Acting Inspector-General of Police, 13 Apr. 1852.

111. IOR P/402/4 (2 Aug. 1837): R.F. Wingrove, Acting Resident Councillor Singapore, 24 Feb. 1837.

112. IOR P/403/15 (31 Jan. 1843): Bonham to Willoughby, 12 Nov. 1842.

113. IOR P/403/19 (21 June 1843): W. Escombe, Secretary to Government Bombay, to Bonham, 16 June 1843.

114. Regulation XVII, Section xii (1817).

115. IOR P/141/3 (13 Dec. 1836): Circular to the Magistrates and Joint Magistrates in the Lower Provinces, 13 Dec. 1836.

116. IOR P/141/66 (9 July 1842): Circular to Session Judges and Joint Magistrates in the Lower Provinces, 10 June 1842.

117. IOR P/132/8 (11 Sept. 1815): Continuation of the list of the Prisoners for transportation intended to have been shipped on board the *Lady Barlow*, but now transferred to the *Helen*, 10 Sept. 1815 (no. 172 Urjaon, convicted of highway robbery, 17 Dec. 1813).

118. IOR P/135/50 (20 Mar. 1823): List of forty convicts to Penang *per Thames*, 9 Mar. 1823 (nos 10, 16, 17, 19).

119. IOR P/132/37 (27 Dec. 1816): List of four convicts to Mauritius *per Friendship*, 24 Dec. 1816 (no. 1).

120. IOR P/141/66 (9 July 1842): Circular to Session Judges and Joint Magistrates in the Lower Provinces, 10 June 1842.

121. IOR P/133/26 (19 May 1818): List of thirty convicts to Penang *per Auspicious*, 10 May 1818 (no. 13 Beng, convicted of robbery by open violence in Rangpur, 23 June 1817).

122. *Report of the Committee on Prison Discipline*, 18 (para. 31). Inspector-General of Prisons, F.J. Mouat similarly described the jail *darogahs* in Sandoway (Arakan) as 'worthless and inefficient': *Reports on Jails Visited and Inspected in Bengal, Bihar and Arracan* (F. Carbery, Military Orphan Press, 1856), 188.

123. James Hutchinson, *Observations on the General and Medical Management of Indian Jails; and on the Treatment of Some of the Principal Diseases which Infest Them* (Bengal Military Orphan Press, 1845), 84–5.

124. See, for example, IOR P/132/13 (7 Nov. 1815): J. Eliot, Superintendent Alipur Jail, to M.H. Turnbull, Secretary to Government Bengal, 16 Oct. 1815.

125. On crime, resistance and transportation, see Anderson, *Convicts in the Indian Ocean*, 28–32.
126. McNair, *Prisoners their Own Warders*, 12.
127. H.L. Adam, *The Indian Criminal* (J. Milne, 1909), 12.
128. IOR P/132/12 (31 Oct. 1815): List of forty convicts to Mauritius *per Lady Sophia*, 28 Oct. 1815 (no. 20).
129. IOR P/132/33 (4 Oct. 1816): List of twenty-five convicts to Mauritius *per Jessie*, 27 Sept. 1816 (no. 25).
130. Jones, *'Stigma'*, 143.
131. IOR P/141/9 (14 Mar. 1837): J. Macrae, Civil Assistant Surgeon Monghyr, to W. Adam, Secretary to Committee on Convict Labour, 29 June 1836.
132. I.B. Lyon, *A Text Book of Medical Jurisprudence for India* (Thacker, Spink and Co., 1889), 20.
133. McNair, *Prisoners their Own Warders*, 12. Adam makes the same point, noting that they were not always successful in covering them: Adam, *Indian Criminal*, 12–13.
134. Mrs Bartrum, *Recollections of Seven Years' Residence at the Mauritius, or Isle of France; By a Lady* (James Cawthorn, 1830), 123–4.
135. Scott, Tehranian and Mathias, 'Production of Legal Identities', 6.
136. IOR P/130/17 (8 June 1810): W.A. Clubley, Acting Secretary to Government Bengal, to T. Brown, Chief Secretary to Government Penang, 10 May 1810.
137. Singha, *Despotism of Law*, 139.
138. Singha, *Despotism of Law*, 248–9, 255 (n. 123), 265.
139. IOR P/141/43 (2 Jan. 1840): Circular of the *Faujdari Adalat*, no no., 11 Oct. 1849.
140. Anderson, *Convicts in the Indian Ocean*, 19–20.
141. IOR P/136/31 (26 Aug. 1824): Minute on the mode of treatment hitherto observed towards convicts transported to Prince of Wales Island from the other Presidencies in India, W.E. Phillips, 15 Apr. 1824 (henceforth W.E. Phillips' Minute).
142. Singha, *Despotism of Law*, 135–6.
143. IOR P/141/53 (30 Mar. 1841): Hawkins to Halliday, 19 Mar. 1841, enclosing Statement exhibiting the number of female convicts, 31 Dec. 1840, in the jails of the several districts in the Lower Provinces.
144. IOR P/145/37 (8 May 1856): Extracts from Returns of Convicts in the Straits Settlements, n.d.
145. Satadru Sen, 'Rationing Sex: Female Convicts in the Andamans', *South Asia*, 30, 1 (1999), 35–6.

146. IOR P/141/53 (30 Mar. 1841): H. Hawkins, Register *Nizamat Adalat*, to Halliday, 19 Mar. 1841, enclosing 'Statement exhibiting the number of female convicts, 31 December 1840, in the jails of the several districts in the Lower Provinces'. See also Singha, *Despotism of Law*, 248–9, 255 (n. 123), 265.

147. *Report of the Committee on Prison Discipline*, para. 25; app. 4, q. 2; Singha, *Despotism of Law*, pp. 248–9, 255 (n. 123), 265.

148. IOR P/136/31 (26 Aug. 1824): W.E. Phillips' Minute; IOR P/142/62 (10 Mar. 1847): Bower to Colvin, 29 Dec. 1846.

149. See, for example, the collection on British colonial ideology edited by Harald Fischer-Tiné and Michael Mann: *Colonialism as Civilizing Mission: Cultural Ideology in British India* (Anthem, 2003).

150. Sen, 'Female Jails', 419.

151. For female convict indents, see for example, IOR P/134/21 (12 May 1820): List of forty convicts to Penang *per Lord Minto*, 12 May 1820 (no. 23); IOR P/142/38 (22 Oct. 1845): List of thirty-four convicts to Moulmein *per Tenasserim*, 9 Oct. 1845 (nos 46–8); IOR P/143/14 (17 Feb. 1848): List of five female convicts to Penang *per Eliza Penelope*, 13 Feb. 1848.

152. IOR P/142/54 (14 Oct. 1846): List of twelve female convicts to Penang *per Fire Queen*, 27 Sept. 1846 (nos 10–12); IOR P/143/4 (28 July 1847): List of ten female convicts to Penang *per Phlegethon*, 22 July 1847 (nos 4–6).

153. Schrader, *Languages of the Lash*, 135–6.

154. IOR P/144/3 (11 June 1851): Statement showing the number of escaped convicts, 1 Jan. 1847 to 1 May 1851.

155. Henrice Altink, '"An Outrage on All Decency": Abolitionist Reactions to Flogging Jamaican Slave Women, 1780–1834', *Slavery and Abolition*, 23, 2 (2002), 107–22; Diana Paton, 'Decency, Dependence and the Lash: Gender and the British Debate over Slave Emancipation, 1830–34', *Slavery and Abolition*, 17, 3 (1996), 163–84.

156. Philippa Levine, 'Orientalist Sociology and the Creation of Colonial Sexualities', *Feminist Review*, 65 (2000), 5–21.

157. CSAS Benthall Papers: Box XXX, part i: *Diaries kept by Mrs Clementina Benthall*, Jan. 1849 – Mar. 1850 (typescript copy at Box XXX, part iii.)

158. Theodore Walrond (ed.), *Letters and Journals of James, Eighth Earl of Elgin; Governor of Jamaica, Governor-General of Canada, Envoy to China, Viceroy of India* (John Murray, 1872), 189 (describing a visit to Singapore in June 1857).

159. IOR P/142/54 (28 Oct. 1846): Bogle to Halliday, 11 Sept. 1846.

160. Sen, 'Female Jails', 419.

161. Mary Carpenter, *Six Months in India, vol. I* (Longmans, Green and Co., 1868), 202. For a detailed interrogation of Carpenter's account of female prisoners, see Sen, 'Female Jails', 428–32.

162. On the colonial ordering of gender identities, see Ashis Nandy, *The Intimate Enemy: Loss and Recovery of Self under Colonialism* (Oxford University Press, 1983), 52–3.

163. Sinha, 'Giving Masculinity a History', 31. On masculinity in the period of high imperialism, see Mrinalini Sinha, *Colonial Masculinity: The 'Manly Englishman' and the 'Effeminate Bengali' in the Late Nineteenth Century* (Manchester University Press, 1995).

164. A concept borrowed from the conceptualization of Australian penal settlements by Raymond Evans and Bill Thorpe, 'Commanding Men: Masculinities and the Convict System', *Journal of Australian Studies*, 56 (1998), 22–4.

165. See, for example, Dr Berncastle, *A Voyage to China; Including a Visit to the Bombay Presidency; the Mahratta Country; the Cave Temples of Western India, Singapore, the Straits of Malacca and Sunda, and the Cape of Good Hope, Vol. II* (William Shoberl, 1850), and Orfeur Cavenagh, *Reminiscences of an Indian Official* (W.H. Allen, 1884), 272.

166. IOR P/403/15 (31 Jan. 1843): Bonham to Willoughby, 12 Nov. 1842.

167. IOR P/403/19 (21 June 1843): Escombe to Bonham, 16 June 1843.

168. IOR E/4/779: India Judicial Department, 31 July 1844.

169. IOR P/403/45 (20 Nov. 1844): Extract from a Despatch from the Court of Directors, no. 6 of 1844, in the Judicial Department, 31 July 1844.

170. IOR P/403/45 (20 Nov. 1844): Minute of the Governor, 8 Nov. 1844.

171. IOR P/404/13 (24 Mar. 1847): J.G. Lumsden, Session Judge Conkan, to W.H. Harrison, Register Bombay *Sadar Faujdari Adalat* [superior criminal court], 1 Feb. 1847; *Ibid*.: Extract from the proceedings, 27 Oct. 1846. For a more detailed account of the case, see Anderson, '*Godna*', 113–14.

172. *Ibid*.: Lumsden to Harrison, 1 Feb. 1847.

173. *Ibid*.: Minutes by Mr Bell and Mr Reid, 9 Mar. 1847.

174. *Ibid*.: Harrison to Escombe, 27 Feb. 1847, enclosing 'Draft of an act for authorizing the branding/marking of convicts sentenced to transportation by any of the courts of the East India Company within its territories subject to the Bombay Presidency.'

175. IOR P/404/13 (24 Mar. 1847): Minute of the Governor, 5 Mar. 1847.

176. IOR E/4/792: India Legislative Department, 14 July 1847; IOR P/ 404/21 (14 July 1847): Resolution on the Honorable Court's Dispatch, 14 July 1847.
177. IOR P/404/40 (27 Sept. 1848): Legislative Department, 12 Aug. 1848. The Government Resolution is worth citing in full:

> Whereas it is thought fit to abolish wholly the practice of branding and publicly exposing convicts throughout the territories under the Government of the East India Company, it is enacted as follows. -
> 1. Section xi regulation iv 1797; section xxxv regulation vii 1813 and clauses 2nd, 3rd and 4th section xii regulation xvii 1817 of the Bengal Code; section xxxv regulation vii 1802 of the Madras Code, clause 1st section iii regulation ii 1807 section ix and i regulation xvii 1817 of the Bengal Code, section iii regulation vi 1811, section v and vi regulation ii 1822 of the Madras Code, and all other regulations or parts of regulations in force so far as they direct that any convicted offenders shall have any words marked or any indelible mark made upon their foreheads, or on any part of their persons, or authorize any sentence of public exposure, commonly called tusheer [*tashir*], and so much of chapter ii regulation xiv 1827 of the Bombay Code, as authorizes any sentence of public disgrace, are rescinded.
> 2. After the passing of this act it shall not be lawful for any court or magistrate within the territories under the government of the East India Company to order that any brand or indelible mark of any kind be made, or renewed on any part of the person of any convicted offender, or to sentence any offender to be publicly exposed by tusheer, or to any other degrading exposure.

See also IOR P/143/30 (28 Feb. 1849): Act II (1849) to abolish the practice of branding and exposing convicts, 27 Jan. 1849; IOR E/4/ 803: Legislative Department, 13 Mar. 1850.
178. IOR P/404/44 (29 Nov. 1848): M. Larken, Register *Sadar Faujdari Adalat*, to Lumsden, 6 Nov. 1848.
179. *Ibid.*: Minute by Mr Reid, 12 Nov. 1848.
180. *Ibid.*: Lumsden to G.A. Bushby, Secretary to Government of India Legislative Department, 28 Nov. 1848.
181. *Ibid.*: Mytton to Halliday, 8 Aug. 1848.
182. Singha, 'Settle, Mobilize, Verify', 172 (n. 123).
183. During a debate on the merits of the rattan against the cat o'nine tails in 1833, the Session Judge of the Conkan, A. Bell, wrote that the rattan left permanent scars, 'which consequently stamps a man's infamy for life'. See IOR P/140/33 (8 July 1833): A. Bell, Session Judge Conkan, to R.J. Webb, Acting Register Bombay *Sadar*

Faujdari Adalat, 6 Feb. 1833. For an illuminating examination of flogging, see Singha, *Despotism of Law*, 247–9.

184. 'CHIRURGUS' to the Editor, *The Times*, 27 Sept. 1851. I thank Jane Caplan for this reference.

185. Adam, *Indian Criminal*, 12–13 (emphasis added).

3

'Surely there is more in this than mere ornament': Ethnography, Surveillance and the Decorative Tattoo

Introduction: Reading the Social Hierarchy

By the last quarter of the nineteenth century, the Government of India had embarked on the collection of information that it believed would smooth the administration of the subcontinent. The most enduring of these projects was the census, first undertaken in 1871 and repeated at ten-year intervals. The thrust of this most Victorian endeavour was initially on counting and later classifying every individual, producing measurable social facts for administrative purposes. It is not difficult to see why historians have used Michel Foucault's power-knowledge paradigm as a tool for its interpretation. As Nicholas B. Dirks has argued, it was in the inscription of colonized spaces that colonial power was transformed into 'usable forms of knowledge'.[1] During the late nineteenth and early twentieth centuries, the government also undertook a series of anthropometric projects. These too were classificatory, and aimed to produce information that would improve colonial administration. This time, however, individuals were physically measured, and produced as biological rather than social data. Anthropometric encounters slotted individuals into explicitly racial hierarchies, according to colonial calculations of the significance of their physical dimensions.

During the early colonial period missionaries, who made observations with Christian conversion in mind, carried out much colonial ethnography.[2] As Felix Padel shows in his illuminating 'anthropological study of anthropologists', during the second half of the nineteenth century ethnography was undertaken by colonial administrators such as district officials and military officers. I share his belief that it is impossible to separate ethnographic accounts (descriptions of culture) from anthropological ones (theories of culture). All colonial ethnographers wrote from their own cultural perspective, which determined both the parameters of their research and the transformation of their human subjects into objects of inquiry.[3] I shall, therefore, use the terms ethnography and anthropology interchangeably. This point is well illustrated when we come to colonial accounts of Indian society, and the mutual exclusiveness of ethnographic and anthropological accounts of it. The focus of much of this colonial writing was on what was widely viewed as the uniquely Indian institution of caste. Administrator-anthropologists held opposing views about its significance; in particular whether it was a simple description of occupation, and was thus cultural, or whether it was a marker of race, perceived as a set of physical attributes. At the same time, they shared a basic assumption. All were looking for the emperors and Lilliputians of the subcontinent: whole social groups who could be fitted into South Asian hierarchies, whether on the basis of cultural or biological difference.

This chapter will focus on a hitherto unexplored yet not infrequent point of departure for nineteenth- and early-twentieth-century ethnographic discussions – the style, frequency and corporal location of decorative tattoos. By the mid to late nineteenth century, colonial administrator-anthropologists used tattooing as a means of creating distinctions between men and women of different caste and tribal groups, and sometimes in tracing the relationships between them. They transformed tattoos into cultural signs, indicators of social, religious and sometimes biological status. Tattoos were like the 'caste marks' noted by Christopher Pinney: one means through which British observers sought to transform India into a fully legible social hierarchy.[4] The missionary Abbé J.A. Dubois, whose 1817 writings on India the British saw as authoritative, mentioned it.[5] Many other colonial ethnographers saw tattoos as an important means of social differentiation, attempting to use marks on individual bodies as a means of constructing collective social ones. Herbert Hope Risley, appointed Superintendent of Ethnography for India in 1901, showed an interest in the meaning of tattooing in his early work on Bengal.[6] He later oversaw an investigation into tattooing in Bengal as part of his larger anthropometric survey (1901–8).[7] Risley's assistant in South India, Edgar Thurston, also called for notes on tattooing from local correspondents during his anthropometric work in Madras.[8]

Popular tradition has it that the English word tattoo (*tatu*) was a colonial import, making its first appearance in Britain after Captain James Cook's Polynesian voyages during the late eighteenth century. As Alfred Gell argues in *Wrapping in Images*, polite society then viewed tattooing as characteristic of either 'the class Other' (the sailor, the criminal) or 'the ethnic Other' (the savage). Tattoos thus became markers of social distinction. The ethnic Other was epitomized in the heavily tattooed man

Omai, brought back from Tahiti by Cook himself in a flourish of exotic colonial display and immortalized in a portrait by Joshua Reynolds.[9] Yet the distance which eighteenth-century society placed between itself and the tattooed Other denied the fact of the existence of decorative tattooing in the British Isles long before Cook set sail. Tattooing was common amongst the insular Celts (the Celtic-speaking populations of Ireland and Great Britain) during the medieval period. Until the seventeenth century, medico-magicians, occult magi and physicians used it. Pre-Reformation pilgrims also returned to Britain wearing tattoos from Jerusalem.[10] As Juliet Fleming shows, Cook's voyages did not so much introduce tattooing to Europe, as is commonly held by writers such as Gell, but reinflected it.[11] Nevertheless, the presence of particular tattoo designs during the late eighteenth and nineteenth centuries marked out their wearers in relation to their ethnicity and/or social position. Harriet Guest asserts that Omai's tattoos both inscribed him with marks of Otherness and removed him from his cultural context, with artistic representations portraying him as the generic 'noble savage'. Reduced to the realms of the exotic, Omai as a colonial subject was rendered culturally illegible.[12]

In a broad sense, in India colonial ethnographers used tattooing practices to distance themselves from the (uneducated) Indian Other. Indian local correspondents too were complicit in this, for they collaborated with British ethnographers like Risley and Thurston.[13] As Arnold argues persuasively, Indian elites became absorbed into the production of British ideas about race. These ideas permitted the Hindu intelligentsia in Bengal to distance itself from 'inferior' social groups.[14] The types of tattoo designs common in India were so different from those found in Europe that they became a general signal of the wearer's Otherness. However, they were not generally exoticizing in the way that Guest argues they were in the Pacific. Discourses of the exotic there rendered colonial subjects into 'singular tokens', their social origins fragmented and incoherent.[15] In India, ethnographers gave tattoos a more functional purpose, using them to mark out the distinctiveness of social (or caste) groups. When colonization met with resistance, they were given another meaning and transformed into marks of 'savagery'. Moreover, Risley, who believed that caste was a biological signifier of race, conjectured that he could use tattoos to delineate the uniqueness of particular sections of the population and, in some cases, to trace racial connections between them. In whatever way anthropologists approached the significance of tattoos, they all worked on the premise that they were a means of comprehending Indian society. Ethnographers thus used tattoos – the most individual and human of marks – to dehumanize, to turn colonial subjects into objects of study.[16]

From the end of the nineteenth century, colonial administrators also saw tattoos as potential marks of criminality and, in the context of the Criminal Tribes Acts, colonial understandings of tattooing practices took on a further dimension. Decorative tattoos – especially those worn by women – were transformed into indicators of criminal tendencies, serving both as an alert against crime and as a means of detecting its perpetrators. My concern here is not to reveal the 'truth' about Indian tattooing practices. Rather, I want to explore how tattooing was used to develop representations of Indian society, and to show how anthropological readings of tattoos fed into the formation of colonial discourses on Indian women, caste, race and criminality. First, however, in order to contextualize colonial writings on tattooing, we now turn to a brief discussion of the anthropometric projects simultaneously underway in the subcontinent.

Communities of Creed or Function: Race, Caste and Anthropometry

During the nineteenth century, there was a split between British adminis-trators who saw caste as a social category, and those who viewed it as a biological one. In the first camp were William Crooke, author of *The Tribes and Castes of the North-West Provinces and Oudh* (1896), John C. Nesfield, Inspector of Schools Awadh, and Denzil Ibbetson, Super-intendent of Census Operations in the Panjab, who believed that caste was little more than a social, occupational category.[17] Nesfield wrote that caste was not a 'community of creed', but a 'community of function': 'Function, and function only, as I think, was the foundation upon which the whole caste system of India was built up'.[18] In the second camp was Risley. He saw caste as a firm indicator of racial origin and hierarchy. For Risley, racial types were revealed through anthropometric analysis of the nose ('the nasal index'), which in turn corresponded to the order of racial precedence.[19] Risley wrote in 1891: 'Everywhere we find high social position associated with a certain physical type and conversely low social position with a markedly different type.'[20] Risley's early followers included James Wise, Civil Surgeon of Dacca and a local correspondent during Risley's first major ethnographic survey. Wise's *Notes on the Races, Castes and Trades of Eastern Bengal* was published shortly after his death (1883).[21] Risley's first Government of India commission, *The Tribes and Castes of Bengal* (1891), was based upon data gathered by Risley and his assistant, Kumud Behari Samanta, between 1885 and 1887. They took 6,000 measurements for eighty-nine population groups.[22] Additionally,

Wise's widow made over his notes on eastern Bengal, and a set of 200 glass negatives.[23] When Risley was appointed Director of Ethnography for India, Edgar Thurston, Superintendent of the Madras Museum (1885–1908), was made Superintendent of Ethnography in the Madras Presidency. R.E. Enthoven held the same post in Bombay. Between them, they undertook an all-India survey, a massive undertaking with a budget of £10,000. Operations were soon delayed beyond the five years originally planned for their completion.[24] The survey was finally published as *The People of India* in 1908.[25]

Risley's main contention was that due to the endogamous nature of caste, it was possible to discern racial typologies within the Indian population. It was the restriction on intermarriage that made anthropometry scientific.[26] Physical appearance provided a clue as to an individual's caste; this impression could then be fixed through the use of anthropometry. As Risley wrote: 'No one could mistake a Brahman for a Kol, but verbal descriptions fall far short of the numerical analysis by measuring.'[27] According to Risley, there were two main racial types found in Indian society: Aryans and Dravidians. The 'intermediate' type, the Mongoloid, was found only in Assam and north-east Bengal, so was largely left unconsidered. The Aryan type was, according to Risley, notable for a long (dolichocephalic) head, a straight, finely cut (lepto-rhine) nose, a long symmetrically narrow face, a well-developed forehead and regular features. Aryan build was slender, but tall. The type's complexion was 'light transparent brown'. The Dravidian type also had a dolichocephalic head, but the nose was thick and broad, the lips thick, the face wide and the features irregular. This type was not as tall as the Aryan and complexion ranged from very dark brown to black. A short cut to discerning the relative position of the castes was the nasal index, a comparison of height and breadth of nose. If castes were arranged according to nasal index, the gradations of racial type and therefore the accepted order of social precedence would emerge. The caste with the finest nose would appear at the top; that with the coarsest at the bottom. For Risley, anthropometry was not simply of scientific interest. It was also a matter of concern for effective colonial administration. More detailed information on caste groups could, he wrote, inform colonial policy on famine, facilitating understandings of who could take food without losing caste. Similarly, an understanding of marriage and divorce customs would help magistrates in settling disputes. Land claims could also be processed more efficiently.

Risley's ideas met with some opposition at the time, even from those sympathetic to anthropometric methodology. Crooke wrote that when anthropometry was applied to caste, there were only very slight differences between the high and low castes. This did not show that anthropometry was flawed, but that 'the present races of India are practically one people.' According to Crooke, Risley's nasal index table for instance showed no appreciable difference between Brahmins and the low caste. Indeed, according to Risley's own figures, the latter were more nasally refined than Rajputs in the North West Provinces. Of course Crooke linked caste to occupational differentiation, rather than distinct racial origins.[28] There have been hints that Crooke's career suffered as a result of his dispute with Risley. Richard Temple, who served as Superintendent of Port Blair (Andaman Islands) at the turn of the century (1894–1903), wrote in his memoirs that Crooke had not received the promotion he deserved, instead remaining Magistrate and Collector in the United Provinces. As Pinney notes, it is not clear whether or not this was because of his animosity towards Risley.[29]

Indian subject populations were rather more sceptical about anthropometry. Crooke wrote of being greeted with the suspicion of being connected to tax assessments or a coming revenue settlement.[30] Thurston also noted the problems he encountered during his anthropometric survey of the Madras Presidency, where whole villages fled when confronted with his measuring equipment. He recounted without apparent irony widespread Indian non-cooperation, and his reminiscences are worth quoting at length:

The Paniyan women of the Wynaad believed that I was going to have the finest specimens among them stuffed for the Madras Museum. An Irula man, on the Nilgiri hills, who was wanted by the police for some mild crime of ancient date, came to be measured, but absolutely refused to submit to the operation on the plea that the height-measuring standard was the gallows . . .

[The Oddes] . . . were afraid that I was going to get them transported, to replace the Boers who had been exterminated . . .

During a long tour through the Mysore province, the Natives mistook me for a recruiting sergeant bent on seizing them for employment in South Africa, and fled before my approach from time to time. The little spot, which I am in the habit of making with Aspinall's white paint to indicate the position of the fronto-nasal suture and bi-orbital breadth, was supposed to possess vesicant properties, and to blister into a number on the forehead, which would serve as a means of future identification for the purpose of kidnapping. The record of head, chest, and foot measurements, was viewed with marked suspicion, on the ground that I was an army tailor, measuring for sepoy's clothing . . .

One man . . . was suddenly seized with fear in the midst of the experiment, and throwing his body-cloth at my feet, ran for all he was worth, and disappeared. An elderly Municipal servant wept bitterly when undergoing the process of measurement, and a woman bade farewell to her husband, as she thought for ever, as she entered the threshold of my impromptu laboratory.[31]

Thurston also noted his subjects' dislike of the procedure on caste grounds. There was only one set of the equipment used to estimate the facial angle. Some castes insisted on being measured by early afternoon, so that they could carry out ritual ablutions before sunset. All this came despite his desperate attempts to persuade people to succumb to his measuring instruments, through offering bribes such as cheroots or money.[32]

Tattooing, Primitivism, Savagery and Social Hierarchies

During the nineteenth century it was not unusual for colonial ethnographers to make references to the significance of tattooing in their analyses of Indian society. Notes on tattoos were frequently made by speakers at the Royal Anthropological Institute, as well as by the compilers of the great regional ethnographies and caste dictionaries produced during the second half of the nineteenth century. 'Tattooing' was often a subsection of the discussion of social structures and religious customs, alongside themes such as 'kin groups', 'marriage', 'birth customs' and 'property'. At one level, administrator-anthropologists used tattoos to divide 'backward' colonial populations from more 'civilized' societies. Indeed, according to one speaker's map of tattooing practices, cicatrization ('gashes') and tattooing were overwhelmingly confined to regions that had at one time fallen under colonial control: Africa, Australasia, much of South East Asia and North America (Figure 3.1).

South Asia was no exception to this juxtaposition of 'backwardness' and 'civilization'. Early ethnographers like Wise linked the origin of tattooing to 'aboriginal' tribal practices.[33] Others wrote of the pain that tattooing caused and its danger to life, which compounded the 'primitivism' of the practice. Their references to barbaric practices in the tattooing of young women in particular can be read as part of the discourse of a gendered civilizing mission. According to James Forsyth, writing in 1872 of the tattooing of Gond women in the Central Provinces, for instance: 'the traveller will sometimes hear dreadful screeches issuing from their villages, which will be attributed to some young Gondin being operated upon with the tattooing-needle.'[34] Crooke reproduced this image in *The Tribes and Castes*.[35] Major-General R.G. Woodthorpe (Royal Engineers) similarly claimed that his survey party in the North East Frontier (1871–6) saw a young women whose newly drawn leg tattoos had become

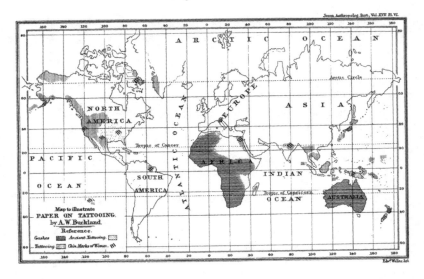

Figure 3.1 'Map to Illustrate Paper on Tattooing'. A.W. Buckland, 'On Tattooing', *Journal of the Royal Anthropological Institute*, 17 (1888), p. 326

infected: 'I went into the house where the poor little thing – sad votary of fashion – lay screaming with pain. The sores were dreadful, both legs apparently rotting away below the knee.' Members of the woman's Naga community had asked Woodthorpe to visit her, presumably in the hope that he could give her the medical attention she needed. However, he wrote that he lacked equipment and expertise, and that there was little that he could do: 'I fear she died a painful death'.[36]

A number of other ethnographic accounts made reference to the simplicity and crudeness of Indian tattoo designs. F. Fawcett (a local correspondent of the Anthropological Institute) noted that Dom tattoo patterns he saw in Vishakhapatnam, Madras Presidency, in the early twentieth century were 'extremely rude'.[37] Risley wrote of the same patterns: 'they compare most unfavourably with the simplest type of line-tatu'.[38] Other administrator-anthropologists made similarly unflattering comparisons, drawing on the difference between tattooing in India and elsewhere. R. Bainbridge, sub-divisional officer of Godda (Bihar), described the tattoos worn by the Sauria Parhaiyas for Risley's 1901–8 survey of tattooing as crude and inelegant, performed by inexperienced friends using inadequate equipment. He compared this to tattooing in Japan, or the intricate designs drawn by the British tattoo artist Sutherland

Macdonald.[39] More frequently, comparisons were made with the supposedly more artistic designs found in Burma.[40] Most anthropologists concluded that tattooing was on the whole confined to low-caste social groups or *adivasi* tribal communities like the Doms and Sauria Parhaiyas. As we shall see, many of these groups carried the additional stigma of criminality with which tattooing also came to be associated.

Beyond symbolizing 'backwardness' or 'primitivism', tattoos were also potential markers of 'savagery' in regions of the subcontinent that proved difficult to bring under colonial control. Notable amongst these were the Naga Hills in the North East Frontier (between Assam and Upper Burma). Between the 1830s and 1880s, the British were engaged in nearly constant conflict there. There were hundreds of casualties on both sides. Shortly after the Naga War (1878–9), at two meetings of the Royal Anthropological Institute, R.G. Woodthorpe spoke of his encounters with tribal groups in the region. The title of his first paper – 'Notes on the Wild Tribes Inhabiting the so-called Naga Hills' – gave a hint of what was to come. He provided a detailed account of social practices in the region, and included descriptions of housing, marriage, religion and so on. He marked the status of each of the 'wild tribes' according to their tattoos. There was not a single reference to tattooing practices amongst the 'kilted' Angami Nagas that he first met: 'The Angamis struck us as a very cheerful, frank, hospitable, brave race, and for hill people wonderfully clean.'[41] It was only as Woodthorpe ventured north-eastwards into hostile territory that he began to make observations about tattooing. At first, he claimed to have seen tattoos only on women (Hatigorias, Dupdorias and Assiringias).[42] There was nothing unusual about this, for women wore tattoos far more commonly than men elsewhere in India. It was when Woodthorpe encountered 'naked Nagas' that he first mentioned men's tattoos. He noted 'we find tattooing beginning to appear among the men, *though not as yet on the face*; only slightly on the arms and breast, a few fine lines running up from the navel and diverging on either side over the breast.'[43]

Woodthorpe next travelled to the Jaipur District. Not long before his visit, in 1875 eighty men belonging to a survey party led by Lieutenant Holcombe had been killed there. Woodthorpe described the tattoos (*ak*) of the men. For the first time during his tour, he noted facial marks: 'They would be good looking as a rule, but for the tattooing which in some cases, when done heavily, makes their faces almost black: in others the tattooing is blue, and then the bare portion of the face, especially in those of fair complexion, appears pink by contrast.' He described four continuous lines running across the forehead, round and underneath the eyes and nose, over the cheeks and round to the corners of the mouth and chin (Figure 3.2).

Figure 3.2 'Soibang, Vangam [Headman] of Chopnu'. R.G. Woodthorpe, 'Notes on the Wild Tribes Inhabiting the So-called Naga Hills, on our North-East Frontier of India, Part II', *Journal of the Anthropological Institute of Great Britain and Ireland*, 11 (1882), Plate XXI

Rows of spots followed the outside lines, and two fine lines made a diamond pattern around the nose.[44] Neighbouring tribes, he continued, had tattoos elsewhere on their bodies: the shoulders, wrists, torso and thighs.[45]

Another paper given to the Anthropological Institute (1897) compounded this image of the naked, tattooed savage. Gertrude M. Godden wrote: 'the Nágás made themselves known to us as barbarous savages; the savage virtues of blood-feud and relentless raiding, and savage ignorance of many of the first principles of the higher civilisation were everywhere apparent.'[46]

The Commissioner of Chota Nagpur, E.T. Dalton, had earlier referred to tattooing in the region in his 1872 *Descriptive Ethnology of Bengal*. The Asiatic Society of Bengal planned to hold an ethnological exhibition in Calcutta, beginning in 1869. However, the society conceded that it would be difficult to persuade individuals to travel to Calcutta, and potentially 'inconvenient political implications' might arise if any of them died, so the exhibition never took place. Dalton's book was based on the information gathered. He linked Naga *ak* to the practice of headhunting, claiming that a young man was not allowed to marry until his face had been tattooed. This was not done until he had successfully taken a human scalp or skull.[47] The ethnographer, S.E. Peal, explained the tattooing of other parts of the body thus: 'All those who got heads won the ák [tattoos] on the face; those who got hands and feet had marks accordingly, for the former on the arms, for the latter on the legs.'[48] Woodthorpe wrote that men were permitted to tattoo their chests after taking their first head, and claimed to have seen skull trophies in Naga villages.[49] The meaning of the illustration of a tree adorned with skulls and entitled 'Golgotha' reproduced by Woodthorpe would not have been lost on his biblically astute Victorian audience.[50] These ethnographers represented tattooing in the Naga Hills as symbolic of a whole society's involvement in the socially sanctioned act of barbarism that headhunting represented. As Padel argues, the Nagas 'represented a new bloodthirsty superstition to suppress in the role of administrator, as well as fresh data to record in the role of anthropologist.'[51] The 1886 Colonial and India Exhibition included representations of their tattoos.[52]

A further feature of colonial discussions of Naga *ak* was its transformation from a broad indicator of 'savagery' to a specific sign of social cohesion. It is worth drawing on an extract from S.E. Peal's account of his visit to the region in 1872:

> When once with a number of Banparas on the road, a large party of Nagas passed, and as neither party spoke, I asked who they were. I was pointed out their hill, and on asking why they did not speak, they said they would not understand one another . . . Both parties passed on, unable to exchange a word, though living within a few miles of each other. A few words did pass, but they were Assamese. I asked how they knew the men, and they said 'by their ák', or tattoo marks.[53]

Peal was not the only ethnographer to use tattooing to signify boundaries between social units. Colonial accounts of other communities also noted tattoos as marks of community. Dalton presented tattooing as a potential mark of difference.[54] Wise also wrote of 'distinguishing stain marks'.[55] In 1935, L.K. Ananthakrishna Iyer, retired Superintendent of Ethnography Kochi, wrote of the designs worn by particular communities.[56] The tattoos he described included those worn by Christians in South India: Syrian Christians tattooed a cross on the forearm, whilst Roman Catholics and Eurasians tattooed a bird on their arms and thighs, a representation of the

Holy Ghost.[57] In keeping with his views on caste, Risley saw tattooing as a clue to establishing the racial origins of some communities. In his early publication *The Tribes and Castes*, he drew on Dalton's work, writing that his conjecture that the Juang were closely related to the Mundas and the Kharias was supported by the fact that the women were tattooed with similar marks: three strokes on the forehead and three on each temple.[58] Crooke, on the other hand, wrote that tattoos were general marks of low status, signifiers of common rather than particular social standing. He noted that although some groups had tattoos on specific parts of the body only, the designs themselves were not socially indicative.[59]

From his early work, it is clear that Risley was trying to use tattooing to locate individuals in relation to their membership of a particular caste or tribe and, according to his perspective, race. He also saw shared tattoos as a means of establishing the common racial origin of seemingly disparate groups. Ten years after the publication of *The Tribes and Castes*, using a network of local British officials and local correspondents, Risley oversaw a study of tattooing practices in Bengal (1901–8). Risley put eighteen questions concerning its meaning, practice and significance to the district commissioners. These were as follows:

1. What are the origins of tattooing?
2. Is it confined to one of the sexes?
3. Is it confined to certain parts of the body and why?
4. At what age and is it done all at once or at various periods?
5. Are there any ceremonies connected with it?
6. Is the tattooing performed by any professional individuals and how do they rank?
7. What pigments are employed and what instruments?
8. Are there any dietary restrictions?
9. Is tattooing considered a sign of manhood?
10. Is it connected with worship or ritual?
11. Is the practice dying out?
12. What are the designs employed? Have they any particular significance?
13. Do the designs vary with the social or family rank of the individual?
14. Are they in any way hereditary?
15. Is the tattooing symmetrical?
16. With what part of the body does it commence?
17. Is the design executed on some preconceived plan and is there any drawing of it prepared beforehand?
18. Is more than one colour employed?

In order to answer these queries, Risley strongly encouraged district officers to submit accompanying illustrations.[60] Questions on tattooing also formed part of the district surveys conducted by Thurston, who compiled detailed notes of regional practices in South India during the same period.[61]

When officials went into the districts, they were met with the same suspicions that greeted anthropometric surveyors like Thurston. R. Bainbridge, a local correspondent in Bihar, wrote of the difficulties of obtaining information. The women were apparently concerned that the practice was under threat and were thus unwilling to answer his questions. Men in the district thought that the questions related to land resettlement or forest clearance, and were nervous of his presence. Bainbridge was forced to resort to compliments, gifts and 'sterner measures' – of what kind he does not say – in order to elicit the details required.[62] A second informant, S.K. Agasti, reported that it was with great difficulty that he found a tattooist to talk to, and even then she gave him only limited information.[63] The unwillingness of subaltern populations to cooperate with the survey reveals something of what has been described in another context as the operations of a *Limited Raj*.[64] Moreover, what local communities did tell ethnographers posed a serious challenge to Risley's preconceived ideas about the relationship between tattooing, caste and race. Local reports on tattooing did not confirm his supposition that tattoos signified shared caste practices.

It is perhaps worth noting at this point that many administrator-anthropologists made ethnographic observations about prisoners in the district jails. Dalton, for instance, thanked J.M. Coates, Superintendent of Jails Hazaribag, in the introduction to his *Descriptive Ethnology of Bengal*.[65] Ethnographers like James Wise, Civil Surgeon of Dacca, later measured and weighed inmates for his *Notes on the Races, Castes and Trades of Eastern Bengal* (1883).[66] Jails were places where Indians had little space to refuse the intimate physical examination that anthropometry entailed. As Arnold shows in his study of state medicine in colonial India, the state had complete access to the bodies of its incarcerated Indian subjects.[67] Imprisoned in relatively small numbers, women seem to have remained untouched by these anthropometric surveys. Colonial practice in this respect was rather irregular, for as we shall see female prisoners were sometimes made subject to minute inspection or anthropometric photography (Chapter 5).

In 1901, Fawcett wrote of his encounter with twenty-five Dom Panos (tribal men) in Vishakhapatnam Jail, South India. He drew twelve line pictures of the tattoos (*bana*) he claimed they had (Figure 3.3).

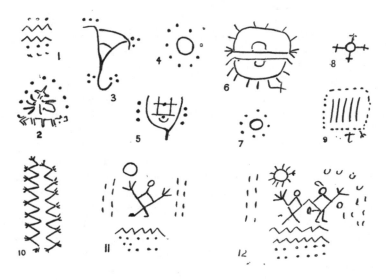

Figure 3.3 'Tattooing'. F. Fawcett, 'Notes on the Dômbs of Jeypur, Vizagapatam District, Madras Presidency', *Man*, 1 (1901), p. 36

From Fawcett's 'Notes' it is possible to deduce that he had actually seen seven of the twelve designs, though it is impossible to tell whether he saw the rest. Though he alludes to having seen tattoos on at least one prisoner's arms, the left shoulder blade of a second man and across the shoulders of another, he includes descriptions of the tattoos of just two of the men in very general terms: 'Tattooed on the right fore-arm' and, simply, 'Tattooed'. One or more of the prisoners may have been persuaded to describe some of the designs to him, or sketch them for his benefit. Indeed, Fawcett constantly alludes to his consultations with the prisoners during his visit to the jail.

Like all local populations who experienced colonial measuring sticks and callipers, these prisoners were of course transformed from individual subjects into objects representing a complex social collectivity. Yet they were also central to the production of colonial knowledge, for they were subjected to close questioning about their social strictures, marriage, religion and so on. This gave them considerable manoeuvre to represent (or re-present) themselves as a social group. This was also the case for those communities interviewed beyond the walls of the colonial prison. Ethnographers made constant complaints about their questions being misrepresented or misunderstood, and the answers to them being misleading. It is difficult to tell whether they had grounds for these complaints, or whether frustrations arose when the answers they expected were not forthcoming. Whatever the case, it was at least partly through recognition of the limitations of their social understanding that disagreements between ethnographers emerged. Risley himself challenged Fawcett's conclusions about the significance of Dom *bana*. Fawcett wrote: 'These patterns *were said to be*, one and all, purely ornamental, and not in any way connected with totems or tribal emblems'.[68] Risley countered with the suggestion that either the Doms had not understood Fawcett's question, had deliberately lied or had misunderstood the meaning of their tattoos. He wrote: 'Surely there is more in this than mere ornament'.[69]

As we have seen, Risley's interest in tattooing arose from his belief that particular types of tattoos could be connected to individuals' racial/caste origins. He linked social groups through similar tattoo patterns, and then used evidence of shared tattoos to make racial connections. In 1902, he aligned the North Indian Doms with South Indian Dombs, for instance, and both with the Pans, an Orissa-based group, on the basis of similar tattoos. This collapsed the diversity of the Dom community across India into a single social category.[70] Risley argued that their tattoos were religious in origin, though he admitted that his contention that they could not possibly be purely ornamental as other writers like Fawcett had claimed was dubious: 'we have no means of gauging the standard of taste among the Dôms.' He also noted that the similarity of their tattoos probably indicated shared caste which, in accordance with his perspective on caste as a marker of 'race', further defined their unique racial origin.[71] Further, Risley was interested in making connections between Indian 'gypsy tribes' and European Roma communities. He believed that tattoos could 'throw some light on the affinities of Indian and European gypsies', though there is no evidence that he ever came to any firm conclusions on this.[72]

Risley's disappointment that the findings of the tattooing survey did not support his approach is almost palpable, and perhaps explains why it was never published. District commissioners put forward various explanations for the origin of tattooing, especially amongst women, and none related to the marking of caste. They said that tattoos curbed women's sexual desire, a tattoo was a disfigurement that would discourage attacks on women, tattoos assured the wearer's place in heaven, they had healing properties, or they allowed the ingress of good spirits into the body. Contemporary ethnographers presented a similar range of explanations. Thurston made frequent references to tattooing in his *Castes and Tribes of Southern India* (1909).[73] He wrote that during his early-twentieth-century anthropometric survey of South India, a man in the Bellary District told him that he had dislocated his shoulder as a child and had the figure of Hanuman (the monkey god) tattooed there in an attempt to relieve the pain.[74] Thurston added that Hindu women were sometimes tattooed over the spleen and liver to avoid having stillborn children. Yet, according to Thurston, branding was more widely used for this purpose. Pregnant Toda women from the Nilgiri Hills were, for instance, branded on the hands.[75]

Other colonial explanations bound tattooing more closely to religious practices. Dubois suggested that some Hindu facial marks were connected with religious fasting and rites of purification, though he was probably referring to the use of coloured dye rather than tattooed inscriptions.[76] In his 1925 *History of Tattooing*, W.D. Hambly noted that tattoos could also record religious pilgrimage. Armenians tattooed in Jerusalem used the same word – *mahdesi* – to mean pilgrim and tattoo, a literal mark of the occasion. Likewise, Muslims tattooed in Mecca used the Turkish word *haji* for both.[77] Drawing on Indian ethnography, Hambly also noted that as tattoos survived death, they would be viewed as evidence of earthly suffering and accepted as penance for sin in heaven, and facilitate the recognition of deceased family members. He wrote that there was a widespread belief amongst Bengali Hindus that those who did not have tattoos would face real difficulties during their journey to the afterlife. Tribal men and women in Assam, for example, had tattoos as they could not afford the jewellery or utensils that would supply them with spiritual prestige and identification after death. Hambly wrote: 'The tattoo is the poor man's identification mark in heaven.'[78] Yet, with tattooing largely confined to women, this need for recognition was also bound up with the gender order within particular communities. Hambly added that tattoo marks were seen to prevent Northern Assamese Tangkhul women from marrying in the next world until her husband came to claim her.[79]

At best, the district commissioners working for Risley presented tattooing as conspicuous bodily adornment. None viewed it as a caste mark, an indicator of occupation or a form of hereditary distinction. Common styles were not seen as exclusive to particular social groups. Their most unequivocal finding was that tattooing was mainly confined to women. There were a few exceptions to this, and in general low-caste and *adivasi* men were far more likely to be tattooed than higher castes. In Hughli and Saran, for example, Santhals and Dosadhs of both sexes wore tattoos. *Hijras* ('dancing boys who act the part of females') also sported designs.[80] In response to the question about tattooists, the commissioners reported that family members, low-caste women or professional *godnawali* performed the role. There was huge diversity in the age at which children were first tattooed, in tattooing styles and where they were drawn on the body.

The commissioners generally agreed that the practice was dying out, and it was here that caste came into play, though not in the way that Risley had foreseen. Though they did not see tattoos as caste marks, the reports outlined a strong association between tattooing and caste status. Few designs indicated high caste, whilst multiple tattoos signalled low-caste or tribal origins. The commissioners' conjecture was that this had probably led to the decline of tattooing, as low-caste groups sought to emulate the higher castes as a way of achieving social mobility. Tattooing was apparently decreasing to such an extent that it had almost died out in some of the districts around Calcutta. They said that the only exceptions to this were in parts of Bihar, Nadia and Dinajpur.[81] This was perhaps due to the concentration of *adivasis* in these areas, where men and women both wore tattoos.

Whilst there was disagreement between colonial ethnographers about whether tattoos were a specific marker of caste and/or race, or generally denoted low status, all viewed them as social signs. Administrator-anthropologists saw tattoos as signifiers of some kind, and Risley and his followers attempted to use designs to make racial connections between seemingly disparate social groups. Yet at the same time colonial observers, including those who fed into Risley's tattooing survey, made the not entirely compatible observation that the practice was strongly gendered. Women mostly wore tattoos, and female tattooists usually inscribed the designs. Their explanations for its origins also frequently related to the gender order. Thus I would argue that ethnographic observations about gender also fed into to the construction of colonial discourses on race, caste and tribe. It is to a discussion of this theme that we now turn.

Gender and Indian Society

In the seventeenth century, a French merchant who made frequent trips to India, Jean-Baptiste Tavernier, wrote of women in Banjera, in eastern Bengal: 'From their waist upwards they tattoo their skin with flowers, as when one applies cupping glasses, and they paint these flowers in diverse colours with the juice of roots in such a manner that it seems as though their skin was a flowered fabric.'[82] Abbé Dubois later wrote that 'Hindu women paint on the arms of their young daughters various figures, chiefly of flowers. It is done by slightly pricking the skin with a needle, and inserting into the punctures the juice of certain plants. These marks are never effaced, and continue imperishable on the skin during life.'[83] Later, colonial ethnographers made many observations about women's tattoos

– and the employment of women as tattooists. Forsyth noted that tattooists in the Central Provinces were usually women, of the Pardhan caste.[84] Wise also wrote about female tattooists in eastern Bengal. He said that in respectable families, the children's nurse was employed. Otherwise, itinerant Bedia women travelled from place to place, with a cupping horn and their tattooing equipment. According to Wise, they also promised to extract worms from decayed teeth, playing tricks by hiding small grubs to produce from their client's mouth. Wise continued that the women made tattooing dye by mixing the juice of the *bhagra* plant with breast milk, pricking out the design, typically in the centre of the forehead, with needles or thorns. They recited a mantra to alleviate the pain and prevent inflammation. He noted that both Hindu and Muslim women had once adopted the practice, but claimed that the recent *ferazi* (Muslim reform) revival meant that Muslim women were no longer tattooed.[85] We shall return to this claim, and the issue of communal differences in tattooing practices, in our discussion later.

The figure of the itinerant female tattooist or trickster elaborated upon by Wise makes multiple appearances in nineteenth- and early-twentieth-century ethnographic literature. Indeed, ethnographers wrote of a close association between non-sedentary communities, tattooing and criminal activity. The district reports on tattooing presented to Risley after 1901 suggested that female tattooists in Bengal were drawn primarily from criminalized groups. Thus Nat, Bedia, Bagdi, Jugi and Mal women all worked as tattooists.[86] Thurston wrote of his interviews with Korava women at about the same time, the name given to the Yerukulas in Tamil-speaking areas of south India. Later, they were brought under the auspices of the 1911 Criminal Tribes Act.[87] In *Ethnographic Notes in Southern India* (1906), Thurston claimed that they told him that they left Madras at harvest time and worked as tattooists in the neighbouring districts. They tattooed women from all social groups: high and low caste, Hindus and Muslims. Their fee ranged from a quarter *anna,* for a dot or line, to twelve *annas* for a more complex design. In the villages, payment was sometimes made in kind. Thurston wrote that the tattoo designs included representations of scorpions, birds, fishes and flowers. These were usually drawn on the arms, legs, forehead, cheeks or chin. Occasionally, names or initials were also tattooed on the arm in Tamil, if the shape of the letters could be drawn out for the (illiterate) women first. According to Thurston, these itinerant women were also engaged in fortune-telling, pilfering and property theft: 'As house-breakers they are expert and burglary is their favourite crime'. Their own tattoos apparently provided an easy means of identifying them,[88] a theme we shall discuss in a moment. Ananthakrishna Iyer also noted female tattooists in Mysore were 'nomadic beggars', who otherwise engaged in putting on puppet shows.[89]

Ethnographers noted the use of similar pricking instruments, dyes and techniques across the subcontinent. Thurston wrote that in South India women prepared ink by rolling a mixture of turmeric and leaves on a thin cloth. They then rolled it into a wick and placed it in an oil lamp. The wick was lit and the lamp covered with an earthenware pot. The lampblack deposited there was then mixed with either water or the breast milk of the woman about to be tattooed. The pattern was selected and traced onto the skin using a blunt stick dipped in the ink. This was then pricked in with the needles and a coat of ink rubbed in, followed by a little yellow turmeric, which brightened the colour.[90] The production of soot using plant products and turmeric, its admixture with water and/or milk, and the use of needles or thorns to prick out designs was, according to British surveys, common throughout India.[91]

Colonial ethnographers were fascinated by these female interventions on Indian women's bodies. There is a palpable sense of titillation in their notes, particularly in the common references they made to the significance of women's breasts during the tattooing process. Many writers – like Wise – stated that breast milk was used to mix the dye. Thurston further noted that women's breasts were never tattooed, as it was feared that they might be punctured.[92] As Dirks has shown, Madras officials were concerned about the sexual content of Thurston's *Ethnographic Notes*.[93] A close reading of Thurston's text reveals that he had never watched tattooists at work, instead writing of their practices from details gleaned through interviews with them, probably in the presence of a local intermediary. The screening of this female world from the gaze of the British male observer, whilst perhaps revealing something of either the ambivalence of colonial power, or women's successful refusal to engage with it, only added to the potentially erotic charge of tattooing. Amongst Thurston's acquisitions for the Ethnological Section of the Madras Museum in 1902–3 was a set of apparatus used by female tattooists in Coimbatore. It included the fruits of the palmyra palm and bael (*ægle marmelos*), in which the powder was kept, the bamboo used to hold the tattooing needles, and half coconut shells in which the ink was mixed.[94] Though the museum's visitors could not watch the tattooist at work, they were made aware of her gender and allowed access to the tools of her trade. This, and the fact that the tattooing equipment consisted of types of natural products unavailable in Europe (palm, bamboo, coconut), rendered the practice utterly exotic.

This seeming exoticism was compounded by the fact that the wearing of tattoos was most prevalent amongst women, unlike in Britain.

Moreover, working-class and aristocratic tattooing practices in nineteenth-century Britain usually entailed the drawing of designs on the body.[95] In contrast, Indian women were often tattooed on the face (Figure 3.4). Colonial ethnographers gave multiple explanations for this, largely relating to their own preoccupations with sexuality and the history of the sub-continent. Few saw it as simple ornamentation. As we have seen, explanations instead included that it signalled a girl's attainment of sexual maturity, enhanced women's sexual attractiveness, curbed women's sexual desires, allowed women to enter heaven and be reunited with family there, cured physical ailments or prevented attacks on Hindu women during the Mughal 'invasion' of the subcontinent.[96]

The tattooing of men in the subcontinent, on the other hand, was said to be relatively uncommon. As we have seen, it was confined to tribal groups, for instance in the North East Frontier. Just as ethnographers saw women's tattoos as a mark of availability for marriage, they commonly viewed men's tattoos as a sign of a boy's transition to adulthood, and a marker of masculinity. E.H. Man (officer in charge of the Andaman

Figure 3.4 'Tatoo Designs'. L.K. Ananthakrishna Iyer, *The Mysore Tribes and Castes, vol. I* (Mysore University, 1935). (Courtesy of British Library, T49126)

Homes, 1875–9) wrote that all boys except those from the Jarawa tribe were first tattooed on the arms at the age of 8, and went on to be tattooed on the back three or four years later. He interpreted these tattoos as a sign of manliness.[97]

In Burma too, where the tattooing of men was far more common, tattooing was seen as part of the transition to manhood. Some of the earliest European visitors to South East Asia wrote about tattooing. In the 1400s, Nicolo Conti recorded how men and women in the Irawadi Valley 'puncture their flesh with pins of iron, and rub into these punctures pigments which cannot be obliterated, and so they remain painted for ever.'[98] In the seventeenth century, Tavernier also wrote of the patterns tattooed on the chest, back, arms and thighs of the Siamese soldiers he saw, brightly coloured flowers and animals which he said gave their skin a fabric-like appearance: 'seeing these soldiers from a distance you would say that they were clad with some flowered silken stuff or painted calico, for the colours once applied never fade.'[99] Two hundred years later, J.G. Scott, who travelled in Burma under the pseudonym Schway Yoe, wrote that such tattooing marked the attainment of the status of adulthood. Burmese tattoos consisted of intricate designs inscribed in black and red, from waist to knee, in what Europeans coined 'breeches' style. Scott wrote that men's ability to endure the length of time taken to complete the complex patterns (often several sittings) and the intense discomfort involved (opium was sometimes smoked to alleviate the pain) were a test of masculinity. He wrote: '[men] would as soon think of wearing a woman's skirt as of omitting to be tattooed'.[100] The pricking instrument used in Burma was about two feet long. The needle (*yat*) had a round, sharp point, divided into four by long splits which held blue coloured dye.[101] A common explanation for the origin of tattooing in Burma was that an ancient Burmese king had directed it as a means of making the sexes mutually attractive.[102] Unlike Indian tattoos, Burmese designs were much admired for their embodiment of artistic skill and beauty.[103] Photographic images of a Burmese men being tattooed whilst smoking an opium pipe were quickly transformed into one of the many exotic colonial images in circulation on collectors' postcards during the late nineteenth and early twentieth centuries.[104] As Saloni Mathur shows, exotic postcards reveal something of the structure of gender relations in colonial India.[105] Such picturesque images were described in Caine's handbook for European travellers. He informed his readers that nothing pleased a Burmese man more than to be asked to show his tattoos.[106]

Almost a century after Risley's work in the Indian subcontinent, late-twentieth-century anthropologists have continued to write about the meaning of tattooing. There are some striking similarities between their approach and that of colonial ethnographers, particularly in the focus on gender relations, marks of identity and the apparent demise of the practice. Nineteenth-century readings of Indian women's bodies have proved remarkably enduring. O.P. Joshi, for instance, writes that women's tattoos now imply particular feminine attributes: chastity and fidelity.[107] Joshi details how non-sedentary traders (*banjara*) and ironsmiths (*gadia lohar*) in Rajasthan wear particular designs ('clan marks') on the face. Names, village names and names of spouses are sometimes also tattooed on the arms. These, Joshi writes, serve as permanent identification marks.[108] Emma Tarlo has noted a similar phenomenon amongst the Bharwads of Gujarat. These itinerant pastoralists have a tradition of providing hospitality to other Bharwads. Their tattoos (and clothes) provide a means of instant recognition. In the past, these have included an image of Hanuman and Lord Krishna on the upper and lower arms.[109]

Tarlo also discusses the prevalence of tattoos (*tajvus*) amongst the Kanbi and Kharak peasant castes in rural Gujarat. Formerly, itinerant Vaghris were employed as tattooists. Girls had a small round tattoo mark on their chin and a cross on their cheek, with designs on the neck, lower arms, lower legs and chest added later on. Traditionally, designs included dots and other often geometrical motifs. These represented a mixture of auspicious and religious symbols, such as the shrine, seeds, flowers, crescents, trees, swastikas and the sun. By the 1970s, designs had come to include desirable objects such as the wristwatch and radio. Other tattoos represented scissors, kitchen implements, aeroplanes or water pumps. Tarlo notes that tattooing is increasingly seen as a sign of backwardness. For this reason, older women are often ashamed of their tattoos. They told Tarlo of the social pressure to have them, because they represent wealth. Although the view that tattoos allowed identification in the after-life was expressed, most of the women denied that they were anything other than decorative, and rejected the idea that they offered protection against the evil eye (*najar*), a view supported by Joshi.[110] As one older female put it: 'They *say* we will be reborn as a camel [if we are not tattooed]. But have you seen it? Have you ever *seen* anyone reborn as a camel? Have you? . . . No? Well, then.'[111]

Tattooing and the Colonial Encounter

By the mid-nineteenth century considerable inter-colonial migration, both within and between Europe and Asia, impacted on tattoo designs. This was fuelled by labour demands and encouraged by improvements in transportation and communications. A large number of men served in British colonial armies, and the culture of the garrison encouraged the acquisition of tattoos. Soldiers for instance might acquire tattoos characteristic of a particular locality, such as an elaborate Burmese design.[112] Sailors too were tattooed during trips overseas.[113] Thurston wrote of a man in Madras who had been tattooed with a European ballet girl whilst in Columbo, Ceylon. The man told him that after his marriage he was ashamed of the design and tried his best to cover it with clothing.[114] With large numbers of Tamil men migrating to Burma throughout the nineteenth century, many returned to South India with elaborate tattoos. By the early twentieth century, tattooists there were even copying Burmese designs.

It is from Thurston's work for the Ethnographic Survey of India after 1901, during which hundreds of South Indian human specimens were surveyed by the anthropometric gaze, that other details about tattooing practices, and their relationship to the colonial encounter, emerge. The Eurasian community was made to remove its clothing, revealing the prevalence of particular types of tattoos. European sailors working the seas between Britain's colonial possessions commonly wore a symbol of hope (usually represented as a woman) and the anchor.[115] Convicts transported from Britain to Australia from the 1780s had all manner of tattoos: the initials of loved ones left behind, hearts, crucifixes, birds, flowerpots, boxing matches, cockfights, and nationalist and unionist symbols such as the thistle and shamrock.[116] These were decorative inscriptions that were produced by migratory experience. Love, loss, memories and, crucially, the promise of reunion were all carried, indelibly, on these transient bodies.[117] Hope for a new future was sometimes also expressed. Frederick Cross, a European jockey turned soldier shipped to Van Diemen's Land (Tasmania) from Bombay in 1845, sported a kangaroo, a man with a spear and a dog, all tattooed above the words 'advancée australia'.[118] This was early Australian nationalist insignia *par excellence*, touchingly inscribed on the body of a man with an ambiguous role in empire building: both as a soldier in India and convict in Australia.

In India too, colonial experiences of one kind or another were written on the bodies of the 130 male members of the Eurasian community who Thurston examined during his South Indian anthropometric forays. The tattoo designs he noted included: a picture of Queen Alexandra (wife of King Edward VII, 1901–11), a steam boat, flowers in a pot, the word 'mercy', royal coats of arms, the crown and flags, a cross (crucifix) and anchor, birds, a dancing girl, a heart and cross, a shepherdess, an elephant, a Burmese lady, a sailing boat, a scorpion, crossed swords, bracelets, initials of loved ones, a lizard and bugles. The tattoos were blue, and sometimes red. Some of them were indistinguishable from those found on Europeans: a partner's initials, the word 'mercy', the dancing girl and heart shapes, for instance. Others – like the anchor, bugle, crossed swords and Burmese lady – seem to record military or seafaring status and exploits. The scorpion and lizard were common Indian designs. The elephant was not, but was perhaps instead a novelty, rather like the dancing girl.

Inscribing cultural experiences in India with European designs, the tattoos embodied the cultural hybridity of a community with a complex relationship to India and Britain in the years before Independence.[119] The exposure and recording of nationalist and Christian designs – royal insignia, flags, birds (symbols of the Holy Ghost) and the crucifix – took place during an anthropometric encounter where the Eurasian body was viewed as a *native* body. Yet their tattoos were mainly European in style. Some of the designs were evidently images common to the military, a common resort of the Eurasian community. Yet at the same time, they seem to speak to what Lionel Caplan refers to as the porousness of the social world Eurasians inhabited.[120] As Fleming has argued in another context, tattooing was sometimes a symptom of the colonial encounter.[121]

Surveying the Criminal Body

The marginality of tattooing as a practice, in Western Europe at least, raises profound difficulties in extracting sources from the archives.[122] In the non-European context there is an additional thorny issue: of how one might move beyond often exoticized and sometimes eroticized ethnographic representations of tattooing towards discerning some sense of the actual nature of the practice. Nowhere is this issue of representation more pertinent than in nineteenth- and early-twentieth-century India, where colonial officials viewed enduring bodily signs like tattoos (and also as we shall see in Chapter 4 transient ones like clothes and hair styles) as firm markers of social difference. Travellers, ethnographers, district commissioners and colonial officials all documented what they believed to be the physical signifiers of India's Otherness.[123] If it is true that, at least to some extent, India was an 'imagined' colonial entity, how can we move beyond the ethnographic representations discussed earlier to discern the nature and frequency of tattooing in the Indian subcontinent in a more tangible sense? This issue becomes all the more pressing when we consider that some of the questions posed by contemporary anthropologists exactly mirror those of nineteenth-century ethnographers, particularly in relation to the significance of tattooing as a mark of identity. Therefore, post-colonial readings of tattooing often echo colonial findings.[124]

Paradoxically, it is the colonial archive that opens up a path through this seeming impasse. In unravelling the actual nature of tattooing in India, we can turn to detailed records of convicts transported overseas during the colonial period. All convicts shipped from India to colonial penal settlements in South East Asia, Mauritius and the Andaman Islands were accompanied by a descriptive roll, or ship indent. These indents include notes of each convict's facial and bodily appearance. The most complete records detailed each convict's name, father's name, place and date of trial, sentence, 'cast or sect' and physical description. Height, physical build, facial description, the presence of absence of a beard or moustache, scars, smallpox scars, inoculation marks, 'burn' and tattoo marks, ear and nose piercings, penal tattoos (*godna*) and any physical deformities were also noted. Occasionally, references to hook swinging (*chuttack*) marks also appear.[125] As Cole has argued, descriptive registers assumed that the body carried its own means of identification.[126]

In theory at least, descriptive rolls enabled the colonial authorities to match bodies to names, and thus recognize individual convicts for the purposes of labour, discipline and control. Effective work assignment, particularly where convicts possessed useful skills, the punishment of the insolent and violent, the capture of escapees and the identification of the dead all depended on the colonial authorities' ability to render individual bodies legible. There was nothing specifically South Asian about this. The compilation of detailed descriptive records of convicted offenders was not unique to colonial administration in the subcontinent. The records were the same as those produced in British prisons, and served exactly the same function. Foucauldian readings of these biodata sets assert that the collection of detailed convict descriptions was bound up with the con-struction of disciplinary knowledge, which allowed the convict to be closely watched, effectively controlled and ultimately reformed. In relation to the penal-economic strategy of transportation, a close reading of Foucault's work reveals a near acknowledgement of the material basis of the web of power relations he describes. Indeed, in *Discipline and Punish*, he writes of the mutual exclusivity of the 'accumulation of men and the accumulation of capital'.[127] This is a useful way of conceptualizing the physical descriptions of inter-colonial transportation convicts found in the archives. Hamish Maxwell-Stewart and Ian Duffield have argued: 'Once paraded, degradingly near-naked, under the omnipotent-seeming official eye, prisoners starkly experienced themselves as humiliated subjects of disciplinary knowledge.'[128] Certainly, it was the desire to know the individual convict within a collectivized group of transportation prisoners that fuelled the need for the acquisition of detailed information about them. And thus marks on the body, including decorative tattoos, came to the attention of colonial officials for surveillance purposes.

Descriptive rolls were far from ideal for these purposes, as they were usually the product of the observations of a single clerk. However, and although transportees were not representative of Indian society more broadly, their indents do provide us with a means of at least partially examining colonial representations of Indian tattooing, especially amongst women. Though female prisoners were not always subject to the general inspections of colonial ethnographers, they were not exempt from minute physical examination prior to their transportation. Of particular value is the indents' simultaneous notation of each convict's 'cast or sect' together with their physical description. They also steer us towards an analysis of colonial perceptions of the relationship between tattooing, caste or race, and criminality. Until the last quarter of the nineteenth century, tattoos were simple signifiers of Indian social groups. Yet with the passage of the Criminal Tribes Acts after 1871, tattoos came to mark something more. Colonial police officers drew on ethnographic writing and transformed tattoos into visual signifiers of hereditary criminal status. They became a potentially useful means for colonial surveillance of individuals designated as members of the so-called criminal tribes.

In the recording of convict tattoos, jail clerks invoked the vernacular language of inscription – *godna/godena* or sometimes the Bengali equivalent *ulki* – and the English translations tattooing and stamping. The records are sometimes ambiguous, with colonial scribes making frequent references to 'marks' on the body, sometimes in reference to moles, scars and warts, and sometimes alluding to boils or sores. Though a precise description of some 'marks' is often absent, their position on the body is occasionally suggestive.[129] Yet the fact that the tattoos worn by convict women – who as we shall see were far more likely to be tattooed than men – were explicitly referred to as such is suggestive of the fact that most of the 'marks' recorded on convict men's bodies did not allude to decorative tattoos.

It is notable that only a tiny proportion (less than 1 per cent) of Indian male convicts transported overseas from the Bengal Presidency before 1857 – which by then extended into Orissa and across Bihar, Awadh, the North West Provinces and the Panjab in North India – sported tattoos. Without exception, tattooed convicts either came from or were convicted in the districts of eastern Bengal, or were Burmese. Otherwise, tattooing did not prevail amongst particular caste or tribal groups. Thus we know that Naffoo, a Burmese convict convicted in Chittagong of murder and plunder, and transported to Penang in May 1818, was tattooed on both legs. Nyatookuree and Wungjyng, both convicted with Naffoo, apparently had 'many marks of godena' on their bodies. Both men were described as Mughs, the designation commonly used for Arakanese living in Chittagong.[130] Almost thirty years later, Sooria Sing Keechuk was convicted of dacoity (gang robbery) in Dacca. He wore a tattoo between his eyebrows, of what design we do not know, when he was embarked for Moulmein in March 1847.[131] Ramdoolub Gope, a Dom convicted of dacoity with murder and arson in Moorshedabad, had a tattoo in the same place, simply described as a mark of 'oolkie' (*ulki*). He was shipped to Singapore on the East India Company's surveillance vessel *Krishna* in June 1851.[132] Mahogoo *alias* Bhowanee was convicted of wilful murder and transported to Moulmein in August 1856. The descriptive roll described him as a 'Hindoo', and recorded the presence of 'somewhat crossed tattoo marks on both his wrists, on top of the right shoulder and also on the back where the dhootee [*dhoti*] ties'.[133] The few surviving Port Blair records reveal that Ramgaiah, who was shipped to the Andamans from Madras in 1862, sported green marks on his forehead and right arm.[134]

The most detailed records of male convicts' tattoos describe flowers (*banfoora*) or pilgrimage tattoos, though both were rare. Three convicts – Damoo Bagdee, Nuffur Howrah and Bhagbut Bagdee – convicted in Hughli and shipped to Singapore in 1855 had floral tattoos, on both ribs and the left arm.[135] A few transportees also had pilgrimage tattoos on their upper and/or lower arms. Thus Meheelaub, convicted of professional dacoity and also transported to Singapore on the *Krishna* (1851), had scars of the 'davi stamp' on the front of both forearms. One of his compatriots, Badul Sewa Singh *alias* Shewlar, had 'dwarka stamps' on the upper and lower parts of both arms. This was a literal embodiment of some visit to the Hindu site of pilgrimage of the same name, the mythical city of Lord Krishna's birth, situated on the far western peninsular of Gujarat.[136] These examples are exceptional, for it was unusual for male convicts to have tattoos, even small ones like these. Burn marks were far more common, particularly on the abdomen (spleen), elbow and knee joints. They point to the widespread use of therapeutic branding amongst Indian subaltern groups during the nineteenth century, as colonial ethnographers suggested.

Burmese convicts were far more likely to have tattoos. Loogele *alias* Sooa, a Burmese convict held in Moulmein Jail (Tenasserim Provinces) in the 1840s, was tattooed on the chest and both arms in red and from the waist to the knees in black.[137] This was the 'breeches' style that so entranced Europeans like J.G. Scott. Before 1857, very few convicts of

Burmese origin appear in the records. After 1884, Burmese life prisoners were transferred to the Andaman Islands, where they were employed in forestry.[138] Systematic descriptive rolls do not survive, so it is not possible to measure the prevalence of decorative tattooing amongst Burmese convicts during this period. However, when Burmese convicts escaped, their tattoos were frequently noted on their descriptive rolls. This was in contrast to escaped Indian convicts, suggesting that decorative tattooing was more widespread in Burma than in any of the Indian presidencies. Of eleven Burmese convicts who attempted to escape from the Islands in 1885, for instance, five were quite extensively tattooed. Nga Saung had 'red tattooed on breast and hands and two spots of black tattooed on both collar bones'. Nga Pyee Moung was tattooed on both thighs and sported red tattoos on his neck. Three others, Gna Ka Yin Gale, Gna Ka Yin Ygi and Gna Shwe Zin, sported tattoos, worn on the jaw-bone, chest, back and thighs.[139] Ironically, that many Burmese sported similar types of tattoos so detailed that it was difficult to record specifics beyond colour (red or black) and bodily location, did not ease individual identification.

When Indian convicts escaped, detailed physical descriptions were swiftly forwarded to the district magistrates in their place of origin, and they were advised to watch out for convicts' attempted return.[140] Tattoos were relatively uncommon, so they provided a less equivocal means for identification than the other physical marks noted on the indents. One man, Narrainsawmy *alias* Doorgia, who escaped from Penang in 1858, for instance, simply had a line tattooed on his forehead.[141] In addition to seeking to avoid ambiguity in the identification of escapees, both tattoos and brand marks were also used to positively identify the dead.[142] This was of no little importance, as it was not unknown for convicts to take on the identity of recently deceased comrades, in an attempt to secure privileges or an early release for themselves. Given that so few convicts were tattooed, however, and only a tiny minority escaped, they were not a particularly useful mark of identification. Brand marks more frequently found their place in the descriptive roles of escaped Indian convicts, together with other details of physical appearance.[143]

The ship indents are much more forthcoming about the tattoos worn by female transportees. As ethnographers suggested, it was more common for women to have tattoos. As we have seen, the number of Indian women transported overseas was very small, never totalling more than 10 per cent of the total number of convicts in any of the penal settlements, even by the latter part of the nineteenth century. Descriptive rolls, however, abound with details of their tattoos. This relatively small number of records can be usefully interrogated for details of the types of tattoos that individual women had. In general, they show less clear patterns than colonial ethnography suggests. Four interesting points emerge. First, tattooing – in substance or style – was by no means uniform between women either of the same caste or from the same region. Tattooing was not, then, any sort of regional or caste mark – something that at the end of the nineteenth century Crooke noted and Risley was forced to concede. Second, women did not have the types of elaborate tattoos later described by colonial ethnographers like Crooke – crocodiles, parrots, shells, bangles, necklaces, leaves, fish, bumble bees and peacocks.[144] In all likelihood this points to the generally impoverished status of transportation women, and the cost of such designs, though it possibly speaks to the situating of the practice in the realms of the exotic. Third, there is no concrete evidence of the demise of tattooing over time, with younger women just as likely to be tattooed as older women. Women from the same region and of the same caste may or may not have sported tattoos. To illustrate this, it is worth a brief look at some of the records: first of a group of nine Hindu women transported from the Bengal Presidency to Penang in 1847. Just three of them wore tattoos. They were each convicted of belonging to a gang of thugs, and were all said to be Nayaks. The two older women – one aged 30, the other 40 – had *godna* marks. The other – aged just 20 – was not tattooed. We do not know if she was married or not.[145] The fourth point to be raised, and one that emerges with great clarity from the ship indents, is that even within the same districts Hindu women were far more likely to be tattooed than Muslims. Large numbers of Muslim women, however, still wore tattoos.

There is just one surviving set of records of female prisoners after transportation to the Andaman Islands began. In 1860, in response to concerns about the emergence of 'hideous vices' – an allusion to homosexual activity – in an almost exclusively male penal settlement, the Andaman authorities sent a proposal for the transportation of female term prisoners to the Superintendent of Alipur Jail in Calcutta. In response, F.J. Mouat, the Inspector-General of Jails in Bengal's Lower Provinces, forwarded a list of the 159 term prisoners in the female jail (Russa) to the Andamans. The list included a physical description of each woman. Of these, 131 were said to wear tattoos. Most common were dots and lines on the face: between the eyes or on the forehead, chin or nose. Less common, but present nonetheless, were similar tattoos on the hands, arms, chest, legs and ankles. Just one woman, Daythary, had more elaborate tattoos: a tree on each arm. What is most notable about the descriptions of these convict women is the predominance of tattooing practices amongst 'Hindus', which seems to add weight to Wise's earlier ethnography of eastern Bengal. However, significant numbers of the Muslim women were tattooed. Of the 117 Hindu convicts, 109 had tattoos. In contrast, 22 out of the 42 Muslim women wore tattoo designs. This may have reflected their place of residence, rather than religion. Of the 5 women from Sylhet, for instance, 4 (all Muslims) had no tattoos. The only woman who did was a Hindu. The age spread of the untattooed women does not differ substantially from the age profile of tattooed women. Indeed, the youngest women, Rookeah, Prayshunoo and Moon Moynee, aged between 12 and 14, were all tattooed. There is thus no clear evidence of a demise in the practice among this limited sample. Sorepah, a Muslim from Mymensingh, was aged 60 and had no tattoos. Jasea, a Muslim from the same district, was 26 and was tattooed on her forehead and left hand.[146]

Such tattoos were not of course recorded for ethnographic posterity, but for surveillance purposes. The use of tattoos as marks of identity reflected developments in Europe, where the police and prison authorities were constantly seeking new ways to register and fix identity. In India too, the police saw decorative tattoos as a means to identify repeat, or habitual, offenders. They also transformed tattoos into a means of identifying members of the designated criminal tribes, especially women. In this way, tattoos were viewed as permanent markers of hereditary criminality.

Marking Hereditary Criminality: Tattooing and the Criminal Tribes

Amongst European criminologists, the meaning of tattoos moved beyond their potential to identify individuals, for they were used in the construction of mass criminal pathologies. From the 1870s, the Italian criminologist Cesare Lombroso focused on 'criminal character' rather than offending behaviour as a means to explain crime. Tattoos figured large in his argument, which was that bodily markings were more prevalent amongst criminals than the general population, as manifestations of their atavistic character.[147] Other criminological schools, such as that led in France by Alexandre Lacassagne, stressed the social factors that informed criminal activity. He argued that the closed jail environment could explain the widespread tattooing of prisoners.[148] In India such discussions did not arise, largely because as we have seen caste was viewed as the most important social determinant. However, as well as being one of many bodily marks used for the identification of individual convicts, tattoos were seen as markers of criminality in a more general sense. A series of police handbooks noted that they were a means to identify social groups –

criminal types – included in the Criminal Tribes Acts. Identification was important so that individuals who ignored the restrictions placed on their freedom of movement could be arrested. Those who failed to appear for registration, often in the form of daily roll calls, or who left the reformatory camps without permission were breaking the law. If particular criminal tribes could be shown to wear particular types of tattoos, an easy, and permanent, method of identification presented itself.

During the late nineteenth and early twentieth centuries, ethnographers and police officials in India made frequent allusions to how members of the criminal tribes could be recognized through their tattoos. Some administrators saw particular types of tattoos as useful in fostering the recognition of those castes and tribes that had what were described as hereditary criminal tendencies. Reflecting ethnographic ambivalence about the meaning of tattoos, others saw them as general signs of low status, rather than marks peculiar to specific social groups. Just one colonial observer attempted to make a direct connection between tattoo styles and criminality itself, unsurprisingly Risley. In 1902, he claimed that a group of Doms in Buxar Central Jail had acted out their criminal rituals for him, and connected these rituals to their tattoos. In a discourse strongly reminiscent of nineteenth-century representations of thuggee, he claimed that their criminal lifestyle had become bound up with their religion. As such, they venerated the 'Sânsari Mâi' (Earth Mother) before going out to commit burglaries. Dom men drew a circle on the ground, and then smoothed cow dung over it. They then squatted in front of the circle, and gashed their left arm with a curved knife. Next, they smeared five streaks of blood in the centre of the circle and prayed for the success of the robbery. Risley noted that several of the men in Buxar Jail had scars on their left arms. In a rather fanciful interpretation of the Dom tattoos drawn by Fawcett (Figure 3.3), Risley claimed that one of the tattoos commonly worn by Doms represented five streaks of blood in an enclosed circular space, with a curved knife lying outside it. However, even he was forced to admit that the 'circle' design was 'not so circular as it might be'.[149]

More usually, police officials interpreted tattoos as marks of community, their handbooks drawing heavily on caste ethnographies. Thurston, for instance, lectured to the Madras police.[150] Police officials carefully noted the position and type of tattoos they said were peculiar to the criminal tribes, especially women. The 1908 *Notes on Criminal Classes* by M. Kennedy (Deputy Inspector-General of Police Bombay) is full of references to the tattoo designs favoured by particular groups. Kennedy wrote of the Mangs, for instance: 'Their hands and arms are profusely tattooed, the figures of a cypress, scorpion and snake being preferred. A mark thus

TTT will often be found tattooed on all fingers of the right hand except the thumb and a sun-flower on the back of the same hand.'[151] The Deputy Inspector-General of Police Bengal, F.C. Daly, made similar references in 1916, writing that Dhekaru women 'generally have four flower pattern tattoo marks on the back of each hand, and invariably one or two such marks on the upper and lower arms. They tattoo their faces also on the chin and between the eyebrows, sometimes extending the pattern down the nose.'[152] Directives given to the Panjab police as late as 1944 noted that Baurias had a particular way of marking themselves. Men could be recognized by three brands on the body, and women by five tattoo marks on the face.[153]

It is difficult to square these representations of tattoos as particular marks of criminality, and the discourses of colonial ethnographers who claimed understanding of Indian tattooing practices, with the fact that the Indian district commissioners who contributed to Risley's survey just a few years before failed to establish any evidence that tattooing was hereditary, that particular castes wore particular types of tattoos, or that tattoos were connected to any form of ritual or worship, or criminal activity. The physical descriptions of many thousands of convicts recorded in ship indents also bear the commissioners' findings out. As we have seen, there is little evidence that Indian male convicts wore any tattoos whatsoever, let alone those which were supposed to denote a particular (later 'criminal') caste or tribal status. Women usually wore dots or lines, and not the elaborate designs noted by police officials.

I argued above that colonial ethnographies sometimes blurred the social boundaries between tattooists, tricksters and criminals. Thurston wrote that Korava women, who worked as tattooists, were well versed in property theft. He added that the men sometimes masqueraded as religious mendicants and went begging. Korava of both sexes could, however, be easily recognized, as they had circular or semicircular tattoos on their foreheads and forearms. Rai Bahadur M. Pauparao Naidu of the Madras police later drew on Thurston's work. Individuals could of course resist this social fixing, and alter their tattoos. Thurston acknowledged this, as did Pauparao Naidu.[154] Ananthakrishna Iyer also wrote that non-sedentary communities would enlarge or change their tattoos if convicted, preventing their recognition as repeat offenders from previous descriptive records.[155] According to Crooke, some dreaded the sentence of flogging, which left more enduring scars of the criminal record on the back.[156]

I would speculate therefore that it is unlikely that particular types of tattoos were ever used for surveillance of the criminal tribes. It is far more likely that any individual with a tattoo was open to suspicion, as marginalized social groups tended to carry out tattooing. Indeed, a few police officials followed the work of Crooke, who made frequent references to 'tattoos common to the aboriginal tribes', arguing that *godna* was a general mark of general low social status.[157] In 1907 the Principal of the Police Training School in Saugor, G.W. Gayer, wrote of the difficulties in identifying the criminal tribes: 'One might easily be deluded into the idea that every tribe has such marked characteristics that anyone could recognize them at sight. Nothing could be further from the truth.'[158] The association between tattooing, low status and increasingly criminality perhaps in part explains the demise of the practice noted during Risley's tattooing survey of Bengal, as social groups abandoned tattooing in an attempt to shake off the stigma of criminality that it implied.

Yet the colonial state continued in its efforts to connect bodily signs with criminality, and to use the body to construct penal hierarchies. In the following chapter, I would like to consider the question of convict dress. First, I shall chart the development of distinguishing clothing for prisoners and convicts in the subcontinent and its penal settlements. This accelerated after the abolition of penal tattooing in 1849. Second, following our discussion of the colonial transformation of decorative tattooing into a meaningful social sign, I shall examine the ways in which ethnographers used clothing as another means of social differentiation. Though an essentially transient sign, the police seized upon anthropological texts and represented clothing as a means of identifying members of the designated criminal tribes.

Notes

1. Dirks, *Castes of Mind*, 107.
2. *Ibid.*, 21–8.
3. Felix Padel, *The Sacrifice of Human Being: British Rule and the Konds of Orissa* (Oxford University Press, 2000), 244–6.
4. Christopher Pinney, 'Colonial Anthropology in the "Laboratory of Mankind"', in C.A. Bayly (ed.), *The Raj: India and the British 1600–1947* (National Portrait Gallery Publications, 1990), 252–63.
5. Abbé J.A. Dubois, *Description of the Character, Manners, and Customs of the People of India; and of their Institutions, Religious and Civil* (Longman, Hurst, Rees, Orme and Brown, 1817), 221. This book

was extraordinarily popular, going through half a dozen editions in the nineteenth century alone. For a fascinating analysis of Dubois's writings, see Dirks, *Castes of Mind*, 21–8.

6. H.H. Risley, *The Tribes and Castes of Bengal: Ethnographic Glossary*, 2 vols (Bengal Secretariat Press, 1891), *passim*.

7. IOR MSS Eur E295/14A-D: District Reports on tattooing in Bengal, received by the Superintendent of Census Operations and the Superintendent of Ethnography [H.H. Risley], Nov. 1901 – Oct. 1908 (henceforth District Reports).

8. See, for example, TNSA Public (23 May 1905), 373: Report of Edgar Thurston, 18 May 1905.

9. Alfred Gell, *Wrapping in Images: Tattooing in Polynesia* (Clarendon Press, 1993), 10. On Omai, see Harriet Guest, 'Curiously Marked: Tattooing and Gender Difference in Eighteenth-century British Perceptions of the South Pacific', in Caplan (ed.), *Written on the Body*, 83–101.

10. Charles W. MacQuarrie, 'Insular Celtic Tattooing: History, Myth and Metaphor', in Caplan (ed.), *Written on the Body*, 32–45; Jennipher Allen Rosecrans, 'Wearing the Universe: Symbolic Markings in Early Modern England', in *ibid.*, 46–60. Roman accounts of tattooing in Britain are also mentioned by A.T. Sinclair, 'Tattooing – Oriental and Gypsy', *American Anthropologist*, 10, 3 (1908), 369. He wrote that by 787 AD the practice was so widespread amongst English Christians that a council in Northumberland banned it.

11. Juliet Fleming, 'The Renaissance Tattoo', in Caplan (ed.), *Written on the Body*, 61–82.

12. Guest, 'Curiously Marked', 84–5.

13. Risley, *Tribes and Castes, vol. II*, app. 4 (List of Correspondents); IOR MSS Eur E295/14A: Report of S.K. Agasti, Magistrate of Mauldi, 16 Jan. 1906 (Local Correspondent Moulvi Abdul Majid) (henceforth Report of Agasti). K. Rangachari assisted Edgar Thurston in Southern India – translating, taking photographs and compiling phonographic recordings: Edgar Thurston, *Castes and Tribes of Southern India, vol. I* (Government Press, 1909), x. Other local correspondents included Ry Narasinga Doss, Ry Sribatso Ratho (who submitted notes on the Oriya castes) and Ry M. Varadaraja Mudaliyar (who submitted a collection of Dravidian death songs). See TNSA Public (4 May 1903): Government Order 432; TNSA Public (10 June 1903): Government Order 517.

14. David Arnold, '"An Ancient Race Outworn": Malaria and Race in Colonial India, 1860–1930', in Waltraud Ernst and Bernard Harris

(eds), *Race, Science and Medicine, 1700–1960* (Routledge, 1999), 123–43.

15. *Ibid.*, 102.

16. On the transformation of colonial subjects into objects, see Padel, *Sacrifice of Human Being*, 244 ff.

17. William Crooke, *The Tribes and Castes of the North-West Provinces and Oudh*, 4 vols (Superintendent Government Printing, 1896); Denzil Ibbetson, *Panjab Castes: Being a Reprint of the Chapter on 'The Races, Castes and Tribes of the People' in the Report on the Census of the Panjab Published in 1883* (Superintendent Government Printing, 1916).

18. Nesfield cited in Crooke, *Tribes and Castes*, cxxxix. See also John C. Nesfield, *Brief View of the Caste System of the North-Western Provinces and Oudh, together with an Examination of the Names and Figures Shown in the Census Report, 1882, Being an Attempt to Classify on a Functional Basis all the Main Castes of the United Provinces, and to Explain their Gradations of Rank and Process of their Formation* (North-Western Provinces and Oudh Government Press, 1885).

19. Risley, *Tribes and Castes of Bengal*, vol. *I*, xxxiii–xxxiv.

20. H.H. Risley, 'The Study of Ethnology in India', *Journal of the Anthropological Institute of Great Britain and Ireland*, 20 (1891), 259.

21. James Wise, *Notes on the Races, Castes and Trades of Eastern Bengal* (Harrison, 1883), 280.

22. The following summary is based on Risley, *Tribes and Castes*, vol. *I*, iii–xxxiv. A discussion of Risley's racial typologies can also be found in Bates, 'Race, Caste and Tribe', 241–5.

23. Risley, *Tribes and Castes*, vol. *I*, xii–ix. The pictures were too expensive to reproduce, and their geographic scope limited, so they were not used to illustrate the book.

24. IOR MSS Eur E295/18: Memorandum on the Ethnographic Survey of India, 23 Oct. 1908.

25. H.H. Risley, *The People of India* (Thacker, Spink and Co., 1908). Separate volumes of anthropometric data were also published. See, for instance, H.H. Risley, *Anthropometric Data: Baluchistan, N.W. Borderland, Burma (Ethnographic Survey of India)* (Superintendent of Government Printing, 1908).

26. Risley, *People of India*, 18.

27. Risley, *Tribes and Castes*, xxx.

28. Crooke, *Tribes and Castes*, cxix. The dispute between Crooke and Risley is also discussed by Christopher Pinney, 'Underneath the

Banyan Tree: William Crooke and Photographic Depictions of Caste', in Elizabeth Edwards (ed.), *Anthropology and Photography, 1860–1920* (Yale University Press, 1992), 167–8.

29. Pinney, 'Underneath the Banyan Tree', 167–8.
30. Crooke, *Tribes and Castes*, v–vi.
31. Thurston, *Castes and Tribes*, xvi–xviii. Aspects of Thurston's study are also discussed by Bates, 'Race, Caste and Tribe', 245–7, and Dirks, *Castes of Mind*, 183–92.
32. Thurston, *Castes and Tribes*, xviii.
33. Wise, *Notes on the Races*, 123.
34. J. Forsyth, *The Highlands of Central India; Notes on their Forests and Wild Tribes, Natural History, and Sports* (Chapman and Hall, 1872), 148.
35. Crooke, *Tribes and Castes, vol. II*, 433.
36. R.G. Woodthorpe, 'Notes on the Wild Tribes Inhabiting the So-called Naga Hills, on our North-East Frontier of India, Part II', *Journal of the Anthropological Institute of Great Britain and Ireland*, 11 (1882), 209. Woodthorpe's tour diaries and photographs of tribes in the North East Frontier (1871–6) and his 1875 Report are held in the Pitt Rivers Museum, Oxford.
37. F. Fawcett, 'Notes on the Dômbs of Jeypur, Vizagapatam District, Madras Presidency', *Man*, 1 (1901), 36.
38. H.H. Risley, 'Note on some Indian Tatu-Marks', *Man*, 2 (1902), 101.
39. IOR MSS E295/14B: Notes on Tattooing Amongst Saoria Paharias [Sauria Parhaiyas] of Godda, by R. Bainbridge, Sub-Divisional Officer, n.d. (henceforth Notes on Soaria Pharias). On Japanese tattooing and Sutherland Macdonald, see James Bradley, 'Body Commodification? Class and Tattoos in Victorian Britain', in Caplan (ed.), *Written on the Body*, 142, 145–6, 152–3.
40. Thurston, *Ethnographic Notes*, 381.
41. R.G. Woodthorpe, 'Notes on the Wild Tribes Inhabiting the so-called Naga Hills, on our North-East Frontier of India, Part I', *Journal of the Anthropological Institute of Great Britain and Ireland*, 11 (1882), 66.
42. Woodthorpe, 'Notes on the Wild Tribes, Part II', 201.
43. *Ibid.*, 204 (my emphasis).
44. *Ibid.*, 207–8. Given the history of European expansion in Australasia, it is no coincidence that when Woodthorpe's 'Notes' were discussed by A.W. Buckland at the Royal Anthropological Institute, she likened Naga tattooing to those worn by New Zealand Maori: A.W. Buckland, 'On Tattooing', *Journal of the Royal Anthropological Institute*, 17 (1888), 322.

45. Woodthorpe, 'Notes on the Wild Tribes, Part II', 207–8.
46. Gertrude M. Godden, 'Naga and Other Frontier Tribes of North-East India', *Journal of the Anthropological Institute of Great Britain and Ireland*, 26 (1897), 162.
47. Edward Tuite Dalton, *Descriptive Ethnology of Bengal* (Asiatic Society of Bengal, 1872), i–ii, 39–40.
48. Cited in Godden, 'Naga and Other Frontier Tribes', 185.
49. Woodthorpe, 'Notes on the Wild Tribes, Part II', 206.
50. *Ibid.*, Plate XVIII, Figure 2 ('Golgotha at Phurima, Lhota Nagas').
51. Padel, *Sacrifice of Human Being*, 254.
52. Buckland, 'On Tattooing', 320, 323–4, 326.
53. S.E. Peal, 'Notes on a Visit to the Tribes Inhabiting the Hills South of Síbságar, Asám', *Journal of the Asiatic Society of Bengal*, 41, 2 (1871), 28.
54. Dalton, *Descriptive Ethnography*, 132.
55. Wise, *Notes on the Races*, 123.
56. Crooke, *Tribes and Castes*; L.K. Ananthakrishna Iyer, *The Mysore Tribes and Castes*, 4 vols (Mysore University, 1935), *passim*.
57. Ananthakrishna Iyer, *Mysore Tribes and Castes, vol. I*, 438.
58. Risley, *Tribes and Castes, vol. I*, 350–1.
59. Crooke, *Tribes and Castes, passim* (see especially the entry for the Agariya: *vol. I*, 9–11).
60. IOR MSS Eur E295/14A-D: District Reports.
61. TNSA Public (23 May 1905), 373: Note of J.D. Samuel, Pleader, District Court Masulipatam, Kistna District, n.d.
62. IOR MSS Eur E295/14B: Notes on Saoria Paharias.
63. IOR MSS Eur E295/14A: Report of Agasti.
64. I refer here to Anand Yang's study of colonial relations in Saran District: *The Limited Raj: Agrarian Relations in Colonial India, Saran District, 1793–1920* (University of California Press, 1989).
65. Dalton, *Descriptive Ethnology*, iv.
66. Wise, *Notes on the Races, Castes and Trades*, 6.
67. Arnold, *Colonizing the Body*, 98.
68. Fawcett, 'Notes on the Dômbs', 37 (emphasis mine).
69. Risley, 'Note on some Indian Tatu-Marks', 101.
70. On the Doms, see K.S. Singh, *The Scheduled Castes, People of India National Series, vol. II* (Oxford University Press, 1993), 483–501.
71. Risley, 'Note on some Indian Tatu-Marks', 97–101.
72. A.T. Sinclair wrote that Risley contacted him in 1902 to suggest such collaborative work: 'Tattooing – Oriental and Gypsy', 362. Their correspondence is reproduced in H.H. Risley and A.T. Sinclair, 'The

Origin of the Gypsies', *Man*, 2 (1902), 180–2 (quote p. 181). Crooke also noted the similarity between the appearance of the Banjara and European gypsies: *Castes and Tribes, vol. I*, 164.

73. Thurston, *Castes and Tribes*, 7 vols, *passim*.
74. Thurston, *Ethnographic Notes*, 383.
75. Thurston discusses branding in depth in *Ethnographic Notes*, 398–406.
76. Dubois, *Description of the Character*, 214–15.
77. W.D. Hambly, *The History of Tattooing and its Significance with some Account of Other Forms of Corporal Marking* (H.F. and G. Witherby, 1925), 53, 70 ff. See also Sinclair, 'Tattooing – Oriental and Gypsy', 362–3.
78. *Ibid.*, 52–4 (quote p. 53).
79. *Ibid.*, 53. On women, tattooing and heaven, see Crooke, *Tribes and Castes, vol. I*, 9.
80. IOR MSS Eur E295/14A: Extracts from the returns of the District Commissioners to the questions on tattooing (henceforth Extracts from the returns); IOR MSS Eur E295/14A: Tattooing in Bengal.
81. IOR MSS Eur E295/14A-D: District Reports. L.K. Ananthakrishna Iyer, who was employed in the Survey, also noted a relationship between tattooing and low-caste status: see *Mysore Tribes and Castes, vol. I*, 438.
82. Jean-Baptiste Tavernier, *Travels in India, Translated from the Original French Edition of 1676 by V. Ball, vol. I* (Oxford University Press, 1925), 34–5. The first edition had been published in Britain in 1889; this second edition was edited by William Crooke. A variant translation is cited in Ananthakrishna Iyer, *Mysore Tribes and Castes, vol. I*, 437.
83. Dubois, *Description of the Character*, 221.
84. Forsyth, *The Highlands*, 148.
85. Wise, *Notes on the Races*, 280.
86. IOR MSS Eur E295/14A: Extracts from the returns.
87. For a detailed analysis of the criminalization of the Yerukulas, see Radhakrishna, 'Colonial Construction of a " Criminal Tribe"'.
88. Thurston, *Ethnographic Notes*, 376–83.
89. Ananthakrishna Iyer, *Mysore Tribes and Castes, vol. 1*, 440.
90. Thurston, *Ethnographic Notes*, 380–1.
91. Crooke, *Tribes and Castes, vol. I*, 9; Ananthakrishna Iyer, *Mysore Tribes and Castes, vol. I*, 439; Wise, *Notes on the Races*, 280.
92. Thurston, *Ethnographic Notes*, 376–83. It is perhaps worth noting that Thurston made further observations about the concealment/exposure

of breasts by women in South India during anthropometric measurement: *ibid.*, 530–1.

93. Nicholas B. Dirks, 'Reading Culture: Anthropology and the Textualization of India', in J. Peck and E.V. Daniel (eds), *Culture/Contexture: Explorations in Anthropology and Literary Studies* (University of California Press, 1995), 291–2.

94. TNSA Education (11 July 1903), 333: Administrative Report of the Madras Government Museum for the Year 1902–3.

95. On the relationship between class and tattooing in nineteenth-century Britain, see Bradley, 'Body Commodification?'.

96. IOR MSS Eur E295/14A: Tattooing in Bengal; Crooke, *Tribes and Castes, vol. I*, 9; Forsyth, *Highlands*, 148; Ananthakrishna Iyer, *Mysore Tribes and Castes, vol. I*, 446.

97. E.H. Man, 'On the Aboriginal Inhabitants of the Andaman Islands', *Journal of the Royal Anthropological Institute*, 12 (1883), 331. For a discussion of the Andaman Homes, see Satadru Sen, 'Policing the Savage: Segregation, Labor and State Medicine in the Andamans', *Journal of Asian Studies*, 58, 3 (1999), 753–73.

98. Ananthakrishna Iyer, *Mysore Tribes and Castes, vol. I*, 437.

99. Tavernier, *Travels in India, vol. II*, 232.

100. Schway Yoe [pseudonym for J.G. Scott], *The Burman, his Life and Notions, vol. I* (Macmillan, 1882), 47. See also C.B. Yule, 'Notes on Analogies of Manners between the Indo-Chinese Races and the Races of the Indian Archipelago', *Journal of the Anthropological Institute of Great Britain and Ireland*, 9 (1880), 294.

101. Yoe, *The Burman*, 47–8.

102. Stanley W. Coxon, *And that Reminds Me; Being Incidents of a Life Spent at Sea, and in the Andaman Islands, Burma, Australia, and India* (John Lane, 1915), 101 (photograph of 'A Burmese "K'nut," showing Tattooed Legs', facing 98).

103. Thurston, *Ethnographic Notes*, 381.

104. IOR Photo 904/(3) 'A Shan Man'; IOR Photo 904/(2, 3) 'Tattooing a Burman'.

105. Saloni Mathur, 'Wanted Native Views: Collecting Colonial Postcards of India', in Burton (ed.), *Gender, Sexuality and Colonial Modernities*, 95–115.

106. Caine, *Picturesque India*, 621–2.

107. O.P. Joshi, 'Tattooing and Tattooers: A Socio-cultural Analysis', in O.P. Joshi (ed.), *Marks and Meaning: Anthropology of Symbols* (RBSA [Raj Books and Subscription Agency], 1992), 17–18.

108. *Ibid.*, 18–19.

109. Emma Tarlo, *Clothing Matters: Dress and Identity in India* (University of Chicago Press, 1996), 273.
110. Joshi, 'Tattooing and Tattooers', 19.
111. Tarlo, *Clothing Matters*, 154, 212–13, 230–1.
112. A.T. Sinclair wrote that the British Vice-Consul in Boston told him of the many British soldiers he had seen who had been tattooed in Burma. Sinclair, 'Tattooing – Oriental and Gypsy', 368.
113. Sinclair, 'Tattooing – Oriental and Gypsy', 368.
114. Thurston, *Ethnographic Notes*, 378–9.
115. Hamish Maxwell-Stewart and Ian Duffield, 'Skin Deep Devotions: Religious Tattoos and Convict Transportation to Australia', in Caplan (ed.), *Written on the Body*, 125.
116. On the tattooing of convicts transported to Australia, see Bradley and Maxwell-Stewart, '"Behold the Man"' and 'Embodied Explorations: Investigating Convict Tattoos and the Transportation System', in Ian Duffield and James Bradley (eds), *Representing Convicts: New Perspectives on Convict Forced Labour Migration* (Cassell, 1997), 183–203.
117. In an interesting parallel, surviving video footage of the penal settlement in French Guiana in the early twentieth century shows convicts who were heavily tattooed with all manner of designs on the upper body (*Behind Bars*, BBC2, 15 May 2000).
118. IOR P/403/47 (30 July 1847): Quarterly return of European convicts transported from the Bombay Presidency to Van Diemen's Land, 1 Apr. to 30 June 1845.
119. Alison Blunt, '"Land of our Mothers": Home, Identity and Nationality for Anglo-Indians in British India, 1919–1947', *History Workshop Journal*, 54 (2002), 49–72; Lionel Caplan, *Children of Colonialism: Anglo-Indians in a Post-Colonial World* (Berg, 2001), chs 3, 4.
120. L. Caplan, *Children of Colonialism, passim*.
121. Fleming, 'Renaissance Tattoo', 68.
122. Jane Caplan, 'Introduction', in Caplan (ed.), *Written on the Body*, xi–xxiii.
123. On orientalist constructions of India, see Ronald Inden, 'Orientalist Constructions of India', *Modern Asian Studies*, 20, 3 (1986), 401–46; Ronald Inden, *Imagining India* (Blackwell, 1990); Thomas R. Metcalf, *Ideologies of the Raj* (Cambridge University Press, 1994).
124. See, for example, B.A. Gupte, 'Notes on Female Tattoo Designs in India', in Joshi (ed.), *Marks and Meaning*, 35–59, which draws on work published by Iyer some sixty years before.

125. On colonial interventions into hook swinging, see Dirks, *Castes of Mind*, ch. 8.
126. Cole, *Suspect Identities*, 29.
127. Foucault, *Discipline and Punish*, 221.
128. Maxwell-Stewart and Duffield, 'Skin Deep Devotions', 120.
129. See, for example, IOR P/136/69 (4 Aug. 1825): List of thirty convicts to Penang *per Bridgewater*, 26 July 1825 (Rammun, convicted of dacoity in Rajshahi, 14 June 1824).
130. IOR P/133/26 (26 May 1818): List of thirty convicts to Penang *per Auspicious*, 26 May 1818; Henry Yule, *Hobson-Jobson: A Glossary of Colloquial Anglo Indian Words and Phrases, and of Kindred Terms, Etymological, Historical, Geographical and Descriptive* (John Murray, 1886), 594.
131. IOR P/142/62 (17 Mar. 1847): List of forty convicts to Moulmein *per Enterprize*, 13 Mar. 1847.
132. IOR P/144/5 (9 July 1851): List of fifty-six convicts to Singapore *per Krishna*, 28 June 1851.
133. IOR P/145/45 (28 Aug. 1856): List of sixty-two convicts to Moulmein *per Fire Queen*, 20 Aug. 1856.
134. TNSA Judicial (23 Jan. 1867), 229–30: Descriptive roll of convict no. 5634 Ramgaiah.
135. IOR P/145/10 (3 May 1855): List of twenty-seven convicts to Singapore *per Soobrow Salam*, 26 Apr. 1855.
136. *Ibid.*
137. IOR P/142/38 (17 Oct. 1845): Return of Bengal convicts who have escaped from the Moulmein Jail from 1836 to this date, 28 Aug. 1845.
138. NAI Home (Port Blair A), Sept. 1902, 6–7: Burmese Convicts.
139. TNSA Judicial (27 May 1885), 1399: Copy of descriptive roll of convict no. 3135B., Nga Saung; Copy of descriptive roll of convict no. 2123B., Nga Pyee Moung; Copy of descriptive roll of convict no. 3044B, Gna Ka Yin Gale; Copy of descriptive roll of convict no. 3038B., Gna Ka Yin Gyi; Copy of descriptive roll of convict no. 3030B., Gna Shwe Zin.
140. This mirrored practice overseas, on which officials in India were well versed. See, for example, IOR P/136/31: W.E. Phillips' Minute; and the correspondence between India and Van Diemen's Land on the subject of the issues raised by the 1838 Prison Discipline Committee: AOT CSO 16/1/8: J.P. Grant, Officiating Secretary to the Government of India, to John Montagu, Colonial Secretary Van Diemen's Land, 1 Apr. 1839; AOT CSO 5/216/5449: J. Spode, Chief Police Magistrate, to Montagu, 10 Feb. 1840.

141. TNSA Judicial (21 Dec. 1858), 49–50: Descriptive roll of a convict who absconded from the Convict Lines, Penang, 28 Oct. 1858.

142. See, for example, TNSA Judicial (17 Dec. 1866), 111–12: Extract from the list of casualties amongst the transmarine convicts at Port Blair, Aug. and Sept. 1866 (D. Ramah and Kadirigah).

143. See, for example, TNSA Judicial (3 Dec. 1887), 2748: Copy of descriptive roll of convict no. 3619B Ditta; TNSA Judicial (24 Mar. 1888), 727: Copy of descriptive roll of convict no. 6642B Onkar.

144. Crooke, *Tribes and Castes, vol. I*, 9. Ananthakrishna Iyer made similar references for South India in *Mysore Tribes and Castes, vol. I*, 439.

145. IOR P/143/4 (28 July 1847): List of ten convicts to Penang *per Phlegethon*, 22 July 1847 (no. 4 Musst Hallee, no. 5 Musst Lalee, no. 7 Musst Puchee).

146. NAI Home (Judicial), 19 May 1860, 41–8: F.J. Mouat, Inspector-General of Jails Lower Provinces, to Rivers Thompson, Junior Secretary to Government of Bengal, enclosing a Descriptive Roll of the Female Life Convicts now confined in the Russa Jail, 7 Mar. 1860.

147. Gina Lombroso Ferrero, *Criminal Man: According to the Classification of Cesare Lombroso. Briefly Summarised by his Daughter Gina Lombroso Ferrero* (Putnam, 1911), 39–48, 232. On Lombroso, see also Pick, *Faces of Degeneration*, ch. 5. For a radical reading of Lombroso's work on the relationship between women, criminality and tattooing, see Jane Caplan, '"Educating the Eye": The Tattooed Prostitute', in Lucy Bland and Laura Doan (eds), *Sexology in Culture: Labelling Bodies and Desires* (University of Chicago Press, 1998), 100–15.

148. Caplan, '"Speaking Scars"', 125–8. Abby Schrader notes that in certain prisons and correctional facilities in the twentieth-century Soviet Union almost three-quarters of all inmates who sported tattoos acquired them in jail: 'Branding the Other/Tattooing the Self', 187–91.

149. Risley, 'Note on some Indian Tatu-Marks', 99–100.

150. Dirks, *Castes of Mind*, 184.

151. M. Kennedy, *Notes on Criminal Classes in the Bombay Presidency with Appendices Regarding some Foreign Criminals who Occasionally Visit the Presidency, including Hints on the Detection of Counterfeit Coins* (Government Central Press, 1908), 110. The Superintendent of Police in the United Provinces, S.T. Hollins, used Kennedy's work in *The Criminal Tribes of the United Provinces*

(Government Press, 1914). See, for instance, Hollins' description of the Baurias, 123.

152. F.C. Daly, *Manual of the Criminal Classes Operating in Bengal* (Bengal Secretariat Press, 1916), 12.
153. IOR MSS Eur F161/157: Note on the criminal tribes in the Panjab, D. Gainsford, Inspector of Police, Panjab (1944).
154. Thurston, *Ethnographic Notes*, 376–7; Rai Bahadur M. Pauparao Naidu, *The History of Railway Thieves with Illustrations and Hints on Detection* (Higginbothams, 1915), 46.
155. Ananthakrishna Iyer, *Mysore Castes and Tribes, vol. I*, 437.
156. Crooke, *Tribes and Castes, vol. IV*, 284.
157. Crooke, *Tribes and Castes, passim* (quote *vol. II*, p. 96).
158. G.W. Gayer, *Some Criminal Tribes of India and Religious Mendicants* (Police Officers' Training School Saugor, 1907), i.

−4−

The Question of Convict Dress

Introduction: Fashioning Identities

On 20 April 1839, three Parsi convicts were placed on board the *Adelaide* for embarkation to the penal settlement at Penang. Dadabhoy Sorabjee had been found guilty of stealing, and Jemsetjee Dadabhoy and Bazonjee Dadabhoy of receiving, five reams of paper taken from the office of the *Bombay Times*. They were each sentenced to seven years' transportation.[1] Shortly before the ship departed, the police constable of the Fort Division, William Read, came on board to check that the fifteen convicts on board were properly provisioned and secured, and had no dangerous weapons. During his inspection, he asked the men to take off their clothes, and put on convict uniforms. They refused. Read began to undress them, starting by unravelling one of the men's turbans. The convicts became angry and abusive, and one of them went to strike Read. When a police officer came to his aid, they did as he asked and changed into the uniforms.

A group of 'Parsi inhabitants' in Bombay discovered what had happened, and later that day petitioned the government on the convicts' behalf. They wrote that by being deprived of their long undergarments (*sadras*), the convicts had been unable to eat or drink anything. The convicts also sent a petition to William Read, through their solicitors Patch and Bainbridge, asking him by what authority he had undressed them. When the Bombay authorities heard what had happened, they immediately took the Parsis' side. J.M. Shortt, the Superintendent of Police, told Read to return the *sadras*. Read claimed that he had been unaware that they were connected to the Parsi religion, or he would never have taken them off. The Sheriff of Bombay promised that there would be no future interference with convicts' 'religious prejudices'. There is no doubt that his sympathy also related to the convicts' social standing.[2] It also reflected the nature of their crime. The men's offence was atypical, as most convicts were transported for violent offences against the person. We know from Read's statement that the men were not housed below deck with the other convicts.[3]

This case throws into sharp relief many of the issues surrounding the question of convict dress in colonial India and its penal settlements. This will be the focus of the first section of this chapter. Following recent cultural studies of clothing, I shall argue that dress is a text that determines perceptions of its wearer.[4] Clothing is a bodily marker, constructing social, cultural and racial identities.[5] It is not simply utilitarian but, as Margaret Maynard puts it in a fine study of clothing in colonial Australia, 'functions on many levels and serves a number of purposes.' These functions and purposes include the establishment and – crucially for a study of penal dress – the negotiation of power relationships.[6] Though clothing can be a means through which individuals have the boundaries of their identity fashioned for them,[7] when they use dress to cross those boundaries, profound social anxieties arise.

Up to the 1830s, there were remarkably few colonial interventions into what prisoners and convicts wore. Dress was a means through which they could display their social standing, perhaps reproducing social hierarchies at the same time. Additionally, clothing was an important means of exchange, and prisoners and convicts used it to engage in contraband trading. It thus gave them both economic and cultural autonomy. The introduction of convict dress during the first half of the nineteenth century was somewhat uneven, but in general terms it was developed in the penal settlements first. By the late 1830s convicts shipped to the Straits Settlements or Burma were expected to wear distinguishing uniforms. Uniforms were also introduced soon after the Andaman Islands were colonized as a penal settlement in 1858. By the second half of the nineteenth century, convict uniforms had developed to provide a nuanced visual display of the penal hierarchy. Yet the government granted concessions to convicts and prisoners if they could show that particular types of clothing were essential to their caste or religion. In practice, few allowances were made, with the example of Parsi *sadras* being the exception rather than the rule. Large numbers of convicts were exempted from having their hair cut or their beards and moustaches trimmed, for instance, though hair cropping remained an important form of secondary punishment, especially for women.

In Chapter 3, we saw how the British tried to anchor their understanding of Indian socio-economic structures to the body, using decorative tattooing as a means to fix identities in relation to caste, race and/or criminality. In the second section of this chapter, I shall show how ethnographers attempted to use clothing in similar ways. At one level, dress was used to effect racialized social boundaries: what Bernard S. Cohn has described as 'social separation', or cultural distancing, between Indians and

Europeans.[8] Yet the British also used it as a means to divide South Asian communities into what they saw as decipherable social units. After the passing of the Criminal Tribes Acts, particular types of clothing became a way in which the police attempted to pin individuals to their legal status as hereditary offenders. Reformers also used new modes of adornment to demonstrate the supposedly successful transformation of the criminal tribes into productive, settled communities.

Clothing as a Cultural Space: Convict Dress, Penal Settlements and Prisons

In nineteenth-century South Asia, men wore a basic or longer waist cloth (*langoti* or *dhoti*). Their upper body was either left uncovered or wrapped with a shawl (*chadar*). In some regions, men wore turbans. Stitched long-sleeved outer robes (*jama*), tunics (*kurta*) and trousers (*pyjamas*) were worn in north India. Women either wore *saris*, long pieces of plain or decorated cloth wrapped around the lower body with one end draped over the torso, or long tunics (*kamiz*) and trousers (*shalwar*), with a veil (*dupatta*). Towards the end of the nineteenth century, blouses were also worn under the *sari*.[9] All were a stark contrast to European dress, which was heavily tailored and often restrictive.[10]

When convicts were first transported from South Asia in the late eighteenth century, they were not issued with a uniform. Instead, they were given standard 'Indian' clothing: a piece of white cloth to be worn as a *dhoti*. Twice a year, they received a new length. The Mauritian penal settlement, for example, imported Patna *chintz* for convicts, issuing six yards of white cloth and a blanket (*cumlie*) twice a year.[11] The East India Company was rather less generous. Bencoolen convicts each received a blanket and half a piece each of white, red and blue cloth annually.[12] In Penang, convicts were issued with a new piece of cloth each year and a coarse blanket every three years.[13] This was said to barely cover them, and it was accepted that those who hired convicts for private purposes would need to buy them additional clothing, 'for decency's sake'.[14] This was first of several references to the indecency of the *dhoti*. As Karen Sayer shows in a nuanced study of dress and the Victorian poor, the middle class saw clothing as a boundary that prevented the body from becoming a source of moral decay. Nakedness was a site of transgression; clothing suggested industry and honest toil.[15] As we shall see, later initiatives covered the Indian criminal body more fully, and at the same time marked it out as distinctive. We know very little of the clothing worn by female prisoners and convicts during the early period. Presumably, like men, they received cloth rations.

There were three reasons for this lack of concern about what transportation convicts wore. First, until 1849 most transportees from the Bengal and Madras presidencies, including women, were tattooed on the forehead with penal *godna* markings. This distinguished convicts from the free population no matter what they wore. Second, as Indian communities were a small minority in the places convicts were sent to, it was easy to recognize them. Before indentured immigration to Mauritius accelerated during the 1830s, for example, there was only a small Indian population on the island, compared to the larger white, creole (Mauritian-born), slave and, later, apprentice populations.[16] The same was true for Bencoolen, the Straits Settlements and Burma. Third, and consistent with ongoing concerns about reducing expenditure on convicts, considerable savings were made if convicts could wear their own clothes. The settlements were responsible for rationing and provisioning convicts, so this kept labour costs down. The failure to develop convict uniforms contrasted with British policy in other penal settlements, where dress was used to distinguish (non-tattooed) convicts from free white settlers.[17]

Given the lack of concern about instituting any sort of distinguishing dress, clothing was a cultural space in which some convicts challenged the distinction between freedom and penal servitude.[18] Up until at least the 1840s, convicts were able to wear other clothes in addition to their standard issue. Many took clothing with them from India. The Superintendent of Police Bombay wrote of the immense quantity of baggage one group of convicts transported in 1839 had with them on embarkation.[19] In 1846, convict luggage actually capsized the boat on which they were being taken to their transportation ship. One convict fell overboard and drowned.[20] However, many convicts were extremely poor and did not own additional clothes; the principle of less eligibility taxed the prison authorities in India as much as it did in Britain.[21]

At a practical level, a change of clothing was very desirable as most convicts worked at outdoor labour, often in cool temperatures or in rain. Before 1839, convicts transported to the Straits were not given any warm clothing. This certainly contributed to high mortality rates there. The Medical Board then recommended that convicts be issued with a coarse wool pair of trousers and jacket upon embarkation, as well as a length of cloth.[22] At the same time, the latitude permitted in relation to clothing allowed convicts to reproduce pre-existing social hierarchies, relating to wealth and status (or lack of them), and cultural identity. The colonial authorities were complicit in this. The permission granted to Parsi convicts to wear their *sadras* is a case in point. It is not surprising, then, that the authorities sometimes saw convicts' choice of clothing as a signifier of religion, though it probably more closely reflected their region of origin. When three Bombay convicts marooned from the Grand River depot in Mauritius, the Head Convict Overseer, William Staveley, noted that they were dressed with a white short gown, had a thin cloth thrown over their shoulders and occasionally wore *cumlies*, 'something like the Musslemen [Muslims]'.[23]

This brings us to another point, the potential use of clothing as a means of identification. This was especially significant for convicts from Bombay, as they were not marked with *godna*. Some of the best evidence we have on convict clothing comes from descriptions of convict deserters,[24] or of convicts tried for secondary offences after transportation. The holdings of the Mauritius Archives in this respect are a particularly rich source. From its records, we know that some convicts possessed a substantial number of garments. During the annual Moharrum celebrations in Mauritius (known as Yamsé), convicts dressed to impress, wearing plain waistcoats, patterned waistcoats, brightly coloured jackets, knee-length trousers and leather belts.[25] Post-mortem records also give clues as to what type of clothing convicts owned. It is clear that even during normal working hours, convicts on the island wore non-standard issue. In place of or in addition to their *dhotis*, convicts wore cotton trousers and shirts, belts, waistcoats and jackets.[26] Convicts also wore coloured turbans, caps or handkerchiefs, something that visitors to the island also noted when they described the appearance of convicts at work.[27] As we saw in Chapter 2, such headgear may have been pulled down low in an attempt to conceal *godna* marks.

Some of the most interesting evidence we have on convict dress relates to their wearing military uniforms. In 1806, Bencoolen convicts were actually employed in British military campaigns, and so the British issued them with uniform coats. These held a symbolic value for the convicts that the British authorities were well aware of. After a campaign had ended, and believing that their military service had won them freedom, the convicts put their uniforms on and went to confront the Resident. He, in turn, removed them, confining the convicts in the fort until they agreed to go back to work. Only then did he give them their jackets back.[28] In Mauritius, commonly convicts were called *sepoys*, a term which the British used to refer to 'a native soldier, disciplined and dressed in the European style'.[29] The use of this descriptive category reflected the mistaken general belief that they were soldiers imprisoned as British political prisoners.[30] In their wearing of army uniforms convicts no doubt perpetuated this image. Golsine, one of the convicts who took part in the Bel Ombre convict rebellion of 1817, the largest convict uprising ever seen on the island, wore a blue waistcoat and cavalry uniform.[31] Another convict, transferred to Madagascar in the 1820s as part of Britain's policy of establishing friendly relations in the Indian Ocean, also had a soldier's jacket, two black jackets, a turban and a piece of white cloth in his possession when he died.[32] The general lack of a distinguishing dress, and the wearing of military uniforms, allowed convicts to reproduce or take on non-penal identities, perhaps relating to a view that they were not under punishment but in service, military or otherwise. In 1824, W.E. Phillips, Superintendent of Convicts Penang, wrote that prisoners no longer feared transportation to what was by then a known penal space, and on arrival called themselves Company Servants (*Kumpanee ke Noukur*).[33] The Malay writer Abdullah Bin Abdul Kadir also referred to them as the Company's convicts.[34]

Clothing was also a means of exchange that convicts could use in contraband trading.[35] The authorities made efforts to contain it, but they were not always successful. Despite an early Bencoolen proclamation banning all persons from trading with convicts, for instance, contraband flourished. In 1806, two convicts were executed for their part in the theft of cloth worth a massive $1,200 (Spanish dollars).[36] The 1825 Bencoolen Rules show a certain resignation to its continuance, instead forbidding individuals from buying goods from convicts worth more than ten rupees.[37] Convicts also sold and bartered their clothes and blankets; in the Straits Settlements, there were several unsuccessful efforts to control this.[38] In Mauritius, convicts were picked up frequently for selling waistcoats, shirts, trousers and buttons on the black market. During the period 1819–40, large quantities of stolen goods were recovered from Mauritian convict camps. These included twill cloth, rolls of silk and cotton, shirts, trousers, jackets, handkerchiefs, shawls, caps, waistcoats, shoes and slippers.[39] The theft of clothing could of course be a hugely symbolic act, depending on what was stolen and from whom. Theft constituted material acquisition, but it could also be retributive. In 1819, a group of convicts burgled the Mauritian Colonial Treasurer. Amongst the stolen items was a pair of epaulettes, an important symbol of his high colonial status.[40] The following year, two convicts, Kalloo Fakir Mohamed and Nacta Redinsing, went maroon – in protest, they claimed, at having been made to work after hours. They attacked and robbed five individuals on the island's roads between 6 and 11 September. Two of their victims died from their injuries. When they were finally arrested, Kalloo was wearing a yellow waistcoat, recognized as having belonged to one of the deceased.[41]

The Mauritian authorities made no attempt to introduce convict uniforms. However, from the early 1840s, convict dress began to be standardized in the penal settlements of South East Asia and in mainland prisons. This was part of the general tightening up of the regulations after the Prison Discipline Committee published its 1838 report, which largely ignored the penal settlement in Mauritius because it was not Company territory. The Committee said little on prison dress, beyond noting that the amount of clothing then given to convicts was more than that possessed by common labourers, and that the 'apparent suffering' of imprisonment could be increased by its introduction.[42] Administrators in Indian jails foresaw prisoner unrest on the issue, and so uniform dress was not actually imposed for some time. In 1851, E.A. Samuells, the Superintendent of Alipur Jail, the largest prison in British India, wrote that if convicts were made to wear uniforms, there would be great discontent.[43] It was not until 1855 that Bengal prisoners were banned from wearing their own clothes. Samuells was proved correct, with inmates making vehement complaints against the prohibition. They were issued with only eight yards of cloth every six months, so they had no dry change of clothing. They had to tear the cloth in half, making two four-yard lengths. Once again the authorities complained about the indecency of their garments, especially for women, who were said to be barely able to cover their bodies.[44] To cite Sayer once again, 'the body that could be glimpsed through disordered/frayed/ragged clothing came to be automatically treated as fluid, sexualized, dangerously unconfined.'[45] Nevertheless, the authorities pushed ahead with the introduction of prison dress. Like *godna*, its form varied. By the 1860s only life convicts in Madras were given uniforms; term prisoners still wore their own clothes.[46] Weaving cloth for prison uniforms was an important part of jail manufacture in the Presidency though.[47]

The penal settlements introduced uniforms a few years before the jails. In 1839, the Bombay authorities ordered that convicts were to be transported with only a limited amount of clothing, to stop them making money by trading it.[48] The authorities in the Straits Settlements introduced new penal dress a few years later. The issue of clothing was to depend on each convict's place in a new class system, outlined in Governor W.J. Butterworth's *Code of Rules*. In this, convicts were divided into five classes. The fifth class was composed of those convicted of serious crimes, and those convicted of secondary offences in the settlement. The fourth class was composed of term convicts and those convicted of less serious offences. The third class contained those promoted from the fourth class. Peons and those working for the Convict Department as overseers (*tindals*) were placed in the second class. First-class convicts had already served sixteen years of their life sentence (term convicts were never transported for more than fourteen years) and were allowed to live out of the convict settlement. Each class had varying privileges, relating to rations and money gratuities. Promotion and demotion between classes provided both positive and negative incentives for good behaviour.[49]

The *Code of Rules* perceived clothing as a way to mark out prisoner classes. Twice a year the second, third, fourth and fifth classes were to be given nine yards of grey shirting, one jail suit, two working suits and a cap. The outfits were to differ slightly according to penal class (Figures 4.1, 4.2 and 4.3). However, the *Code* was not introduced immediately. In 1847, the Superintendent of Convicts at Singapore complained that convicts were still given lengths of cloth. They did not make them into clothes, as they should have done. Instead, they rolled the cloth into a sort of cummerbund. Once again, convict garments were described as 'almost an offence to public decency'. The Superintendent suggested that convicts be issued with stitched black clothing and a red cap, both to cover them and to make them more conspicuous.[50]

It seems likely that women were given the same ration of cloth, though the records are not forthcoming on this point. As we have seen, this was

Figure 4.1 'Chetoo, an Incorrigible Convict of the Fifth Class'

Figure 4.2 'Convict of the Second Class and Munshi (writer)'

the case in Indian prisons, and was also the case later on in the Andaman Islands. Broadly speaking, the rules for the management of convicts in Arakan and the Tenasserim Provinces followed those devised for the Straits. Fourth-class convicts there wore regulation prison uniform, and the fifth class a distinctive red prison dress.[51]

Until the 1850s, convicts who worked as overseers had been issued with a 'belt' alone, of what kind we do not know.[52] The first attempt to clothe first-class convicts – from which the *tindal* class was drawn – differently came in 1850 when Butterworth provided them with special uniforms. Some convicts initially refused to wear them. Butterworth put their reaction down to 'caste prejudices', a typical colonial reading of convict resistance at this time.[53] Some high-caste convicts may have been concerned about the loss of particular garments a uniform entailed, though the general response may have been related to other factors. Convict *tindals* were perhaps concerned about losing the autonomy to dress as they pleased, or at being so obviously differentiated from ordinary convicts. In relation to the second point, it was later claimed that Andamanese tribals

Figure 4.3 'Head Tindal, Maistri (foreman) of Cart Makers and Wheelwrights'. J.F.A. McNair, *Prisoners their Own Warders: A Record of the Convict Prison at Singapore in the Straits Settlements Established 1825, Discontinued 1873, together with a Cursory History of the Convict Establishments at Bencoolen, Penang and Malacca from the Year 1797* (Archibald Constable, 1899)

targeted convict overseers in the Andaman Islands during their attacks on working parties. Convict overseers thus often removed the visible symbols of authority – turbans, badges and belts – when going out to work.[54] Whatever the case – and subaltern voices are typically absent from the account – the objections of convict *tindals* were eventually overcome. Together with peons (orderlies) and *munshis*, they were issued with various belts and brass plates. Additionally, first-class Indian convicts otherwise employed were permitted to wear clothes of their choice. A demonstration of a lengthy period of good behaviour, this enabled them to find work with private employers – a step in the right direction for their rehabilitation, integration into the free population and subsequent removal from the coffers of the convict system.

The initial difficulties Butterworth faced in introducing penal dress raise a number of issues relating to convict negotiation of relations of power.

One obvious implication of the standardization of dress was to ignore the possible significance of religion and/or caste to prisoners and convicts. Yet, as Arnold shows, in mainland Indian jails religion and caste did impact upon prison discipline, whatever the authorities claimed.[55] Jail administrators wanted to standardize punishment, but they also wished to avoid accusations that they were interfering in questions of caste, which could and did lead to episodes of prison unrest. These imperatives were essentially incompatible; officials acknowledged that the close social contact integral to incarceration had a different impact depending on caste. In 1823, for example, the Commissioner of the Deccan, in response to Brahmin prisoners' complaints about the lack of caste differentiation in the Ahmednuggur Jail wards, wrote: 'If [Brahmins] are not separated at all from the inferior castes their punishment by this admixture may be deemed to be greater than was contemplated, since degradation or perhaps pollution is added [to] the penalty of imprisonment.'[56] The Secretary to Government Bombay added that mixing castes within the jails 'may even be so repugnant to native manners that it should not be admitted into a sentence.'[57]

As the number of petitions referred to government from the 1820s reveals, defence of caste or religion was an issue for large numbers of prisoners. In some jails prisoners' concerns were taken more seriously than in others, and their preferences informed prison management. Until the mid-1820s, particular regimes divided prisoners according to their own desires relating to caste. Others ignored prisoners' wants in this respect altogether and segregated inmates according to their crime or sentence.[58] In Calcutta's Alipur Jail, which had no system of classification at all, jail administrators often expressed the sentiment that mixing castes prevented mass escapes.[59] During the first half of the nineteenth century, the Bombay Presidency was by far the most willing to accommodate caste in its jails. In 1824, the administration directed that if Brahmins risked loss of caste they should, where possible, be accommodated separately. At the very least, they should not be placed in the same cells as Muslims or low-caste Hindus and they should be allowed to prepare their food separately.[60] The 1838 Committee of Prison Discipline, whilst acknowledging the diversity of jail classification throughout India, criticized Bombay in this respect.[61] Officially at least, 'caste prejudices' were not to affect prison discipline. In practice, from the 1840s they were viewed as too important to ignore.[62]

What of the privileging of caste amongst transported convicts? Broadly speaking, the Mauritian and South East Asian penal settlements followed the Indian pattern. During the early period, convicts were left to organize themselves. In Mauritius, convicts were issued with rations with which to prepare their own food. Indeed, when in 1835 a convict sentenced to twenty years' hard labour for a secondary offence committed on the island refused to eat his ready-prepared food, he was given permission to prepare it himself in future.[63] Colonial understandings of caste also informed the allocation of labour. Attendants on the Civil Hospital's convict wards, for instance, were low-caste men.[64] Brahmins were asked to read out Convict Department notices in the convict camps.[65] In the Tenasserim Provinces convicts ate together on caste lines until the 1840s.[66] In 1846 the authorities instituted common messing there. It met with the same level of convict resistance it had in mainland jails. The Principal Assistant Commissioner Ramree (Arakan) reported that had he not chained the convicts together at night, there would have been considerable bloodshed.[67] The Magistrate of Moulmein Jail wrote that the comparatively high number of escapes that year could be put down to convict responses to the introduction of common messing.[68] However, mixing castes was a deliberate policy that the British, as in Alipur Jail, saw as a safeguard against revolts. Governor W.J. Butterworth and Comptroller-General of Convicts J.F.A. McNair both echoed earlier opinions in India, writing that in the Straits Settlements it prevented threatening combinations.[69]

With the drive towards uniformity of discipline in mainland Indian jails, questions of caste became inextricably linked to questions of dress. As we have seen, an 1855 prison circular directed that Bengal prisoners should be in possession of only the jail allowance of clothing.[70] In Chittagong jail, Muslim prisoners were ordered to remove their caps. This caused uproar amongst the prisoners. The Inspector-General of Prisons Bengal, F.J. Mouat, later condemned the magistrate of the district, writing: 'The skull cap is an essential part of the dress of a Mahomedan; and to be without it is, in their estimation, to be unsuitably clothed . . . No good in jail discipline and punishment can be effected by interference in such matters.'[71] Other communities were given similar concessions on dress. In keeping with its more accommodating attitude to prisoners' socio-religious status, in the Bombay Presidency Brahmins were allowed to wear their *sowla* cloths when eating.[72] As we shall see, further concessions were granted on the issue of haircutting and beard trimming.

From the late 1830s, as more standardized prison uniforms were developed in the penal settlements, conflicts on the question of caste or religion and dress inevitably occurred there too. Concessions on dress were, on occasion, also granted to transportation convicts. As we have seen, upon embarkation, transportees were issued with standard convict dress. Yet, at least in theory, they were allowed to keep clothing connected with religious duties or customs. There was of course considerable space for convicts to manipulate colonial perceptions about religion or caste to their own advantage. In seeking concessions on dress, the problem for convicts was to convince officials that their clothing had a specifically religious as opposed to social status connotation. Shreerustna Wassoodewjee, a Bombay convict transported to Singapore in 1846, petitioned that he was 'a member of a high class of Hindu and not capable of wearing a cap and trousers'. He wished to be dressed in a manner 'suitable to his caste'.[73] By this time, a more standardized uniform was in place in the settlement. The authorities were still willing to grant concessions to high-caste communities, but Wassoodewjee claimed only that he was a 'high class of Hindu'. The convict authorities countered that he was not a Brahmin and thus no better entitled to sympathetic treatment than many others.[74]

Though the issue of the jail allowance of cloth taxed the Indian administration during the 1850s, uniforms themselves were not introduced until the 1860s. At first, they were not standardized and varied across the districts. In 1860, F.J. Mouat, Inspector-General of Prisons Bengal, recommended the use of 'special prison dress', a check-patterned jacket and *dhoti* which he hoped would not affect caste.[75] After the 1864 Jail Committee recommended the division of prisoners into classes according to their offence and 'character', dress was more widely used as a distinguishing tool. Across India – in the North West Provinces, Awadh, the Central Provinces, Mysore and Coorg and British Burma – prisoners were given coloured badges, the colour distinguishing the penal class to which they belonged.[76]

By the 1880s, Indian jail officials made moves towards the special treatment of habitual offenders. As we shall see in the next chapter, in some regions, such as in Madras, this included their being photographed and worked separately, in order to prevent them contaminating other prisoners with their supposed criminal propensities. Habitual offenders were also issued with distinctive dress. Those imprisoned in Bombay wore a different uniform. In the Panjab, after 1885, all persons who were suspected of having given a false name or refused to reveal their identity – and thus suspected of being habituals – were made to wear special jackets and hats. The jackets had two dark blue stripes, three inches wide, running down each side. The caps had one central blue stripe, also three inches wide, woven into the fabric of the clothes.[77] Later, in the Madras Presidency, a new 'penal stage' was designed as a harsh three-month introduction to prison life. As well as separate sleeping compartments and hard labour like the treadmill, inmates wore clothing made from rough gunny cloth. Habitual thieves were made to wear a blue cap.[78]

Dress, Status and Sexuality: Convicts in the Andaman Islands

The British established the Andaman Islands as a penal settlement after the 1857 Uprising and, within a decade, it had replaced South East Asia as the destination for Indian transportation convicts. At the time of colonial settlement, tribal (*adivasi*) communities inhabited the Islands. The need for a socially differentiating uniform was therefore even less apparent than it had been in the South East Asian settlements and Mauritius. During the early years, convicts were given a small amount of cash – one *anna* nine *paise* per year – to clothe themselves.[79] Robert Napier's report of 1864 noted the generally 'miserable appearance' of the convicts, remarking that 'most appear scarcely to have a rag to cover them'.[80] It was suspected that convicts were not spending their allowance on clothing, but on stimulants like tobacco and opium instead.[81] After Napier's report, the authorities began to issue clothes rather than money gratuities. They gave convicts a short *kurta* and *dhoti*, and in what was the first attempt to fix convicts individually to their dress, each suit was stamped with the convict's number. At first, the clothes were made of thin American drill cloth, but the authorities later imported cloth manufactured in the Agra Central Prison.[82] After 1883, the settlement itself was able to meet its need for clothing. Women worked the looms in the Female Factory (women's jail), which by the end of the nineteenth century were capable of producing 24,000 suits of convict dress each year. Invalids and convalescents made blankets and blanket coats from imported Indian wool.[83]

By the 1870s, the Andamans settlement had become more socially complex. Large numbers of convicts had been given tickets-of-leave on the condition that they settle on the island as self-supporters. However, with no uniform dress in place there was no way of differentiating between them and convicts under sentence of transportation. Superintendent D.M. Stewart then made the first attempt to formulate a uniform, trying unsuccessfully to dye the cloth received from India (with what colour we do not know) before it was issued to the convicts. Nevertheless, at the time of J.S. Campbell and H.W. Norman's report in 1874, though there were no proper uniform garments both separated convicts from self-supporters and crudely expressed the penal hierarchy, which was based on Butterworth's 1845 *Code of Rules*. The bottom three classes of convicts wore what Campbell and Norman described as jail clothing, and the top class their own garments.[84]

A decade later, the authorities developed more refined convict uniforms to differentiate between the penal classes. The government issued all new arrivals with two *dhotis*, two *kurtas* with sleeves, two cloth bags (*gumchas*), two blankets and one blanket coat. They received a replacement supply of *dhotis*, *kurtas* and *gumchas* annually, and a new blanket coat every other year. Third-class convicts who worked outdoors received an additional suit. Second-class convicts were allowed to wear their own clothes in addition to government issue, a privilege expressly forbidden to third-class men. As in India, Mauritius and South East Asia, the latitude that convicts were allowed with respect to clothing facilitated the replication of Indian social hierarchies. Convicts brought clothing with them from India and wealthier convicts had better garments.[85] Brahmins were allowed to wear the sacred threads.[86] The authorities issued women with two *saris*, two *kurtas*, coloured white with a blue stripe, and a country blanket (Figures 4.4 and 4.5). Women undergoing secondary punishment were provided with an altogether different type of dress.

In keeping with earlier Indian penal settlements, the Andamans authorities promoted some convicts to the position of overseer (*jemadar*). On board transportation ships, they wore a distinguishing red cloth stripe around the right sleeve, just above the wrist.[87] In the settlement, convict

Figure 4.4 'Verteilung der Rationen' (Issuing the Rations)

Figure 4.5 'Verbannte Weiber' (Exiled Women). Robert Heindl, *Meine Reise nach den Strafkolonien, mit vielen originalaufnahmen* (Ullstein, 1913)

overseers wore completely different uniforms from their convict charge: white dress, red turbans, badges and coloured belts. They had to buy their cotton dress, out of their gratuity money, though the government provided the badges and belts.[88] Female petty officers wore distinctive red *chadars*.[89]

Prison clothing was the property of the state and not convicts. Though, as in the 1860s, items were anchored to individuals by stamping with the convicts' numbers, they also had government marks. This was supposed to prevent convicts hoarding or bartering their clothes, something that an 1883 Settlement Order had also prohibited.[90] Convicts were not allowed to have more than three blankets or two blanket coats in their possession at any one time. If they were found without their clothing ration, they would be obliged to pay for a new set themselves out of their cash gratuity. When convicts became self-supporters, they had to mark any convict clothing in their possession with a 'distinctly and durably marked' S.S., if they wished to continue wearing it.[91] Self-supporters and convicts dressed completely differently. A 1913 murder trial hinged on whether the accused self-supporter, Sardar, had worn the bloodstained convict *kurta* found at the scene. He was found guilty, but on appeal said that he had been a self-supporter for too long to possess such a garment. His conviction was overturned.[92]

When Lyall and Lethbridge inspected the settlement in 1890 they recommended that in addition to the measures already in place habitual thieves should be visibly distinguishable from other convicts, on the grounds that they were more likely to reoffend than those convicted of serious crimes. This distinctive clothing would be removed if they kept a clean record for five years.[93] An early-twentieth-century visitor to the Islands wrote that dangerous offenders such as gang robbers (*dacoits*) wore a shirt and *dhoti* marked with red cotton thread. Thieves wore a small red badge on their chests.[94]

Though clothing successfully distinguished individuals as convicts, and delineated their place in the penal hierarchy, it did little to assure the recognition of individuals. Indeed, though the clothing of suspected escapees could be checked for government stamps or a convict's number, it did not fix them to individual identities. With clothing open to barter and exchange, it was a permeable sign. There was a lengthy correspondence about the clothing of one convict picked up at sea in 1872, for instance, and whether the '104' sewn onto it in copper thread was the convict's number, or a trade mark.[95] The administration did, however, find an alternative means of fixing individuals to their criminal record, though unlike *godna* it was temporary. They issued convicts with metal tickets that they were obliged to wear like a necklace. These were the same as those worn by prisoners on the mainland. The Andaman tickets detailed each convict's number, section of the Indian Penal Code under which convicted, date of sentence and date release was due. Such information was similar to that previously inscribed in *godna* markings, though the tickets added further details. If of 'doubtful' character, the ticket was also marked with a 'D'; if a member of a gang in India, with a star; and, if a life prisoner, with an 'L'. Convicts wore the tickets during the first five years of their transportation, and if they were well behaved they could remove them. Petty officers did not wear neck tickets.[96] If convicts committed a secondary offence after their removal, the authorities reissued them with one bearing the letter 'D'.[97] There were some problems with the tickets. Iron was a valuable exchange commodity for the Islands' indigenous inhabitants, and colonial relations with them were often strained, particularly during the early years of settlement. In 1860, for instance, eight Andamanese raided a working party between Atalanta Point and Navy

Bay, stealing tools and the convicts' tickets.[98] Convicts also bartered them. For this reason, from 1896 iron tickets were replaced with wooden ones. Convicts already in the settlement retained their iron tickets, which explains why contemporary observers and secondary commentators offer conflicting descriptions of them.[99]

Clothing was part of the disciplinary regime in the Islands, but it was also a way in which convicts could counter it. As we have seen, when convicts were given a money allowance to buy clothes, the authorities suspected that they spent it on other goods instead. Convicts employed at indoor labour, and thus protected from the elements, were able to hoard or barter spare clothes. In 1890, one Madras convict, who had been in the settlement for less than two years, was found to have five suits of good clothing in his possession.[100] In addition, convicts were often caught wearing non-standard clothing, and they were punished for doing so.[101] They were also punished for refusing to wear their neck tickets. The opportunities to remove them were heightened if they were stationed at some distance from the main headquarters of the settlement, for example in the neighbouring Nicobar Islands.[102]

The wearing of the tickets, and uniform convict dress more generally, later became a focus of outrage for the political, nationalist prisoners incarcerated in the notorious Cellular Jail in the Andamans in the early twentieth century. Their clothing distinguished them from ordinary transportees. A large 'S' was sewn on the clothing of those convicted of sedition; a 'C' denoted those convicted in conspiracy cases. All nationalist prisoners also wore neck tickets inscribed with a 'D', for 'dangerous'.[103] This was quite unlike arrangements made for the reception of the Manipuri political prisoners, received in 1891, who had their own clothing sent from Assam.[104] The Manipuris were transported to the Andamans after a revolt against the British. Most were members of the royal family, which perhaps explains the more accommodating attitude towards their dress. For twentieth-century political prisoners, contact with each other at work or mealtimes became difficult. One political prisoner, Nanigopal, refused to wear prison clothing and broke his wooden neck ticket so many times that it had to be replaced with an iron one.[105] Another, Barindra Kumar Ghose, wrote in his memoirs: 'I understood that here there was no such thing as gentleman [*sic*], nor such thing as man, here there were just convicts'.[106]

By the second half of the nineteenth century, the Andamans authorities were so concerned about imbalanced gender ratios that they appointed a committee for the 'elimination and identification of men addicted to this nefarious practice', a veiled reference to homosexual activity. As Sen shows to effect, the concern was that it took place when the eyes of the state were averted.[107] These concerns eventually fed into the development of distinctive dress. Juvenile convicts were seen as particularly vulnerable to the attention of older men. At first, they were locked up in lattice cages at night, in an attempt at segregation.[108] This presented obvious safety risks, so by the 1880s all men and boys labelled 'habitual recipients' (catamites) were instead confined in altogether separate barracks in Aberdeen, where they worked separately at stone-breaking.[109] Convicts caught indulging in homosexual acts were given a public flogging, in an attempt at deterrence.[110]

In 1890, Lyall and Lethbridge reported that juveniles 'habitually given to unnatural offences' wore coloured coats.[111] This referred to the issue of brown-coloured clothing to catamites, a measure designed to enhance their visibility and thus close supervision. Yet this distinctive dress also drew attention to them. W. Birch, assistant to Superintendent T. Cadell, argued that there were 'great disadvantages attendant upon marking out by a distinctive dress (and thus advertising) habitual recipients'.[112] It is interesting that known sodomites were not clothed differently. As cultural historians have shown, homosexuality is a culturally specific construction. At particular historical junctures, the focus was on particular acts rather than identities.[113] Here it is clear that the colonial eye looked at catamites differently from sodomites. This was to do with the perceived vulnerability of juvenile convicts, rather than the sanctioning of particular types of sexual behaviour.

Race, Dress and the Penal Hierarchy

We have seen how the colonial authorities used convict dress in an attempt to enact boundaries of criminality, penal status and sexuality. Prison uniforms were also used to mark racial divisions between convicts. I would like to discuss this in relation to the European and Eurasian convicts transported to penal settlements in Mauritius, South East Asia and the Andamans. Eurasians were invariably shipped to Indian penal settlements. Though the usual destination for Europeans convicted in India was one of the penal settlements in Australia (New South Wales, Van Diemen's Land or Western Australia), during the first half of the nineteenth century they too were occasionally sentenced to transportation to the Straits or Burma. The issue was whether or not they had been born in India, and thus whether they could be legally classified as Europeans. Those of Indian birth (known as East Indians) were invariably sent to South East Asia or Mauritius, not Australia. The few exceptions to this were black or Portuguese men born outside the subcontinent and shipped to Van Diemen's Land.[114] On arrival in South East Asia or Mauritius, Europeans and Eurasians formed a small minority of convicts, and as on the mainland[115] were treated entirely differently from Indians. They were a means through which the racial hierarchy of the penal settlements could be bolstered. The authorities gave them separate accommodation and different food rations. They were not put to hard labour, but employed as clerks, hired out privately, or worked as overseers to Indian transportees.

European and Eurasian convicts in South East Asia were issued with a much larger quantity of clothing than Indians, and it was European in style. Until the early 1840s in the Tenasserim Provinces, they were given two white jackets, two white shirts, two pairs of white trousers, a pair of shoes, a straw hat and a black neckerchief. 'Native Christians' fell somewhere between the two allowances, receiving a loose drawers (*jangeah*) and an undershirt (*banyan*).[116] In 1843, G. Broadfoot took over as Commissioner of the Tenasserim Provinces. He immediately set about tightening up convict discipline there. One of his first measures was to remove all privileges from European convicts. Broadfoot ordered that they be issued with the same rations and clothing as Indians, and put to hard labour. They felt this to be a considerable hardship and when they brought it to the Government of India's attention it agreed, ordering that their former privileges be restored immediately.[117] European convicts in the Straits Settlements also wore different dress from Indians. McNair wrote that the Straits authorities issued European convicts with a light blue loose coat and a cap bordered with lace. They also wore a distinctive badge to indicate their grade. Artificer overseers, for instance, might be given a picture of a crossed hammer and chisel.[118]

In the Andamans, European ticket-of-leave convicts were used as convict overseers. Imprisoned in India, these men were selected for transfer (rather than transportation) to the Andamans on licence, on the basis of their fitness, labour skills or ability to speak an Indian language. The fact that they enjoyed considerable privileges once again illustrates the contingency of colonial categories of criminality and race, and the relationship between them. Europeans were accommodated separately to the bulk of Indian convicts, in the Christian Barracks. They were given different food rations and a dram per day of rum. They were exempted from wearing prison dress, and instead wore what might be described as standard working-class garments. Until the 1870s, they were issued with four cotton or flannel shirts, trousers and socks (according to the season), two wool coats, one straw hat and two pairs of strong shoes.[119] The 1886 *Andaman and Nicobars Manual* regulated that twice a year they would then receive three blue jackets, three pairs of trousers, three white shirts, a straw hat, a country blanket and a pair of shoes.[120] As Sen argues, the men enjoyed a 'promotion within a demoted society'.[121]

In 1871, a licensed prisoner called James Devine murdered a convict, Alkana, when 'maddened with drink'.[122] The scandal made the pages of *The Times* in London.[123] Other than the liberal issue of rum (the monthly ration could be drawn all at once), what shocked the colonial authorities on the mainland most was the fact that Eurasian convicts lived together with European licensed prisoners in the Christian Barracks. To their dismay, this challenged their vision of the appropriate racial order in the settlement. The secretary to the Government of India, E.C. Bayley, wrote that one man, Thomas Fernandez, dressed like a European and professed to be a Christian, but was in fact Indian. He lamented: 'being treated at Calcutta as a native and at Port Blair like a European, he practically escaped all punishment.'[124] Officiating Superintendent F.L. Playfair reassured him that though Fernandez lived in the barracks, he was not a licensed prisoner. He worked in irons, did not receive any pay and wore jail clothing. After the 1871 scandal, the Andaman authorities tightened up the rules, but according to local articulations of categories of race and criminality Eurasian prisoners were allowed to remain in the barracks.[125]

The contingency and instability of colonial categories of race, class and criminality (and the multiple interactions between them) were further complicated by discourses of gender. One Eurasian convict shipped to Mauritius was a woman named Maria Davis, who arrived in 1828 with her daughter Emma. The government at first refused to accept them, but eventually agreed to accommodate them separately from Indian convicts. They gave the women an extraordinary amount of clothing: six pairs of shoes, cloth for blouses, sixty yards of 'gown stuff' and a dozen pairs of stockings.[126] A second Eurasian woman, Victoria Adelaide Hassey, was transported to Singapore in 1855,[127] and her arrival provoked a similar response to that of Maria Davis. According to Governor W.J. Butterworth, there was 'much sympathy and compassion here especially among the ladies of the community – This person is young, educated, and a Christian, yet she is mixed with heathen females, and no instructions have been sent to me to treat her otherwise than an ordinary native female criminal'.[128] Both women had committed murder (Davis had beaten her servant to death whilst in a drunken stupor).[129] Yet like male European and Eurasian convicts, the colonial authorities viewed them first as *British* rather than as *criminals*. Within the penal spaces thus created, these men and women were then adorned with the appropriate cultural markers.

The Long, Greasy, Dirty Elf-locks in which They so Delight

In 1875, there was a disturbance in the Central Jail Tiruchchirappalli (Trichi) in the Madras Presidency, during which five Burmese inmates attacked a fellow prisoner so brutally that he nearly died. In his report to government, the jail superintendent claimed that the only jail regulation that the men had ever complained about was that on haircutting. The Inspector-General of Jails Madras, T.E. Tennant, concluded that the convicts had carried out the assault because, unlike them, the man had allowed his hair to be cut.[130] The Madras Presidency had been receiving transportation convicts from Burma since 1870. By 1876, there were 176 Burmese convicts in the presidency, imprisoned in the central jails at Rajahmundry, Vellore, Salem, Cannanore and Coimbatore, and in the Madras Penitentiary.[131] After the attack, the government called for a report on haircutting in Burmese prisons.[132] Meanwhile, Tennant conducted his own report on the treatment of Burmese convicts in the presidency, finding that policy differed widely. In some jails, convicts were allowed to wear their hair long. In others, they were close shaven or their hair was cut short. He found nothing 'offensive or degrading' about either practice.[133] The Inspector-General of Prisons Burma later reported that once appeals against sentence had been rejected, all prisoners had their hair cut once a fortnight.[134] This had been the case since 1871.[135]

During the nineteenth century, the close cutting, shaving and cropping of hair was normal practice in Indian prisons and penal settlements. Like penal dress, short hair created physical uniformity amongst male prisoners. Short hair bestowed a stigma, which was a punishment in itself. Penal administrators on the Indian mainland and in the penal settlements also saw haircutting as a hygienic way to keep prisoners clean, and to control the spread of head lice. In addition, they used hair cropping or shaving to control unruly female prisoners and in this sense it was a gendered form of punishment. Hair was thus a visual tag through which male prisoner and convict status could be marked and the conduct of women controlled, judged or predicted. Yet as the response of Burmese transportation prisoners in Madras hints at, some convicts played an active role in setting boundaries around what was acceptable, refusing to have their hair cut and retaliating against prisoners who did.

After 1856, the Bengal Presidency jail rules directed that as soon as appeals against sentence were concluded, male prisoners should have their hair shaved and beard trimmed every fifteen days. In keeping with earlier concessions on dress, the rules would be applied only if they caused no personal disgrace or degradation. Muslims' beards would be trimmed only to the length of a closed fist; Sikhs, Kols and Faraizis (Muslim reformists) were not to have their hair or beards cut at all. In what Arnold describes as an 'elaborate lexicon of bodily signs and ritual practices', Bombay jail manuals made similar provisions to those in Bengal.[136] Nevertheless, the introduction of the Bengal rules caused unrest in some jails, particularly those with large Muslim populations like Shahabad, Noakhali and Bankura.[137] Rajashahi prisoners petitioned the magistrate and judge of the district, asking for exemption from the rule:

> It is written in the Koran that, if the Mahomedans shave their beard after it has once grown, they should be excommunicated from the pale of Mahomedanism. If in opposition to this they be now forced to shave their beard, then they will be excommunicated from their religion, and when released from imprisonment, they will not be admitted to the society of their family and relatives.[138]

The Muslim Association of Calcutta also became involved in the dispute, writing to Mouat to express their concerns.[139] He replied that they had misunderstood the rules, which called for the trimming rather than shaving of beards. Whilst he was sympathetic to religious objections, he wrote, he would not take into account 'prejudices which I know to be unconnected with religion . . . in bar of the rigid discipline which I am resolved to maintain.'[140] He would prefer hair to be reasonably short, but only if there were no religious sanctions against it. Otherwise, he did not want prisoners to grow 'the long greasy, dirty, elf-locks in which they so much delight.'[141]

As for prison dress, the problem for jail officials was to unravel the reason for prisoners' objections, and whether they were based on religion or caste, or other factors. Inevitably, there were disagreements about this. In January 1857 prisoners in Mymensingh refused to take a meal until they were reassured that they would not have their beards trimmed at all. The District Magistrate subsequently suspended the practice on the grounds that the men were Muslims. Mouat on the other hand saw this as a moral victory for the prisoners, not a religious one, which would make the future enforcement of jail rules difficult.[142] Whilst claiming to be sympathetic to prisoners, Mouat rarely conceded to their protests where they conflicted with points of discipline. Thus, by his own account and despite their objections he refused to allow Goalla prisoners in Behar Jail to divide into their own messes, prisoners in 'two or three other' jails to wash their own clothes, sweepers in Mymensingh Jail to subdivide themselves, or to cave into a Burdwan silk weaver's objection to weaving gunny cloth. Prisoners' protests on these matters were, he claimed, 'dignity objections', not in reality based on caste grounds.[143] Other colonial officials were nervous of the effect that this outright dismissal of caste might have on jail order. The Junior Secretary to Government, C.J. Buckland, urged Mouat to make further inquiries about religious practices in eastern Bengal, writing 'religious prejudices are not always to be set aside, merely because they are mistaken.'[144] It is difficult to avoid the conclusion that these perceived religious infringements fed into the uprising that swept across India in 1857, for we know that one of the first acts of the rebels was the breaking open of the jails.[145]

Convicts sentenced to transportation were subject to the same rules as ordinary prisoners, and so had their hair and beards cut prior to embarkation for the penal settlements. Later photographic evidence (Figures 4.1, 4.2 and 4.3) shows the use of haircutting in delineating the penal hierarchy, with convict overseers being allowed to wear their hair long. This was totally in keeping with regulations on dress. Head shaving marked out notorious convicts. The convict assassin of Viceroy Mayo, Shere Ali, for instance, had his head newly shaved before his execution in the Andamans in 1872 (Figure 5.4). It is also worth noting that one of the issues that persuaded the European prisoners in the Tenasserim Provinces to petition against Commissioner Broadfoot's tightening up of jail rules was their subjection to head shaving. In their eyes, this put them on a par with Indian convicts, thus challenging the racial order and, given their former employment as overseers and so forth, its relationship to the penal hierarchy.[146]

I would like to return to the 1856 sanction against cutting prisoners' hair until all avenues of appeal had been exhausted. This was a direct reference to the stigma that cropped hair caused. Shaved hair marked ex-prisoners, making it difficult for them to find work and likely they would end up back in jail for some petty offence. The best evidence we have of this relates to European prisoners in Calcutta. Normal practice in the Presidency Jail was based on that in British prisons and houses of correction. Every prisoner sentenced to hard labour (usually habitual offenders) had their hair cropped, no matter how short their sentence. In March 1870, a European named Edward Ward was fined two rupees for being 'drunk and incapable'. When he did not pay the fine, the authorities sent him to jail for seven days, where his hair was cut short. His complaint that this disfigured him, made before the Magistrate of the Southern District, is worth quoting at length:

Ward – On admission to the jail my hair was cut . . . Dr Lynch [the jail surgeon] visited me on the day after I was put into the cell, and he ordered my hair to be cut again, and the barber was immediately sent for and without a comb but only with scissors he cut my hair and jagged it as you see close to the scalp. I have been laughed out of the [Seamen's] Home. No captain will look at me, they say 'it is clear where you came from, stand back.' Why should my hair have been cut twice in seven days' imprisonment? Why should I be disfigured and be prevented from shipping?

Magistrate – Perhaps your head was found to be unclean.

Ward – I think my head was clean, but no one could know it was dirty, to order the second cropping of my hair, for no one looked at my head to see. When it was first cut, they only left just enough to lay hold of. Dr Lynch did not charge me with doing any thing wrong, I had not broken the jail rules; he just said 'send for the barber immediately and cut this man's hair.' I said it was cut once, Dr Lynch said 'it will be cut again,' and it was then and there cut again as you see Sir.[147]

The Bengal government agreed that it was a harsh punishment that prevented ex-prisoners from finding work. The case led to revised rules on cutting the hair of European inmates. If sentenced to less than one month's imprisonment, they would not have their hair cropped, and all would be allowed to let their hair grow during the last month of their imprisonment.[148] Showing one of the overlaps between the treatment of Indian and European offenders, in 1886 the *Amended Rules on the Subject of the Cropping or Shaving of Hair of Convicts in Jail* extended the same sanction to Indian prisoners. They also bound haircutting, like dress, more closely to the prison hierarchy. Prisoners sentenced to simple imprisonment and convict warders did not have their hair cropped or shaved at all.[149]

Unlike male prisoners, women did not have their hair cut when they went into jail or after appeal. Their hair was only ever cut or trimmed for two reasons: 'health and cleanliness' or 'flagrant or continued misbehaviour'.[150] Hair cropping was a gendered punishment, a means for the disciplining of female prisoners. According to the colonial authorities, it was remarkably effective in this respect. In his *Note on Jails and Jail Discipline in India* (1868), A.P. Howell wrote that it was extremely difficult to punish women effectively. 'Personal vanity' meant that the only punishment they really dreaded, and therefore the threat of which was the only way good conduct could be encouraged, was haircutting. It is difficult to square this with his other claim: 'This is not a permanent source of injury, is not attended with cruelty or personal degradation.'[151] This was perhaps a coded reference to the fact that it did not mark the body, but rather temporarily changed its appearance. Certainly, interpretations of the practice in early colonial Australia point to the way that head shaving defeminized, disgraced and shamed British convict women.[152] In India, head shaving was not used very often: just twice in the whole Bombay Presidency between 1887 and 1892, for instance. Yet it was the *threat* of head shaving that made it so effective. In 1893, the Inspector-General of Bombay Prisons echoed Howell's earlier comments, adding that it was a more effective disciplinary tool than solitary confinement or strict rationing, the only other options open to punish female prisoners. He lamented its potential withdrawal as a punishment.[153]

Nevertheless, in 1893 the head shaving of women was banned in Indian jails, though it remained a secondary punishment for another twenty years in the Andaman Islands. Campbell and Norman had noted that female convicts' hair could be cropped in their 1874 report.[154] The 1886 *Andaman and Nicobar Manual* codified the practice.[155] Mrs Talbot Clifton, who visited the Islands in 1910, reported seeing a 'sullen-looking female' having her hair cut in the Female Factory. Echoing her contemporaries in India, she noted that it was 'the greatest punishment which can be inflicted upon a woman'.[156] Men too were subject to hair cropping for misconduct. Another contemporary visitor to Port Blair, C. Boden Kloss, wrote that he saw some of the inmates at Viper Island, where convicts were sent for secondary punishment, having their hair close cut.[157] The practice was not abolished until 1915.[158]

Cultural Distancing, Clothing and the Criminal Tribes

As we have seen, the British used clothing in the Indian penal settlements as a means of establishing racial boundaries. During the nineteenth century more generally, the British viewed dress as a marker of separation – between free Europeans and Indians.[159] The army is a good example of patterns of change. Before the 1857 Uprising, locally raised East India Company troops wore 'native fashion' and military coats. They became gradually 'Europeanized' in appearance, wearing tight coatees with long tails. After 1857, however, the army reverted to its Indian appearance. *Sepoys* wore turbans, and their clothing became looser in style.[160] Yet Indians of all social classes continued to wear British-style dress and cast-off official uniforms. Entertainers, musicians and bandsmen in Calcutta all wore old police and army jackets, coats, hats, buttons and pantaloons. There were frequent auctions, where unlined military coats typically sold for between twelve and fourteen *annas*. If they were lined, they went for as much as one rupee, four *annas*. English police coats fetched even more: one rupee, six *annas*.[161] In Calcutta, there was even a shop where uniforms could be hired.

When Indians took on markers of British authority, they transgressed European boundaries of rule. W.H.H. Vincent, an official in the Twenty-Four Parganas district, reported in 1896 of the '*foofoo* bandsmen' who paraded in Calcutta, 'dressed up like slovenly soldiers'. This, he said, was a direct challenge to British prestige.[162] J.A. Bourdillon, the Commissioner of Burdwan, also wrote of the 'disreputable raggamuffins' who worked as musicians in Calcutta. He too was worried about the threat they posed to British 'dignity'. Bourdillon also wrote of increasingly common theatrical representation of Europeans, where actors were dressed up in European clothing, 'made the butt of the piece, and treated with every kind of indignity amidst the uproarious applause of the audience.'[163] When Indians wore (or ridiculed) European garb, the boundaries between colonizer and colonized began to break down.[164] Edgar Thurston, Superintendent of Ethnography, Madras, wrote with contempt in 1906 of the 'change for the worst [*sic*] in native male attire'. The examples of declining standards that he cited included Indians wearing brightly coloured caps instead of turbans, Bengali clerks donning patent leather boots and Indian cricketers' bright blazers, reminiscent of those worn by English public school teams.[165]

As we saw in Chapter 3, when the British colonized India they were faced with a society that seemed both complex and elusive. Administrator-anthropologists used various mechanisms in trying to make sense of the subcontinent's socio-economic structures and hierarchies, and in exploring the meaning of caste and its relationship to race. These included the types of tattoos individuals wore. They also gave similar meanings to clothing, and colonial interpretations of both were quite similar. Like tattoos, the British used dress in an attempt to divide the South Asian population into decipherable units. Lyon's 1889 *Medical Jurisprudence for India* noted the ways in which clothing could be used to differentiate between Hindus, Muslims, Jews and Parsis, for instance.[166] Photographers working on the compilation of ethnographic dictionaries during the late nineteenth and early twentieth centuries dressed their subjects in what they believed to be 'typical' garments. This clothing became a visual signifier of collective religious, caste or tribal status.[167] As Pinney has argued, the work of ethnographers like Crooke was part of the systematic recording and ordering of 'the peoples of India'.[168] Photographers also attempted to capture the essence of 'timeless' India, as they believed that the modernizing colonial project would soon transform it beyond all recognition. They even took to clothing their photographic subjects in garments long since abandoned by them. E.T. Dalton's *Descriptive Ethnology of Bengal* (1872) included a lithograph of Tosco Peppé's photograph of two young Juang women, scantily clad in leaves. When Risley reproduced the image in 1908 he noted that Manchester saris had replaced them.[169] Nevertheless, the photograph both sexualized and infantilized the Juang (the caption accompanying the image referred to 'Juang girls'). As Willem Van Schendel has shown in a study of colonial photography in the Chittagong hills, nudity signified primitivity, closeness to nature and indecency, and sexually titillated its audience.[170]

Given this collectivization of the Indian social body, it was perhaps inevitable that the same props would also be used for the purpose of identifying members of the criminal tribes. As we have seen, the first Criminal Tribes Act was passed in 1871, and by the mid-twentieth century the Acts encompassed over 13 million people. At the end of the nineteenth century, police handbooks drew on contemporary ethnography to detail the types of clothing supposedly worn by particular criminal tribes. Central to this discourse of criminal typology was the idea of individuals disguising themselves, and thus passing themselves off as other social groups such as merchants, the police and, frequently, holy men (*sadhus*). Ethnographers and police handbooks noted that disguises were virtually undetectable to all but their own community, a visual slipperiness that made assiduous policing of them all the more necessary. Their secret pointers included the ways in which the turban or *dhoti* were tied, or the type of knot in the sacred thread. If disguises were not adopted, then the face was instead covered.[171] Echoing Crooke's *The Tribes and Castes*, in 1914 the Superintendent of Police in the United Provinces, S.T. Hollins, wrote a handbook for district officers detailing the secret dialects and slang – a criminal *patois* – unique to many criminal tribes. He added that particular body odours could also be a tell-tale sign of criminality.[172] Another means of detection was the 'generalized look' – rather vague ideas about collective morphology that remained ill defined. One pamphlet published for students of criminology in 1915 shows middle-class Indian collusion in such notions when it noted: 'There are certain physical characteristics in instinctive criminals which may be true to some degree, but to invest them with any scientific value would be premature as they often occur in persons of unimpeachable character. Heavy protruding chins, small shifting eyes, heavy dark hair and beards *may* be some of the features of a natural offender.'[173]

Handbooks also commonly detailed the types of clothing particular groups wore, and included photographs of designated criminal tribes in their supposed disguise (Figure 4.6). These were always taken outside jail buildings, which is evident from the barred windows that are frequently in view in the pictures.

Figure 4.6 'A Dehliwal Bauria Disguised'. S.T. Hollins, *The Criminal Tribes of the United Provinces* (Government Press, 1914). (Courtesy of British Library, V9405 OIOC)

Typical of such descriptions are those of Deputy Inspector of Police in Bombay, M. Kennedy, which were reproduced by Hollins. They claimed that Oudhias wore particular types of clothing, and carried an umbrella, a stick and a padded quilt. They painted caste marks on their foreheads, and carried a begging bowl, in order to disguise themselves as religious mendicants.[174] Another group, wrote Hollins, the Bauria, wore caste marks on the forehead, 'which differ so subtly from the regular *tika,* that the wearers are able to pass themselves off as devout men, but which at the same time reveal him to be a Bauria to other members of his fraternity.'[175] The Inspector-General of Police in the Panjab, D. Gainsford, added in 1944 that Baurias left one end of their *dhoti* dangling, a telling sign to other members of the same criminal fraternity. He made the following general comments on the disguises of the criminal tribes:

Most criminal tribes have particular forms of dress and particular ways of distinguishing themselves, and photographs taken immediately after their arrest would prove of great value to other officers . . . Individuals should be photographed at the earliest possible moment. Should the gang or any individual among them appear to be in disguise, the photograph should be taken immediately, so that the peculiarities of the disguise can be noted.[176]

As well as representing photography as a useful means of detection, Gainsford also called attention to the fact that fingerprinting was a useful means to counter disguise, a theme we will discuss later in the next chapter.[177]

In 1882, the British Salvation Army extended its activities to India, where after initial scepticism on the part of government, it embarked on collaborative projects to 'reform' the criminal tribes. In 1908 its officers took over their first reformatory in the United Provinces, extending their activities later on. Reform centred on changing the habits and dispositions of the criminal tribes, teaching them order, industry and discipline. As Tolen argues, many of the Salvation Army's efforts focused on changing modes of ornamentation on the body. Reformed women and men wore saris and turbans in what was a 'reconstruction of Indian "tradition".' Though there was some resistance to these efforts, only those with 'neat appearances' were granted passes to leave the reformatories, which assured their eventual compliance. This was part of what Tolen describes as their transformation into 'productive and subjected bodies'.[178]

In Chapter 5, I would like to explore further the theme of criminal photography. Photographs of criminal tribes were meant to be representative of whole social groups, and were printed to aid collective identification. From the third quarter of the nineteenth century, the colonial state also began to photograph thousands of individuals – prisoners, habitual offenders and transportation convicts. The aim of these pictures was quite different. The photographs were meant to ease the recognition of old offenders and convict absconders, so that both could be punished appropriately. However, as Chapter 5 will show, photography was a field of power that encompassed colonial tensions between the construction of social collectivities and individual identities, and subject negotiation of the images. The colonial state might have been able to *see*, but it was not necessarily able to *know*.

Notes

1. *The Bombay Gazette*, 3 Oct. 1839, 5 Oct. 1839 (Supreme Court, 29 Sept. 1838).

2. On the special status accorded to Parsis during the colonial period see T.H. Luhrmann, *The Good Parsi: The Fate of a Colonial Elite in a Postcolonial Society* (Harvard University Press, 1996).

3. IOR P/402/33 (1 May 1839): Petition from Manockjee Sorabjee Cursetjee Manock Soortee and others, Parsee inhabitants of Bombay, without date; Statement of W. Read, Head Constable Fort Division, Bombay Police, 26 Apr. 1839; Messrs Patch and Bainbridge to Willoughby, 23 Apr. 1839; J.L. Johnson, Sheriff of Bombay, to Willoughby, 17 May 1839.

4. J. Entwistle, *The Fashioned Body: Fashion, Dress and Modern Social Theory* (Polity Press, 2000), 7–8.

5. Karen Sayer, '"A Sufficiency of Clothing": Dress and Domesticity in Victorian Britain', *Textile History*, 33, 1 (2002), 112–22.

6. Margaret Maynard, *Fashioned from Penury: Dress as Cultural Practice in Colonial Australia* (Cambridge University Press, 1998), 2.

7. Tarlo, *Clothing Matters*, 8, 318.

8. Bernard S. Cohn, *Colonialism and its Forms of Knowledge: The British in India* (Oxford University Press, 1997), 111. See also E.M. Collingham, *Imperial Bodies* (Polity, 2001), *passim*. On Hindu women's dress, note O.P. Joshi, 'Continuity and Change in Hindu Women's Dress', in Ruth Barnes and Joanne B. Eicher (eds), *Dress and Gender: Making and Meaning* (Berg, 1992), 214–31.

9. Tarlo, *Clothing Matters*, 28.

10. Cohn, *Colonialism*, 130.

11. See indents on the Commissariat: MA RA54 (Sept. 1817); MA RA1067 (Jan. 1850).

12. IOR MSS Eur D742/46: Regulations for Convicts, Bencoolen (Regulation I 1824).

13. IOR P/136/31 (26 Aug. 1824): W.E. Phillips' Minute.

14. IOR P/136/66 (19 May 1825): President's Minute (R. Fullerton), 8 Mar. 1825.

15. Sayer, '"A Sufficiency of Clothing"', 118.

16. The first Mauritian census (1826) recorded a composite category of 14,000 Indians, Chinese and creoles, 9,000 whites and 63,000 slaves. Given the island's history as a slave colony, one must assume that creoles formed the largest proportion of the composite category. PRO CO172/42: Baron d'Unienville, *Tableaux de Statistiques*, tableau no. 6.

17. Maynard, *Fashioned from Penury*, ch. 1.

18. For a similar cultural reading of slave clothing, see Shane White and Graham White, 'Slave Clothing and African-American Culture in the

Eighteenth and Nineteenth Centuries', *Past and Present*, 148 (1995), 149–86.

19. IOR P/402/32 (17 Apr. 1839): J.M. Shortt, Superintendent of Police Bombay, to Willoughby, 3 Apr. 1839.

20. IOR P/142/52 (19 Aug. 1846): Mytton to Halliday, 10 Aug. 1846.

21. *Report of the Committee on Prison Discipline*, 50–1.

22. IOR P/402/37 (18 Sept. 1839): J. Glen, Secretary to the Medical Board, to L.R. Reid, Acting Chief Secretary to Government Bombay, 12 Aug. 1839.

23. MA Z2A36: Descriptions of three Bombay convicts who marooned from the Depot of Grand River, 25 Mar. 1827. The convicts were named as Heringa Vulud Donepa, Hooloorah Bedur and Shree Newas Achary.

24. White and White also note that American slave runaway adverts detailed the clothing worn by absconders: 'Slave Clothing', 151.

25. MA JB332: Trial of Massooben Ramjee, Luckoo Puddhoo, Arribapou and Ragoo. Evidence of the Court of First Instance, 4 May 1843. These four Bombay convicts were acquitted of murdering a non-convict Indian, Soulal, in an alleged dispute over an Indian woman named Singui.

26. MA JI11: Post-mortem of Bhelo Kalipa, 21 July 1831; MA JI1: Post-mortem of Renbella, 18 Apr. 1831; MA JI13: Post-mortem of Fugur Chund, 18 Apr. 1838.

27. Bartrum, *Recollections of Seven Years' Residence*, 123–4.

28. IOR P/129/22 (3 Apr. 1806): Extract Public Department Proceedings (Walter Ewer, Late Commissioner Bencoolen, to Marquis Wellesley, n.d.), 27 Mar. 1806.

29. Yule, *Hobson-Jobson,* 809.

30. François J.M.A. Billiard, *Voyages aux colonies orientales, ou léttres Ecrit des Iles de France et de Bourbon pendant les années 1817, 1818, 1819 et 1820* (Librarie Française de l'Advocat, 1822), 30–1. On the crimes for which convicts were actually transported, see Anderson, *Convicts in the Indian Ocean*, app. B1, B2.

31. For a detailed analysis of the uprising, see Clare Anderson, 'The Bel Ombre Rebellion: Indian Convicts in Mauritius, 1815–53', in Gwyn Campbell (ed.), *Abolition and its Aftermath in Indian Ocean Africa and Asia, vol. II* (Frank Cass, 2004).

32. MA RA387/415: R. Lyall, Political Agent Madagascar, to Barry, 26 Dec. 1828, 1 Sept. 1829, enclosing a 'Memorandum respecting the Sepoys [convicts] in Madagascar'.

33. IOR P/136/31 (26 Aug. 1824): W.E. Phillips' Minute. On convict views of transportation and loss of caste, see Anderson, 'Politics of Convict Space', 41–6.
34. A.H. Hill, *The Hikayat Abdullah: The Autobiography of Abdullah Bin Abdul Kadir (1797–1854), an Annotated Translation* (Oxford University Press, 1969), 176, 223, 282–3.
35. This was also the case in slave societies and other penal settlements. See White and White, 'Slave Clothing', 150; Parliamentary Papers 1822 (449) XX.539: Committee of Inquiry into State of Colony of New South Wales (Bigge Reports).
36. IOR P/129/32 (1 Jan. 1808): Extract from a letter from the Resident at Bencoolen, 15 Aug. 1806.
37. IOR MSS Eur D742/46: Regulations for Convicts, Bencoolen (Regulation I 1824).
38. TNSA Judicial vol. 326A: Bonham to Chamier, 21 Apr. 1837; IOR P/142/37 (17 Sept. 1845): Butterworth to Turnbull, 26 Feb. 1845. In 1856, convict Ramun was punished for selling his clothes: TNSA Judicial (30 July 1885), 1964: List of a convict sentenced to transportation for life who is eligible for release. When the Straits penal settlement closed in 1873, Ramun was transferred to the Andamans. Documents like this detail the local offences of time-expired convicts.
39. On convicts and contraband trading in Mauritius, see Anderson, *Convicts in the Indian Ocean*, 99–105.
40. MA JB136: Trial of Ruttunah, Ramsook, Sobah, Turée, Kehurée and Madow. Interrogation of Torée, Court of First Instance, 5 May 1820.
41. MA JB133: Trial of Kalloo and Nacta. Judgment of the Court of Appeal, 6 Oct. 1820.
42. *Report of the Committee on Prison Discipline*, 95. The 1837 Committee on Convict Labour noted the annual allowance for prisoners employed on the roads as two blankets, two *chadars* and two *dhotis*. See IOR P/141/9 (14 Mar. 1837): Second and Concluding Report of the Committee of Convict Labour, 28 Jan. 1837.
43. IOR P/144/21 (29 Apr. 1852): Samuells to Grant, 2 Jan. 1852.
44. IOR P/145/13 (14 June 1855): A. Sconce, Session Judge Nadia, to W. Grey, Secretary to Government Bengal, 25 May 1855; Memorandum of Mouat, 6 June 1855.
45. Sayer, '"A Sufficiency of Clothing"', 118.
46. TNSA Judicial (13 Sept. 1864), 82–3: R.S. Ellis, President Sanitary Commission, 13 Aug. 1864.
47. TNSA Judicial (27 May 1868), 284–5: W.S. Drever, Acting Commissioner of Police and Superintendent of Jails, 27 Apr. 1868.

48. IOR P/402/32 (17 Apr. 1839): J. Farish, Governor of Bombay, to Shortt, 3 Apr. 1839.
49. IOR P/142/37 (17 Sept. 1845): Butterworth to Turnbull, 26 Feb. 1845.
50. IOR P/143/16 (22 Mar. 1848): H. Man, Superintendent of Convicts Singapore, to J. Church, Resident Councillor Singapore, 19 Oct. 1847.
51. IOR P/145/64 (25 June 1857): Mouat to E.H. Lushington, in charge of the office of the Secretary to Government Bengal, 13 Apr. 1857.
52. IOR P/142/37 (17 Sept. 1845): Present system of management and discipline of convicts at Singapore, Superintendent D.A. Stevenson, 9 Jan. 1845.
53. IOR P/143/56 (9 Oct. 1850): Butterworth to J.W. Dalrymple, Under Secretary to Government Bengal, 14 May 1850.
54. M.V. Portman, *A History of our Relations with the Andamanese, vol. I* (Superintendent Government Printing, 1899), 277–8.
55. Arnold, 'Colonial Prison', 170–5.
56. IOR P/399/33 (12 May 1824): W. Chaplin, Commissioner of Deccan, to H. Pottinger, Collector Khandesh, 25 Dec. 1823.
57. *Ibid.*: J. Farish to W. Chaplin, 6 May 1824.
58. *Ibid.*
59. IOR P/399/36 (4 Aug. 1824): J.E. Grant, Register *Sadar Adalat* Bombay, to Farish, 17 July 1824.
60. *Ibid.*: Farish to Grant, 29 July 1824.
61. *Report of the Committee on Prison Discipline*, 24, 66.
62. Arnold, 'Colonial Prison', 170–1.
63. MA Z2A79: E.A. Williams, Acting Procureur Général, to Finniss, 21 Mar. 1835.
64. MA RA601: A. Montgomery, Surgeon-in-Charge of the Civil Hospital, to Charles St John, Chief Medical Officer, 21 Oct. 1840.
65. MA RA915: Report of the Committee on Convicts, Memorandum, 30 Aug. 1847.
66. *Report of the Committee on Prison Discipline*, 263.
67. IOR P/142/61 (8 Apr. 1846): H. Hopkinson, Principal Assistant Commissioner Ramree, to Bogle, 27 Feb. 1846.
68. IOR P/142/61 (10 Feb. 1847): Bower to Colvin, 21 Jan. 1847.
69. IOR P/142/37 (17 Sept. 1845): Butterworth to Turnbull, 26 February 1845; McNair, *Prisoners their Own Warders*, 53–4, 123.
70. IOR P/145/31 (24 Jan. 1856): Mouat to A.W. Russell, Under-Secretary to Government Bengal, 26 Dec. 1855.
71. *Ibid.* On the Bengal government's criticism of the local withdrawal of Bihari prisoners' *lotahs* (drinking vessels), which triggered riots during the same year, see Yang, 'Lotah Emeutes'.

72. Arnold, 'Colonial Prison', 174.
73. IOR P/404/3 (6 Aug. 1846): Petition of Shreerustna Wassoodewjee, 1 Aug. 1846.
74. *Ibid.*: Minute of Willoughby, 2 Aug. 1846.
75. IOR P/146/30: Mouat to R. Thompson, Junior Secretary to Government Bengal, 9 Aug. 1860.
76. IOR P/436/45: Notes on Jail Administration in India, 9 Jan. 1869.
77. NAI Home (Judicial A), Dec. 1886, 117–219: Measures for the organization of reconvicted prisoners, 16 Aug. 1886.
78. NAI Home (Jails A), Feb. 1898, 32–4: G. Stokes, Chief Secretary to Government Madras, 27 June 1898.
79. NAI Home (Port Blair A), Nov. 1871, 1–6: Annual Sanitary and Medical Report on Port Blair, 1870.
80. NAI Home (Port Blair A), 1 Apr. 1864, 5: Report of Robert Napier.
81. NAI Home (Port Blair A), Nov. 1871, 1–6: Annual Sanitary and Medical Report on Port Blair, 1870.
82. NAI Home (Judicial A), 12 Aug. 1871, 18–19: Supply of clothing to Port Blair; Nov. 1875, 1–3: Annual report, 1874–5.
83. IOR V/10/600: Andaman and Nicobar Report, 1883–4 (333 women worked 215 looms); NAI Home (Port Blair A), June 1896, 1–2: Money allowance for female convicts.
84. NAI Home (Port Blair A), Aug. 1874, 51–84: Report on the Penal Settlement in the Andamans by Mr J.S. Campbell and Major-General H.W. Norman (henceforth Report of Campbell and Norman).
85. NAI Home (Port Blair A), June 1890, 74–8. Report on the Andamans by C.J. Lyall and A.S. Lethbridge (henceforth Report of Lyall and Lethbridge). For more details of this extensive report, see Sen, *Disciplining Punishment, passim.*
86. Portman, *History of our Relations, vol. I*, 303, 318.
87. NAI Home (Port Blair A), Mar. 1875, 43: Rules for transportation.
88. W.B. Birch, *Andaman and Nicobar Manual, as in Force on the 1st January 1886* (Superintendent of Government Printing, 1886), 67–70; Report of Lyall and Lethbridge.
89. Birch, *Andaman and Nicobar Manual*, 67–70.
90. *Ibid.*; IOR V/10/599: Andaman and Nicobar Report, 1882–3.
91. Birch, *Andaman and Nicobar Manual*, 67–70. On convict dress, see also Report of Lyall and Lethbridge.
92. NAI Home (Port Blair A), Aug. 1913, 32–5: Setting aside death sentence of life-convict Sadar (murder).
93. *Ibid.*

94. Mrs Talbot Clifton, *Pilgrims to the Isles of Penance: Orchid Gathering in the East* (John Long, 1911), 77.
95. NAI Home (Judicial A), Oct. 1872, 247–50: Report of R.M. Hughes, Secretary to the Strangers' Home for Asiatics, West India Dock Road, Limehouse, 24 Aug. 1872.
96. Clifton, *Pilgrims to the Isles of Penance*, 91.
97. NAI Home (Port Blair A), Aug. 1896, 39–45: Superintendent R.C. Temple to J.P. Hewett, Secretary to Government of India; NAI Home (Port Blair A), Sept. 1896, 79–84: Settlement Order no. 910, 31 Mar. 1896.
98. Portman, *History of our Relations, vol. I*, 303. Portman also notes a captured Andamanese had a convict's ticket in his possession. *Ibid.*, 318.
99. NAI Home (Port Blair B), Feb. 1896, 64–6: Reversal of a sentence of death passed on a convict. Majumdar, *Penal Settlement in Andamans* and Aggarwal, *Heroes of Cellular Jail*, claim that the tickets were wooden, in contrast to contemporaries Rosamund E. Park, *Recollections and Red Letter Days* (private circulation, 1916), 52, and Clifton, *Pilgrims to the Isles of Penance*, 91.
100. Report of Lyall and Lethbridge.
101. See, for example, NAI Home (Port Blair A), Nov. 1888, 90–4: Memorial of W.B. Birch.
102. See, for example, NAI Home (Port Blair A), Aug. 1872, 1–2: Roll of summary punishments awarded to convicts stationed at Nancoury, June 1872. Seven convicts were fined two *annas* each.
103. Ujjwal Kumar Singh, *Political Prisoners in India* (Oxford University Press, 1998), 55.
104. NAI Home (Port Blair B), June 1892, 76–80: Petitions from Manipuri prisoners requesting relatives and friends may send them goods.
105. Kumar Singh, *Political Prisoners*, 57. See also V.D. Savarkar, *The Story of my Transportation for Life* (Sadbhakti, 1950), 238–42.
106. Barindra Kumar Ghose, *The Tale of my Exile* (Arya Office, 1922), 53, cited in Singh, *Political Prisoners*, 56.
107. Sen, *Disciplining Punishment*, 173–4, 214–15.
108. NAI Home (Port Blair A), Apr. 1875, 16–19: Juvenile convicts.
109. Report of Lyall and Lethbridge.
110. NAI Home (Port Blair B), Dec. 1880.
111. Report of Lyall and Lethbridge.
112. NAI Home (Port Blair A), Mar. 1888, 101–19: Suspension of W. Birch, First Assistant Superintendent.

113. Jeffrey Weeks, *Sex, Politics and Society: The Regulation of Sexuality since 1800* (Longman, 1992), ch. 6.
114. AOT CON 35/1: George Morgan *per Guillardon*, 26 Sept. 1829; Peter Shields *per Waterlily* and *Sarah*, 2 Sept. 1844; Joachim Marks *per Waterlily* and *Sarah*, 2 Sept. 1844.
115. Arnold, 'Colonial Prison', 170.
116. IOR P/143/6 (1 Sept. 1847): Memo of Half-Yearly Clothing Issue, Major H. Bower, Magistrate Mergui Jail, 22 July 1847.
117. IOR P/142/5 (8 Aug. 1843): J.H. Quigley and other East Indian convicts, to Bushby, 15 July 1843, enc. Petition of the Undersigned Convicts [J.H. Quigley, Thos Leonard, W.H.G. Halford, Peter Letang, Wm Pendleton, J.C. Johnson, C. Abott, A. Barriman, J. Gomes, F. Philips] at Moulmein Jail, 6 July 1843; Turnbull to G. Broadfoot, Commissioner Tenasserim Provinces, 8 Aug. 1843.
118. McNair, *Prisoners their Own Warders*, 94–5.
119. NAI Home (Port Blair A), Mar. 1875, 43.
120. Birch, *Andaman and Nicobar Manual*, 67–70.
121. Sen, *Disciplining Punishment*, 226.
122. NAI (Judicial A) 20 May 1871, 21–2: Murder by James Devine, a licensed convict. C.C. Macrae, Clerk of the High Court, to E.C. Bayley, Secretary to Government of India, 9 May 1871.
123. *The Times*, 13 Feb. 1872.
124. NAI (Judicial A) 20 May 1871, 21–2: Murder by James Devine, a licensed convict. Bayley's note, 16 May 1871.
125. NAI (Judicial A) 19 Aug. 1871, 9–10: Report on the laxity of discipline at Port Blair. Officiating Superintendent F.L. Playfair to Bayley, 7 June 1871, enc. Rules to be observed by the Christian prisoners in their Barrack.
126. MA RA417: Finniss to Barry, 19 Nov. 1829.
127. IOR P/145/10 (3 May): List of thirty-eight female convicts for Singapore *per Soobrow Salam*, 26 Apr. 1855.
128. IOR P/145/22 (8 Nov. 1855): Extract from a letter from W.J. Butterworth, 12 July 1855.
129. IOR P/145/10 (3 May): List of thirty-eight female convicts for Singapore *per Soobrow Salam*, 26 Apr. 1855; IOR SM46: *The Government Gazette* (and *Supplement*), 7 Aug. 1828.
130. TNSA Judicial (29 July 1875), 190–2: T.E. Tennant, Inspector-General of Prisons Madras, to D.F. Carmichael, Chief Secretary to Government Madras, 10 July 1875.
131. TNSA Judicial (15 Feb. 1876), 68–70: Tennant to Huddleston, Chief Secretary to Government Madras, 22 Jan. 1876.

132. TNSA Judicial (29 July 1875), 190–2: Government Order 1681, 29 July 1875.
133. TNSA Judicial (15 Feb. 1876), 68–70: Tennant to Huddleston, 22 Jan. 1876, enc. Summary showing the Practice regarding the Cutting of the Hair of Burmese Convicts in the several Jails in this Presidency.
134. TNSA Judicial (1 June 1876), 7–9: W.P. Kelly, Inspector-General of Prisons Burma, to A. Eden, Chief Commissioner British Burma, 3 May 1876.
135. NAI Home (Judicial A) 16 Sept. 1871, 15: C.B. Cooke, Assistant Secretary to the Chief Commissioner of Burma, to Bayley, 17 Oct. 1871.
136. Arnold, 'Colonial Prison', 174–5.
137. IOR P/145/51 (27 Nov. 1856): Mouat to C.J. Buckland, Junior Secretary to Government Bengal, 13 Nov. 1856.
138. *Ibid.*: Petition of Moulvee Jamaloollyal Alee Mundle, Aheer Mundle and Goribullah, prisoners, 9th Kartick 1263.
139. IOR P/145/64 (25 June 1857): Mahammud Muzhur, Secretary to the Unjoomuni Islamee (Muslim Association), to Mouat, Calcutta, 9 Dec. 1856; Memorial of the Members of Unjoomuni Islamee or the Mahomedan Association, Calcutta, 28 Mar. 1857.
140. IOR P/145/64 (25 June 1857): Mouat to Muzhur, 10 Jan. 1857.
141. IOR P/145/51 (27 Nov. 1856): Mouat to Buckland, 13 Nov. 1856.
142. IOR P/145/64 (25 June 1857): C.E. Lance, Magistrate of Mymensing, to Mouat, 15 Dec. 1857; Mouat to Buckland, 8 Jan. 1857.
143. *Ibid.*: Mouat to Buckland, 11 Feb. 1857.
144. *Ibid.*: Buckland to Mouat, 31 Jan. 1857.
145. Arnold, 'Colonial Prison', 153. This is also implied by Yang, 'Lotah Emeutes'.
146. IOR P/142/7 (16 Oct. 1843): Broadfoot to Turnbull, 26 Sept. 1843; IOR P/142/27 (29 Jan. 1845): Turnbull to Bushby, 29 Jan. 1845.
147. IOR P/433/44: S. Hogg, Commissioner of Police Calcutta, to A. Eden, Secretary to Government Bengal, 25 Apr. 1870, enc. Memorandum by Messrs Miller and Roberts, Official Visitors of the Presidency Jail.
148. IOR P/433/44: Draft Rules on Cutting and Cropping the Hair of European Prisoners, 6 May 1870.
149. NAI Home (Judicial B) Aug. 1886, 183–4: Amended rules on the subject of the cropping or shaving of hair of convicts in jail.
150. *Ibid.* Chatterjee has noted the extension of this particular penal practice (like *godna*) into the private sphere, in the instance of a slave being shorn by her mistress: 'Colouring Subalternity', 50–1 (n. 5).

151. A.P. Howell, *Note on Jails and Jail Discipline in India, 1867–68* (Superintendent of Government Printing, 1868), 84–5.
152. Joy Damousi, '"What Punishment will be Sufficient for these Rebellious Hussies?" Headshaving and Convict Women in the Female Factories, 1820s–1840s', in Duffield and Bradley (eds), *Representing Convicts*, 204–14; Joy Damousi, *Depraved and Disorderly: Female Convicts, Sexuality and Gender in Colonial Australia* (Cambridge University Press, 1997), ch. 4.
153. NAI Home (Jails A), Dec. 1893, 117–19: T.M. Filgate, Inspector-General of Prisons Bombay, to G.C. Whitworth, Acting Secretary to Government Bombay, 13 Sept. 1893.
154. Report of Campbell and Norman.
155. Birch, *Andaman and Nicobar Manual*, 49.
156. Clifton, *Pilgrims to the Isles of Penance*, 127–8.
157. C. Boden Kloss, *In the Andamans and Nicobars: The Narrative of a Cruise in the Schooner Terrapin* (John Murray, 1903), 20.
158. Mathur, *Kala Pani*, 64.
159. See also Christopher Breward, on how descriptive accounts of clothing were instrumental in negotiating a sense of national identity and membership of the 'imperial race' in the metropole: 'Sartorial Spectacle: Clothing and Masculine Identities in the Imperial City, 1860–1914', in Felix Driver and David Gilbert (eds), *Imperial Cities* (Manchester University Press, 1999), 238–53.
160. Thomas S. Abler, *Hinterland Warriors and Military Dress: European Empires and Exotic Uniforms* (Berg, 1999), 112–20.
161. NAI Home (Public A), July 1896, nos 139–67: Note by W.E. Young, Collector of Customs Karachi, 18 Feb. 1896.
162. NAI Home (Public A), July 1896, 139–67: W.H.H. Vincent, Officiating Magistrate Twenty-Four Parganas, 14 Nov. 1895.
163. *Ibid.*: J.A. Bourdillon, Commissioner of Burdwan, 22 Jan. 1896.
164. Deborah Sutton has also noted how the 'Travelled Toda' 'introduced a threat of reverse, of inversion', through their appropriation of metropolitan material culture, including clothing: 'Horrid Sights and Customary Rights: The Toda Funeral on the Colonial Nilgiris', *Indian Economic and Social History Review*, 39, 1 (2002), 68–9.
165. Thurston, *Ethnographic Notes*, 520.
166. Lyon, *Text Book*, 20.
167. For an overview of ethnographic photography in India, see Pinney, 'Colonial Anthropology'; Christopher Pinney, *Camera Indica: The Social Life of Indian Photographs* (Reaktion, 1997), ch. 1.
168. Pinney, 'Underneath the Banyan Tree', 166–7.

169. Dalton, *Descriptive Ethnology*, Plate XXXIII; Risley, *The People of India*, Plate XX. See also Pinney, *Camera Indica*, 48–9.

170. Willem Van Schendel, 'A Politics of Nudity: Photographs of the "Naked Mru" of Bangladesh', *Modern Asian Studies*, 36, 2 (2002), 346.

171. Daly, *Manual of the Criminal Classes, passim*; E.J. Gunthorpe, *Notes on Criminal Tribes Residing in or Frequenting the Bombay Presidency, Berar and the Central Provinces* (Times of India Steam Press, 1882), 66–7; Kennedy, *Notes on Criminal Classes, passim*; Rai Bahadur M. Pauparao Naidu, *The History of Professional Poisoners and Coiners of India* (Higginbotham and Co., 1912), 2–3. See also Naidu's *The Criminal Tribes of India, No. II: The History of Korawars, Erukulas or Kaikaries* (Higginbotham and Co., 1902).

172. Crooke, *Tribes and Castes, passim*; Hollins, *Criminal Tribes*, 62–3, 83, 99, 103.

173. Dr Sanjivi, *Criminology and Detection* (Tinnevelly Institute of Criminology, 1915), 3 (my emphasis).

174. Hollins, *Criminal Tribes*, 83; Kennedy, *Notes on Criminal Classes*, 220–3.

175. Hollins, *Criminal Tribes*, 18.

176. IOL MSS Eur F161/157: Inspector-General's Standing Order No. 62, note on the criminal tribes in the Punjab, 1944.

177. *Ibid.*

178. Tolen, 'Colonizing and Transforming', 117–20 (quotes 119, 120). On the Salvation Army's activities in India, see also Radhakrishna, 'Colonial Construction', 137–47

Voir/Savoir: Photographing, Measuring and Fingerprinting the Indian Criminal

Fragments of History: Contextualizing the Photograph

In *Camera Indica*, Christopher Pinney describes the development of photography in colonial India in terms of its 'indexicality'; its superiority over more equivocal signs in a country where nothing was what it seemed.[1] Contemporaries believed that photographs offered an objective record of subject matter, free from the interpretation of either the photographer or the audience. It was a scientific form of knowledge that, for the first time, facilitated the accumulation of what can be described as 'visual facts'. Lorraine Daston and Peter Galison have usefully conceptualized this as 'mechanical objectivity'.[2] Indeed, Henry Fox Talbot, the author of the first book of photography, tellingly entitled *The Pencil of Nature*, wrote on taking his first picture of a building in 1835 that it had 'drawn its own picture'. In his eyes, natural objects delineated *themselves* through photographs.[3] This gave photographs what the Reverend Joseph Mullins referred to at the Photographic Society of Bengal as a 'stern fidelity'.[4] Photography thus shifted the boundaries of what registered as visual truth, and overtook earlier artistic interpretations of places and people, like those produced in the early nineteenth century by the Flemish artist F. Baltazard Solvyns.[5]

Accordingly, theorists of visual culture have situated photography within the power/knowledge (*pouvoir/savoir*) paradigm described by Michel Foucault. Here, a 'carceral network' of productive power surveys, classifies and disciplines groups of individual bodies in order to objectify and, ultimately, subjugate them through its panoptic gaze.[6] David Green argues that photography was crucially important to the investment of power in the body by nineteenth-century anthropologists.[7] Suren Lalvani writes that photography organizes relations between power, knowledge and the body in such a way as to render the body visible and thus permeable to disciplinary regimes.[8] According to James R. Ryan, photographs were 'expressions of the knowledge and power that shaped the reality of Empire'.[9] It is not difficult to see why the camera has been conceptualized as a mode of productive power. In the colonies, it was a potential means of categorizing populations for the purpose of effective administration, and created what we might term representational vision. As Chris Jenks points out, the terminology of *pouvoir/savoir* itself accords, at least implicitly, some significance to the importance of 'seeing'. He writes: 'the *voir* in *savoir* speaks through our daily knowing and through our tacit rules of agreement'.[10]

Though photographers like Fox Talbot and his contemporaries made claims about the objectivity of photography, photographs do not, of course, transcend the social context in which they are produced. Cultural, economic and political forces all determine both their content and the way they are interpreted.[11] Despite the 'dream of perfect transparency', photography requires human agency and thus enters rather than ends the debate over objectivity.[12] Moreover, the very essence of a photograph is a paradox. As Elizabeth Edwards underlines, photographs record a present moment, but immediately imply the past. They present 'a timeless vision', suggesting that the specific can be taken for the general. Photographs therefore reproduce a 'repetition of arrested time', becoming 'a symbol for wider truths, at the risk of stereotyping and misrepresentation'.[13] Photographers' choice of photographic objects and subjects, their composition of the images and the ways in which those images were read indeed combined to form new spatial and ethnographic representations of the Indian subcontinent. However, as Edwards – and Ryan – demonstrate with considerable nuance, photography was not an unflinching arm of the state's apparatus. Photographs are what we might describe as fragments of history, unsettling the past as much as they fix its truth. In Ryan's words, they are 'dynamic objects with entangled histories'.[14]

In this chapter, I want to take up these issues of historicity, fragmentation and dynamism in examining nineteenth-century colonial experiments with the photographing of Indian criminals. Historians have explored the multiple interactions between nineteenth-century photography, criminality and identification in the European and North American context.[15] However, these interactions have received scant attention in India or British colonies more generally. There is a much broader literature on ethnographic photography in India, and the way in which it created or consolidated social categories of various kinds. The genesis of criminal photography was different. It aimed to enhance the visibility of individual bodies rather than whole social groups. Far from constituting an effective technological panoptican, however, photography failed to anchor individuals to images. Photographs were difficult to read and even harder to index. Though convicted in relatively small numbers, colonial sensibilities precluded taking pictures of female offenders at all. Subsequently, penal administrators looked for other ways to fix criminal identities, and turned to an anthropometric system designed in Paris by Alphonse Bertillon. Bertillonage was developed to include and was eventually superseded by a system of classification by fingerprinting. Only then did the colonial authorities seem to have found a solution to the problems of the mutability of the body and the shielding of women from their classificatory gaze.

Ethnographic Photography in Colonial India

Photography was first introduced in India in the 1840s and soon became popular with amateurs and professionals alike.[16] During the second half of the nineteenth century, they took thousands of photographs of Indian landscapes and people, many of which were reproduced in ethnographic texts. Individuals, or groups of individuals, were presented as expressive of particular social categories, relating to region of origin, religion, caste or tribe, or sometimes a somewhat inconsistent combination of all four. Seated or stood before the camera in supposedly traditional dress, and sometimes with signifying occupational props, the images presented these individuals as representative of broader social groups. The text accompanying the pictures reinforced their meaning in this respect, and photography became an important means of fixing social categories.

Surgeon John McCosh began to photograph Indian and Burmese 'types' from the early 1850s. Captain Houghton and Lieutenant Tanner made a photographic collection of Sindh in 1861, on the orders of the commissioner there.[17] Many of their photographs were incorporated in the most famous photographic project of its day, *The People of India*, compiled under the direction of the Political and Secret Department of the India Office, and published in eight volumes between 1868 and 1875. It contained almost 500 prints. Pinney describes *The People of India* project as an historical moment that signalled a move from interest to intent. In the wake of the 1857 Uprising, the colonial authorities saw accurate knowledge of the Indian population as crucial to the effective administration of a vast, seemingly elusive subcontinent. The social unrest that had spread over large areas of North India had raised the issues of subject loyalty and betrayal, not for the first time, but to a greater extent. The need to understand the Indian population in order to exert more effective control over it became more pressing.[18]

Pinney also contends that two different photographic forms emerged in nineteenth-century India. The first was the 'salvage paradigm', which aimed to capture the last remnants of the so-called dying races.[19] In 1872, for instance, the Asiatic Society of Bengal brought out E.T. Dalton's *Descriptive Ethnology of Bengal*. It was illustrated with lithographic portraits copied from photographs, including that of the two Juang women discussed in Chapter 4. Dalton described the sight of a group of Juang returning from work as 'like a dream of the stone age'.[20] The most famous example of 'salvage' photography is undoubtedly M.V. Portman's collection of photographs of Andamanese tribals, taken during the 1890s.[21] Portman was driven by the belief that they were on the verge of extinction, and the images were accompanied by details of his subjects' sex, age and language, and their physical characteristics, including their weight, colour of skin and length of ears. He also traced the hands and feet of each individual. Portman's position as officer in charge of the Andaman Homes between 1879 and 1900 gave him unique access to his photographic subjects, and it seems that he was able to pose and photograph them with ease.[22] This was an institution of confinement – like a jail – where colonized bodies could be easily observed.

The second mode of photography described by Pinney was the 'detective paradigm', which stressed the value of photography for the future identification of dynamic social groups, who were changing rapidly beyond recognition. Crooke's *The Tribes and Castes of the North-Western Provinces and Oudh* (1896), for instance, was illustrated with ethnographic prints taken by Sergeant Wallace in Mirzapur. Unlike Risley, Crooke believed that caste changed over time. New endogamous groups were constantly being created, particularly in areas where the gender ratio was imbalanced. The mutability of caste meant that distinct racial typologies could not be discerned. Rather, as we have seen, caste was simply a 'community of function'. The photographs Crooke chose to illustrate *The Tribes and Castes* reflected his views, with occupational props strongly in evidence. In one image, two leather workers (*chamars*) hold a pair of shoes. Crooke also named each subject, and noted his or her caste, occupation and place of residence. As with all these prints, the text accompanying each picture was crucial for its effective reading.[23]

Though they had their own distinctly South Asian agenda, such photographic projects were not exclusive to the subcontinent. Across the globe, photographs set up or confirmed existing classificatory and racially charged frames of analysis.[24] J. Beddoe's *The Races of Britain* (1885) was subtitled 'a contribution to the anthropology of Western Europe'. H.N. Hutchinson's *The Living Races of Mankind* (1900) was a more popular publication, coming out as a fortnightly magazine. It attempted to categorize socio-national groups in Europe and elsewhere and included photographs of 'typical' individuals.[25] Carl Dammann's *Anthropologisch-Ethnologisches Album in Photographien* (1873–6) reproduced 600 images from around the world, arranged first by geography and then racial and cultural types. The album is best conceived as 'a series of illustrations onto which precise taxonomic readings could be projected'.[26] Other colonial projects subjected marginalized peoples in Australasia, Africa, America, Papua New Guinea and Samoa to the scrutiny of the camera's lens.[27] Yet photography was also part of the orientalization of Europe, and the objectification of its underclass, often through the establishment of links with the 'savage Other'.[28]

Photographing the Individual: Old Offenders and Transportation Convicts

In *The Pencil of Nature*, Fox Talbot wrote that photography had the potential to transform criminal investigations.[29] In 1856, the Secretary to the Medical Board at Fort William, Norman Chevers, noted that the British authorities were using photography for the identification of old offenders. He predicted that in India it would soon become such an invaluable means of recording crime scenes and identifying murder victims that it would demonstrate the inexorable nature of colonial policing: 'no measure would afford more aid to police inquiries in India, or impress more vividly, even upon the minds of the ignorant and superstitious common people, a conviction of the difficulty of eluding our vigilance and of our accuracy in the detection of crime'.[30] Chevers was correct on both counts. After the passing of the 1869 Habitual Criminals Act in Britain, all convicted offenders were indeed registered and photographed. The biweekly *Police Gazette* included descriptions and photographs of unknown prisoners.[31] By 1870, as Chevers had said, photography was being used for police and medico-legal inquiries in India, though the development of its use (and indeed the use of fingerprinting) in forensic investigations is outside the scope of this book.[32] By the 1870s, the police authorities were also taking photographs of suspected old offenders, or habitual criminals, in the belief that a visual image was a more accurate representation of an individual than a written description.

In one of the earliest references to the photographing of convicts, in 1856 the Commissioner for the Suppression of Dacoity in Bengal, J.R. Ward, asked for a grant of 300 rupees so that he could photograph fifty thug approvers under his control.[33] Six weeks before Ward made his request, an approver named Sona Fukeer had escaped. Five men had been brought in for identification, but Fukeer remained at large. Ward added that though his main motive was the identification of suspected escapees, the portraits would 'form an interesting collection', an opinion echoed several times later on.[34] As we have seen, the colonial authorities viewed thuggee as ritual murder committed by hereditary criminals. Those thug approvers who agreed to give evidence against other thugs had part of their sentence remitted, but if they eluded police surveillance, they avoided punishment altogether. Ward's request was quickly sanctioned.[35]

From the late 1860s, it became more common for police authorities across the subcontinent to photograph prisoners. Twice-convicted offenders automatically received more stringent sentences, making the identification of every person tried in court important. Defendants with past convictions, however, often remained unrecognized. They used aliases or simply refused to tell the police who they were or where they lived. Improvements in communications meant that travel between the districts was easier than ever before. Some police and jail officials saw photography as a way to tag their identity, together with that of 'dangerous' offenders who had been convicted of murder or violent crime. They saw the reconviction of old offenders, or the recapture of dangerous ones in the event of escape, as a matter of urgency.[36] As Inspector-General of Jails Bengal, F.J. Mouat, later put it, 'nothing impressed me more strongly than the need of some unerring test of the identity of habitual criminals'.[37]

By 1868, the Lahore jail authorities photographed all persons they considered to be professional criminals, all persons sentenced to more than five years' imprisonment, and all those whose previous convictions were for serious offences. In order to catalogue changes in appearance, they took felons' pictures both on entering and when leaving the central jail. An annual list was published in the *Police Gazette*, so that District Police Superintendents knew whose pictures were on record.[38] The prison authorities in the Central Provinces also photographed all old offenders.[39] From 1869, the Burmese authorities photographed particularly 'dangerous' offenders and circulated pictures of those arrested under suspicious circumstances.[40] By this time, all twice-convicted offenders in Madras were also photographed. They were pictured dressed in their own clothes, shortly before their release. Copies were distributed to all the Police Divisions in the town, where they were pasted into the Old Offenders Registers. By 1874, the jail authorities had photographed about 200 habitual criminals. The Inspector-General of Jails Madras, T.E. Tennant, wrote that the pictures were of great use in the identification of previously convicted offenders, and prevented them from successfully using aliases.[41] Photography was used even more in Bengal. By the start of the 1880s, the photographs of 760 criminals were on record in the presidency.[42]

Photography was not, however, an extension of the all-seeing colonial eye. Many officials disagreed with Tennant and, far from constituting a panoptican gaze, criminal photography reflected practical and techno-logical limitations and the resistance of colonized subjects to it.[43] In part, problems with photography were related to the sheer number produced. It was impossible to identify an individual within a large batch of prints, and there was no foolproof system of classifying them to narrow the search down. Identification depended on chance recognition when browsing through police registers.[44] Indeed, in 1877 the Indian Prison Conference described the use of photography as a means of identifying old offenders as completely 'useless'.[45] The problems that emerged were related to these limitations. First, many colonial officials viewed photographs as expensive, especially in relation to their practical value. The initial proposal to photograph systematically all jail inmates, made by the Inspector-General of Jails Bengal in 1867, was rejected due to worries about the expense.[46] Even as photography became more widespread in Indian jails towards the end of the 1860s, many officials in the provinces refused to sanction it on the grounds of cost. The potential scale of the operation was huge. In the North-West Provinces alone there were over 3,000 prisoners who had previous convictions. The Inspector of Jails there wrote in 1869 that any possible benefits did not outweigh the expense.[47] The Inspector-General of Police in Hyderabad agreed.[48] Many repeat offenders did not travel beyond their home locality, and were well known to their local communities and police, making photographs unnecessary.[49] In addition, it was often difficult to find willing photographers, substan-tially pushing up the price per picture.[50] As in the case of penal tattooing, this of course raises further questions to do with local resistance to incorporation by colonial technologies of rule.

A second problem was concerned with the interpretation or reading of photographs. Their purpose was of course to individualize their subjects, tagging them with an identity that could be easily recognized. Yet photographs did not provide the 'stern fidelity' they seemed to promise, recording only a moment in an individual's lifetime rather than some immutable essence of them. Photographs sometimes faded. An indi-vidual's appearance might change, especially after repeated periods of incarceration and indoor labour. Weight could be lost or gained, the colour of the complexion might change, or hair, beard or moustache be altered.[51] E.R. Henry of the Bengal Police noted that by 1892 just 68 out of 1,728 unidentified criminals photographed in Bengal had been recognized from their portraits.[52]

Third were multiple claims that uneducated Indians were incapable of identifying individuals from photographs, or not to be trusted in doing so.[53] On the first point, the General Superintendent of Operations for the Suppression of Thuggee and Dacoity, C. Hervey, noted in 1869 that Europeans too found it difficult to identify individuals from their portraits, especially if they did not know them.[54] During the same discussion, the Acting Police Commissioner in Bombay's Southern District put it like this: 'the eye requires a certain education before it can perceive a likeness even of the most marked character; the Police have not had this education, and the most ludicrous consequences would result.'[55] The Commissioner of Police in Sindh agreed. He wrote that his officers were 'indifferently educated men, who cannot recognize a likeness, and in whose hands a photograph would be of as little use as a blank card.'[56] The poor quality of many of the photographs did not help, and things did not necessarily improve over time in this respect. Almost twenty years later, E.V. Westmacott, Officiating Inspector-General of Jails Bengal, wrote: 'Not only are natives generally incapable of recognising a photograph, or even, as one officer says, of telling the top of the face from the bottom, but the photographs that have been circulated are such that I am assured that European officials cannot recognise criminals from them when they have them in their hands.'[57] Indeed, these problems were not unique to India and the British police noted similar problems in recognizing offenders from their portraits. The 1906 *Criminal Investigation: A Practical Textbook for Magistrates, Police Officers and Lawyers*, based on Hans Gross' *System Der Kriminalistik*, catalogued numerous difficulties in using photographs to identify suspected offenders. 'Enormous difficulty', it noted, 'is always experienced in recognising persons from photographs, especially when the person recognising is a simple-minded fellow who has rarely seen photographs and has never before tried to find resemblances.'[58] Havelock Ellis, in his discourse on *The Criminal*, similarly asserted in his 1910 edition: 'Photography alone, or the assertion of a policeman, constitutes a hopeless method of identifying a criminal, and the majority of criminals have not only been allowed to escape recognition, but in some cases grave injustice has been done through imaginary recognitions.'[59] The effective reading of photographs was a question of the quality of the print and the education of the reader; both were frequently inadequate. In India, only the Superintendent of Alipur Jail recorded any degree of success in using photographs to identify offenders and, even then, by 1886 only half a dozen times.[60]

The second point, the supposed untrustworthiness of Indians, was something that had exercised colonial officials since the late eighteenth century, for instance when framing early *godna* regulations for perjurers and forgers.[61] Colonial officials wrote that their dishonesty, compounded with the size of the Indian presidencies, made it almost impossible to use photographs to track down individuals. In 1879, the Inspector-General of Prisons Bombay, O. Probyn, put it like this:

> In England the photograph of any noted offender placed in the hands of clever detectives might assist in tracing the person wanted, because something is know of him to start with, and the public are against him to a man. In this country it is quite different. In our own Presidency (Bombay), which is upwards of 180,000 square miles in area, and is still but a very small part of our Indian possessions, how difficult it often is to trace a person who has no reason to hide or disguise himself after he has left his usual place of abode. What can be done in more civilized countries cannot always be accomplished in this, and it would be a hopeless task to endeavour to trace an escaped convict amongst the millions of inhabitants of India.[62]

Probyn was not alone in his assertion that the Indian public were not against wanted persons 'to a man'. Earlier on, colonial officials had despaired of Indians' responses to photographs. In 1869 Hervey presented a police approver with several photographs of suspected dacoits. He wrote, apparently without the irony that had characterized the approver's tactic of non-recognition: 'He exultingly, and to the delight of the men around me, selected the photograph of quite another man, or one who had lost one eye, while his man had both eyes perfect.'[63] He saw this as evidence of the uselessness of photographs for identificatory purposes, rather than as evidence of the agency of the approver, a point we shall return to later. It is difficult to say to what extent the approver's actions deliberately played on British assumptions about the 'pre-modern native', but it is worth noting that the British authorities too were nervous of corruption and collusion between prison warders and the police in identifying offenders.[64]

In the mid-1870s, the colonial government extended criminal photography to transportation convicts. From the very beginning of transportation the authorities in the penal settlements, including the first 1793 Andamans settlement, made complaints to mainland jail officials about the accuracy of the descriptive rolls that accompanied convicts to their destination.[65] These rolls were compiled by 'native writers' (clerks) in the presidency transportation holding jails, at Alipur (Bengal), Chengalpattu (Madras) and Thane (Bombay). They drew on descriptions sent with convicts from their place of trial. As we have seen, these ship indents were designed to individualize convicts and facilitate their identification, for the purposes of surveillance, management and control. The degree of Indian involvement in producing these records is clear from those descriptions that are clearly translations from the vernacular. Thus 'wheaten complexion' (which Risley later noted meant 'light transparent brown'),[66] 'copper complexion', 'high nose', 'cat's eyes' and 'sheep's eyes' all appear. There are echoes of Johann Lavater's eighteenth-century *Physiognomische Fragmente* (*Essays on Physiognomy*) here, which claimed scientific, 'optic power' in reading the face for indications of character.[67] During the first half of the nineteenth century it was unusual, though, for contemporaries to interrogate convicts' appearance for signs of their criminality. James Wathen's description of Penang transportees with 'villainy in every feature' is rare in this respect.[68] It was only later on that there was what Shruti Kapila describes as coalescence between the physical sciences and ideas about race, criminality, heredity and degeneration.[69] The indents' careful detailing of limb, head, nose, forehead, ear and eye shape and size was however the antecedent of later anthropometric practices. The scientific discourses of phrenology, craniology and anthropometry sought to establish, predict or record individual and collective character on the basis of physical measurements.

Much of the information contained in even the most detailed rolls was, by its nature, highly subjective. Judgements about a convict's physique and facial features inevitably varied from one observer to another. Other descriptions were so lacking in detail that their use was limited and, throughout the transportation period, the penal settlements were not slow in calling for greater accuracy in convict rolls.[70] By the early 1880s, all Andaman convicts were inspected on arrival at Port Blair, and their appearance checked against that recorded in their indent. If necessary, the rolls were altered. As for prisoners incarcerated in Indian jails, transported convicts' appearances sometimes changed after long periods at hard labour. Convicts also aged and sickness took its toll. For this reason, after 1883 new descriptive rolls were prepared for all released Andaman convicts.[71] Throughout this period penal administrators were keen to promote the recording of more permanent bodily signs on the rolls. In 1874, the Inspector-General of Prisons North West Provinces called attention to recording the condition of convicts' teeth, adding that the position of vaccination marks could also be included in descriptions.[72] Other suggestions included measuring prisoners from the tips of the fingers across the chest, and the use of colour guides to record skin tone.[73]

Though it had been banned in 1849, penal administrators suggested the reintroduction of penal tattooing and branding several times. Almost immediately after the 1858 British settlement of the Andaman Islands, a large number of convicts escaped. Superintendent James Walker suggested that in order to ease their recapture convicts should be branded before their departure. He suggested that the letters 'P.B./L' (Port Blair Life) denote life convicts and 'P.B./T' (Port Blair Term) term convicts. Walker proposed that after they arrived, convicts' numbers – which he described as the key to tracing their name, caste, crime and sentence – be branded underneath the letters, producing a mark such as: 'P.B./L/1085'. Given its recent abolition, the Government of India refused to adopt the proposals.[74] After two cases of convicts escaping from the Islands in 1870, Superintendent H. Man again suggested that life prisoners be branded. This time, the idea was that a broad arrow would be burnt on one shoulder or forearm and, as proposed in 1858, 'P.B.' on the other. Despite the fact that soldiers could still be branded, again the Government of India refused to sanction what they described as a 'barbarous practice'.[75] The issue was raised once again in 1873, during discussions about criminal photography. The Inspector-Generals of Prisons in Madras, the North West Provinces, Panjab and Awadh all recommended that transportation prisoners should be tattooed before their embarkation to the Andaman Islands. It was photography, however, that won the support of the Government of India.[76] Three years later, the 1877 Prison Conference dismissed the permanent marks created through penal tattooing as cruel.[77]

The Straits Settlements made the first systematic attempt to photograph all transportation convicts when they arrived there. J.F.A. McNair (Comptroller-General of Convicts, 1857–77) wrote in his memoirs that he taught photography to two literate convicts, who worked in a specially constructed photographic studio inside Singapore Jail.[78] Though these pictures do not survive, McNair's memoir reproduces a unique collection of convict photographs. The pictures include various categories – or 'types' – of convicts, from 'fifth-class incorrigibles' to first-class overseers, timekeepers and clerks (Figures 4.1, 4.2 and 4.3). In many ways the photographs mirrored ethnographic projects simultaneously underway in the Indian subcontinent, and for this reason we might term the collection penal ethnography. Convicts were individually posed, full frontal, their faces expressionless. McNair does not name them. Instead each convict forms part of a collective category within the penal hierarchy. The inclusion of various props is the prime indicator of which category that is. Fetters on the legs, clothing, turbans and caps or the (red) sash of authority all indicate a convict's status. Clearly, these photographs were not taken in order to facilitate the recognition of individuals, in case of escape, but instead to represent the collective categories to which convicts belonged.

The implicit juxtaposition of those who resisted the penal regime against those who collaborated with it in these pictures provides a neat representation of the basis of the settlement's organization. The importance of hard labour and incentives to the successful running of the system – and potentially 'reformative' nature of the punishment of transportation – both emerge through this set of prints.

Yet there is one crucial difference between the penal classifications captured in Singapore and other photographic projects underway in India. Although both were concerned with recording the appearance of 'types', the penal ethnography reproduced by McNair never acknowledged convicts' caste, in bold contrast to the significance accorded to it by ethnographic photographers in the Indian subcontinent. There, individuals were usually collectivized on the basis of their caste, and this was noted in the caption displayed beneath the print. This was at least partly because the punishment of transportation was predicated on the supposed loss of caste it caused. As we saw in Chapter 4, from the 1840s administrators in the penal settlements made greater interventions in their organization of convicts, and rejected convicts' own penal groupings, based on caste or other factors. McNair's prints symbolized the possibility of moving up or down the penal hierarchy, an implicit contrast to the fixity of caste expressed through ethnographic photographs.

I would argue that once photographs attempted to represent the individual criminal, rather than the penal or ethnographic collective, their meaning shifted. Allan Sekula writes that in Europe: 'photography came to establish and delimit the terrain of the *other*, to define both the *generalized look* – the typology – and the *contingent instance* of deviance and social pathology'.[79] I am less sure that criminal sociology in India successfully expressed the contingent instances of deviance than the 'generalized look' that Sekula describes. As we saw in Chapter 4, photography was effective in communicating colonial perceptions of the general appearance of the criminal tribes. If photographs of the criminal tribes expressed criminal typologies, McNair's collection represented penal ones, successfully illustrating convict placement on the rungs of the penal ladder in the Straits Settlements. The photographing of individual offenders, however, was clearly not a great success on the mainland, and this was also the case when it was extended to convicts shipped to the Andaman Islands. It would seem that colonial discourses in India could not move beyond a reading of social, criminal or penal 'types'. These were closely aligned to expressions of the meaning of caste and race, and the relationship between them.

The expression of the 'generalized look' is typified in the tale of two convicts who escaped to London in 1872. The Norwegian barque *Gazelle* picked them up 100 miles west of the Andaman Islands. The ship called at Antwerp and then London, where the men were placed in the Strangers' Home for Asiatics on West India Dock Road, Limehouse. During three interviews – with the captain of the ship, the British Consul at Antwerp and then the secretary of the Strangers' Home – the men, Loham Sing and Teeluck, gave the same story. Loham Sing claimed that he was on a pilgrimage to Benares and the Jugannath Temple in Puri. He said that he had met Teeluck on the road and they had travelled there together. After attending a festival, they hired a canoe to go and collect shellfish. They had accidentally drifted out to sea and were on the verge of starvation when they were picked up by the *Gazelle*, six days later.[80] The men's story aroused suspicion. The captain reported that despite their proximity to the Andamans – in itself suspicious – the men were not willing to go to the Islands. On arrival in London, they were apparently anxious to change their clothing. Moreover, the particular festival that the men claimed to have attended had taken place two months *after* their rescue at sea. Assuming that, if they were escaped convicts, they would have given false names, both men were photographed and the pictures sent to Dr King, a former medical officer on the Islands, who had since returned to England. Dr King wrote: 'I cannot say I recognise either of the men positively from their photographs, but their *general appearance* is exactly like that of many of the convicts at the Andamans.'[81] This negation of the particular in favour of the general was enough corroborating evidence to have the men shipped back to Calcutta.[82] According to *The Times*, both men were retransported to the Andamans, though one of them again escaped, never to be seen again.[83]

By the early 1870s, when all Indian transportation convicts were sent to the Andamans, administrators made regular complaints about the inaccurate information detailed in convict descriptive rolls. They called for the more precise recording of identifying marks, such as the exact position of bodily scars and moles, suggesting that each should by measured from the nearest joint.[84] During a 1906 visit to the Islands, Risley noted 'particularly absurd' descriptions on the rolls of convicts transported some years earlier: 'keeps company with gymnasts', 'not loved by his neighbours', and 'he is a bad man'.[85] Also during the 1870s, the Superintendent of Alipur Jail, S. Lynch, reported that there were always convicts in prison who were supposed to be escaped convicts from the Straits Settlements or Port Blair. The descriptive rolls sent from the settlement for use during police inquiries were, he said, absolutely no help in identifying

them. Lynch saw photographs as a means of 'easy detection'.[86] Given that
the authorities were already photographing old offenders on the mainland,
and following McNair's Straits Settlements project, photography was,
perhaps inevitably, extended to transportation convicts in the Andamans.

Proposals to photograph all life transportation convicts were floated in
1874, when the Government of India first asked the authorities in the
Bengal, Bombay and Madras presidencies for their opinions on it.[87] They
favoured the idea, and photography began on an experimental basis the
following year. The Government of India drew up the following set of
rules, based on a draft produced in Bombay. All male prisoners were to be
photographed before their departure for the Andaman Islands. The convicts
would be dressed in their own clothes, and the pictures would be of *carte-
de-visite* size, showing either their full figure or their profile. On the back
of each photograph, a note would be made of their name, time and place
of being photographed, caste, race, height, age, distinguishing marks,
native place, crime and 'other particulars of conviction'. The photographs
would then be numbered consecutively, and kept in the Inspector-General
of Prisons' office in a specially prepared and indexed register. Seven
further copies would be made, and distributed to the Commissioners of
Police in Calcutta, Madras and Bombay, the Superintendent of Port Blair
and the Inspector-General of Police. The two remaining copies could be
kept for identificatory purposes without upsetting their records. Finally,
the rules made provision for convicts who resisted the process, warning
that any prisoner who opposed being photographed, gave unnecessary
trouble, or caused any obstruction at all would be guilty of a breach of
prison discipline and thus liable to any punishment that the jail superintendent had the power to inflict.[88] We shall return to the theme of convict
resistance in a moment.

The Government of India recommended that the carbon process be
adopted, noting that it was easy to reproduce negatives from carbon prints.
As carbon prints are more chemically stable than silver prints, this reflected
its desire for the longevity of the pictures. The government also favoured
the single transfer method. This reversed the print, but was much cheaper.[89]
Its other suggestion, that money be saved through the use of jail officials
as photographers, was not taken up everywhere. Madras Presidency
convicts, for instance, only spent a day or two in Chengalpattu before
transportation, which meant that their pictures had to be taken quickly.
Prisons also lacked the necessary equipment, though in Alipur prisoners
employed in the Jail Press Establishment mounted and trimmed the cards.
Equally, the carbon process was not adopted across the presidencies; in
Madras, photographers were said to be unsure about it.[90] Nevertheless

Secretary A.P. Howell was very pleased with the initial results (Figures 5.1 and 5.2).[91] The convicts were not named in the correspondence.

The Madras authorities commissioned a professional photographer, and he took every convict's picture before their embarkation to Port Blair (Figure 5.3). He charged five rupees per convict, for eight copies and the negative, photographing between twenty and thirty convicts in batches. He numbered the photographs consecutively, and a descriptive roll was attached to each.[92] This was very detailed, noting each convict's number, name, caste and religion, occupation, place of residence, an estimate of their age, height, previous convictions, particular distinguishing marks, offence, calendar case number, sentence, sentencing authority, date of sentence, education, health, weight, conduct in jail and any 'other remarks'.[93] The notation of caste and religion was a measure that the Government of India thought would enhance the additional 'ethnographic utility' of the photographs, something that it mentioned several times.[94]

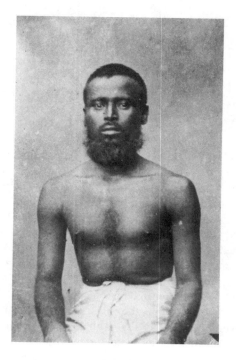

Figure 5.1 'Photographing Life Convicts by the Carbon Process'. (Courtesy of National Archives of India: Home (Port Blair A), Feb. 1876, 5–13)

Figure 5.2 'Photographing Life Convicts by the Carbon Process'. (Courtesy of National Archives of India: Home (Port Blair A), Feb. 1876, 5–13)

Copies were indeed sent to the Museum of the Asiatic Society in Bengal and to the India Office, London.[95]

It is unclear whether this or other photographic schemes included female offenders. The issue was never properly discussed, and I have yet to find a *carte-de-visite* of a convict woman. Lynch was the only official who mentioned women, arguing in 1874 that only male convicts should be photographed, though he did not specify why.[96] I would speculate that the intimate contact necessary for the correct positioning – and possibly unveiling – of female subjects was deemed unacceptable, creating problems in the authentication of female identity. Indeed, the Bengal police later exempted women from anthropmetric measurement.[97] Because so few women were transported, this probably caused few practical difficulties in the Andamans. The screening of women from identificatory practices was probably more of an issue for repeat offenders who drifted in and out of jail.

Figure 5.3 'Chungamma Naidu'. (Courtesy of Tamil Nadu State Archives: Judicial, 24 Sept. 1877, 166–9: 'Descriptive Roll of 2 male convicts sent to Port Blair on the Steamer Asia on the 25th April 1877')

At the end of 1875, J. Waterhouse, Assistant Surveyor-General in charge of the Photographic Branch in Calcutta, had calculated that eight pictures would cost one rupee.[98] However, they turned out to be much more expensive than this. In Bombay, the cheapest tender for photographing convicts (by Messrs Ritter and Mokenteller) was a hefty eight rupees for six copies. Bourne and Shepherd's studio bid had been even higher: ten rupees for the same quantity.[99] It was only after a Mr Blees, a guard on the Great Indian Peninsular Railway who claimed he had formerly been in business as a photographer in Karachi, agreed to match the Madras rate (by then five rupees for eight copies plus the negative) that the project even got underway.[100] The cost of photographing Bengal convicts was also more expensive than the initial forecast. Messrs O. Mallite charged three rupees for just four copies of each picture.[101] The Bengal authorities later calculated that if they had photographed all convicts transported from Alipur Jail to the Andamans between 1875 and 1876 (they had not), it would have cost a massive 3,600 rupees, much higher than the Government of India's allowance for the whole subcontinent.[102]

In 1876, the government asked the presidencies whether transportation convict photography should continue. They had mixed views. The Bengal government reported that the practical advantages of photographing convicts were unlikely to outweigh its expense. The Madras government, on the other hand, wanted to continue with it. The Bombay authorities felt unable to judge what had been only a short-lived experiment. The Government of India therefore decided to continue with transportation convict photography for another year, and asked the Superintendent of Port Blair for his particular opinion on its value. It authorized the Bombay and Madras presidencies to spend 1,000 rupees each and Bengal 1,500 rupees for the next year.[103] In 1878, the government reviewed transportation photography, and they decided that only the most 'conspicuous offenders' would be photographed. To some extent, their decision paralleled reservations about photographing old offenders. It was difficult to recognize individuals, and the pictures were more expensive than had been anticipated. Moreover, the Port Blair authorities received convict photographs only some months after they had been taken. Meanwhile, the photographs faded somewhat, and as in India some convicts' appearances changed. Neither the pictures nor the convicts represented in them were static.

The decision also reflected the fact that transportation convicts were shipped off the mainland to serve long sentences. Most convicts never escaped and so the photographs were very rarely needed, unlike those of old offenders, who spent only short terms in prison.[104] In any case, if a person was picked up on suspicion of being an escaped convict, the usual practice was for his photograph to be taken and sent to the Islands for identification. In 1881, for instance, a conditionally released convict named Kirpa Naik turned up in Mauritius. Presumably, he knew about the island's booming sugar economy, and tried to sign a contract of indenture. Unfortunately for him, he raised the suspicions of the Emigration Agent. The agent photographed the man and sent the picture to the Bengal government. It forwarded the print to the Andamans and, though we know nothing of her account of events, his wife identified him from it. On his return to the Islands, Kirpa Naik claimed that he had drifted out to sea accidentally, and had been picked up by a passing vessel en route to Mauritius.[105] In another 1890 case, three suspected escapees – Abdulla, Nawab and Ghapur – were picked up at sea and taken to Kochi. Their pictures were taken, and in an illustration of the uncertainty that characterized the reading of photographs, were sent to the Andamans together with full physical descriptions. Abdulla had lost the sight of one eye, and Ghapur had an injured nose, which eased their identification. Other incriminating evidence found on the men included a letter bearing a Port Blair postmark. The men were swiftly returned to the Islands.[106]

Criminal Photographs as Dynamic Objects

In this section, I want to explore the meaning of photographs to old offenders and transported convicts. Methodologically, I would like to follow the work of Edwards on photographic archives here. She asserts that the language of the colonial gaze is not appropriate to describe the multiple meanings of these 'little narratives'.[107] This approach must also inform discussions of criminal photography in colonial India. To cite Ryan once again, photographs are 'dynamic objects'.[108] We have already discussed official perspectives on photography, and seen glimpses of Indian agency in the reading of photographs and, through the rules framed for photo-graphing transportation convicts, in its performance. However, as subaltern responses to photography emerge only through colonial reports and memoirs, if at all, we cannot give precise meanings to photographs. These will always be, to some degree, unknowable.[109]

Subaltern responses to the camera may have reflected one of several things: excitement, fear or ideas about an appropriate presentation of the self that clashed with those of Europeans. M.V. Portman wrote that the Andamanese assisted him when taking and developing photographs, though his project meant that many Andamanese were used to the process.[110] In 1902, C. Boden Kloss mocked the lengths that a group of Andamanese women went to in dressing up for the camera: 'So absurdly comical did they appear, that it was only by much perseverance I was able to photograph them'. However, he also noted that some Andamanese were rather nervous of the camera. Other pictures he took in the neighbouring Nicobar Islands were spoiled after a boy peeked at the plates before he had removed them from the slides.[111] More usually, ethnographic photo-graphers noted that the subjects of ethnographic projects did not under-stand or appreciate the camera's function. Samuel Bourne, a professional photographer of some renown, wrote of his attempts to photograph a group of Kashmiris in the 1860s: 'By no amount of talking and acting could I get them to stand or sit in an easy, natural attitude. Their idea of giving life to a picture was to stand bolt upright, with their arms down as stiff as pokers, their chins turned up as if they were standing to have their throats cut.' He went on to add that this affected the composition of the print.[112]

Captain Cookesley (Royal Artillery) faced similar problems in his attempt to photograph the Lushai during an 1871–2 expedition, apparently because they did not understand how to pose for a photograph.[113] A.C. Newcombe, in *Village, Town and Jungle Life in India* (1905), similarly noted: '[Hill people] did not know what was going to be done to them, and evidently were rather frightened, as shown in the photograph by their putting their hands together. When the cap was taken off the first time, they all bobbed their heads as if they expected they were going to be shot.'[114] Dalton too wrote that Tosco Peppé had persuaded the two young Juang women to pose only after 'many a tear'.[115] These interpretations of subaltern responses to the camera served to bolster the superiority of European technology, and exclude them from the colonial modernity that the camera represented.

Similar views were expressed about the photographing of criminals. In 1869, the Bombay Commissioner of Police wrote of the photographing of a man on suspicion that he was the fugitive Nana Saheb, who had been responsible for the 'Cawnpur Massacre' in 1857 but had since disappeared: 'Had the man been sentenced to be hung [*sic*], he could not have exhibited greater fear.'[116] At the beginning of the twentieth century, a visitor to the Andaman Islands, Mrs Talbot Clifton, tried to photograph some convict women working in the Female Factory. She wrote that when she brought out her camera and tripod, the women 'all howled simultaneously'. Talbot Clifton attributed this to their belief that they were about to be beaten with the legs of the tripod.[117] The photographic subjects themselves do not speak to this point, but who is to say that their response to the camera was not based on other factors to which the photographers were oblivious? The photographic process was certainly a powerful enactment of colonial technological superiority. Richard W. Ireland catalogues prisoners' fear of the camera in Britain at about the same time, and suggests that part of the reason they dreaded being photographed was their lack of knowledge about what would happen to the print.[118] There is other evidence that in India photographic subjects deliberately sought to disrupt the process. Lady Dufferin noted in her journal that when she tried to take a group photograph in Darjeeling in the 1880s, one boy did a headstand, and others 'began to shake and gesticulate in the most bewildering fashion'.[119] In this, we begin to see how subjects attributed different meanings to photographs, at variance with those of the photographer.

In the next chapter, we shall explore William Marshall's phrenological experiments amongst the Todas of the Nilgiri Hills in South India. Here, I would like to note his exasperation at their response to the prospect of being photographed. He noted with annoyance that one young woman put her hair into 'curl-papers' in preparation for the sitting. This of course obscured Marshall's observation of her cranial form, his reason for taking her picture. He also noted that the Todas greased their hair with butter, something he found highly unpleasant when taking calliper measurements.[120] There is no evidence that Indian prisoners or convicts had their own photographs, though by the later nineteenth century some of the better off surely did.[121] Certainly, British transportation convicts possessed them. When a convict named William Burkinshaw escaped from Western Australia to Calcutta in 1867, he was identified after a photograph of a woman was found in his pocket. The print was sent to the penal settlement at Swan River and recognized as a picture of his wife, Christina.[122]

The colonial authorities were also highly sensitive about the potential use of photographs intended to identify offenders, recognizing that they could be harnessed and used by colonial subjects in a completely different way. In 1872, convict Shere Ali murdered Viceroy Mayo during his visit to the Andamans. There were allegations at the time that the assassination was part of a wider Wahabi (extremist anti-colonial) plot.[123] In his biography of Mayo, W.W. Hunter wrote that Shere Ali had been 'childishly vain of being photographed as the murderer of a Viceroy'. Recognizing his potential to become an anti-colonial martyr, Hunter refused to publish any details of his identity.[124] Three photographs of Shere Ali are now held in the India Office Library. He is named as the subject of just one of them, the others noting simply that the pictures were of the (unnamed) murderer or assassin (Figure 5.4).[125]

Singha has also noted how in the late nineteenth century, photographs of political militants turned up in the 'disturbingly adulatory medium of the vernacular press.'[126] In 1909, colonial hackles were raised once again when matchboxes and handkerchiefs bearing portraits of Indians convicted of sedition were discovered in two cases of imported Japanese goods.[127]

As in Britain and North America, criminal offenders sometimes refused to be photographed, or resisted the process in some way.[128] In India, there is evidence that they deliberately moved, pulled faces or refused to sit still, potentially successful tactics during a process that could take some time. In part, this was related to the technological limitations of photography, as individuals had to sit perfectly still during the long exposures. The 1874 *Rules Regulating the Photographing of Prisoners Transported to the Andamans* are suggestive of experience of a range of convict tactics. They stated that convicts resisting photographs would be guilty of a breach of prison discipline and punished appropriately.[129] For this reason, the Inspector-General of Jails Madras recommended that photographs be taken in profile or against a grid, 'to reduce the yielding flesh to unchangeable proportions'.[130] Nevertheless, F.J. Mouat, Inspector-General of Jails

Figure 5.4 'Assassin of Lord Mayo'. (Courtesy of British Library, Photo 127/[99])

Bengal and first president of the Photographic Society of Bengal (1856–7), later wrote how 'a clever culprit' could change subtly his expression whilst being photographed, and so prevent his recognition later on.[131] It is impossible to read the response of the convicts to photography into some of the surviving prints we do have (Figures, 5.1, 5.2 and 5.3). That the photographs were taken at all indicates their ultimate compliance to the process. However, their and other convicts' feelings about it remain indiscernible.

The Body as a Legible Text: the Bertillon System of Identification and Fingerprinting

By the end of the nineteenth century, then, the limitations of photography for the identification of old offenders and convicts were apparent. In 1891, E.R. Henry was appointed Inspector-General of Police Bengal. He wrote that photography was only really useful in identifying those criminals, like forgers and cheats, who gave their victims the chance to recognize them.

They might then be able to pick them out from a set of photographs. Otherwise, photographs were taken only if a suspect's name was unknown. The system of identification in Bengal at this time largely consisted of the circulation of police registers and descriptive rolls, the weekly visits of district police officers to the prisons, and chance recognition by jail warders. It was not a provincial system, and other districts did not keep such good records. Henry noted the example of one man, Guru Dayal, who was convicted eight times in eight districts, using various aliases. On each occasion, he was given a lighter sentence than his first, three years and eight months imprisonment. The need to identify individuals was linked to the enhanced punishments twice-convicted offenders faced for some offences.[132]

By the end of the nineteenth century, a further dynamic in developing less equivocal means of identification was the passing of the Criminal Tribes Acts. The criminal tribes were always suspects in criminal investigations in their home localities; moreover absence from their settlements was punishable.[133] Henry later wrote: 'The importance of being able to fix human personality, of being able to give to each human being an individuality differentiating him from all others, under conditions which will ensure that this individuality can be convincingly and quickly ascertained in spite of all efforts that may be made to confuse it, cannot be overestimated.'[134]

Henry recommended that the Bengal authorities adopt a new method of criminal identification that had been trialled in Paris: Alphonse Bertillon's system of anthropometry (Bertillonage).[135] In 1891, the Government of India had already introduced a basic anthropometric system into Bengal jails. Anthropometry promised, it said, a valuable means of verifying the identity of old offenders. By April 1892, 'every prisoner of any importance' had been measured.[136] According to Henry's calculations, Bertillonage was a far more accurate system. The chances of misidentifying any of his 1,000 sample of prisoners when using it were just 870,911 to 1.[137] Henry drafted detailed instructions of the system, adapted to India, for the use of district superintendents. If individuals were arrested for crimes that carried additional penalties for a second offence, trained police officers would take six measurements of them. The measurements were: length of the head, width of the head (Figure 5.5), length of the middle finger of the left hand, length of the forearm, length of the left foot, and height. The combinations were said to be almost unique, and to remain stable over time.

Before taking the measurements, police officers would check the accuracy of their callipers and rulers against a standard metal gauge.

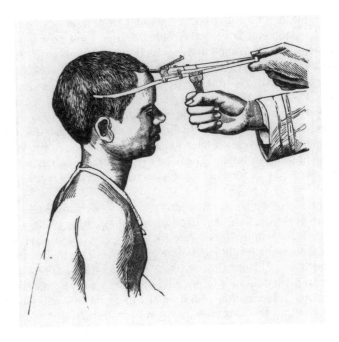

Figure 5.5 'Measuring Width of Head'. (Courtesy of National Archives of India: Home [Police A], June 1893, 129–45)

Ideally, individuals would be measured twice and, if there was more than a 2 millimetre difference between the two measurements, they would be retaken. Henry's instructions also ordered the compilation of descriptive rolls, containing details of the individual's religion, caste, mother tongue, complexion, build ('stoops, humpbacks, inverted toes and other deformities will be noted'), type and amount of head and body hair, and the size, nature and position of marks and scars in relation to two fixed points, such as the shoulder and elbow. Those on the head and neck would be noted first, followed by those on the right arm, left arm, front, back, right thigh including buttocks, right leg below the knee, right foot, left thigh including buttocks, left leg below the knee and left foot. Birth marks, disease marks (such as smallpox scars), accidental marks (injuries, burns and so on), artificial marks (vaccination marks, tattoos) and marks of age (baldness and loss of teeth) would also be recorded. Those marks that were particularly prominent would be indicated through an asterisk. Finally, each card would contain enough space for two photographs, one taken facing the camera and the other of the right-hand-side profile. Henry instructed that lighting come from the left for the full face shot, and from above for the profile. A graduated ruler would be held against the face to show the relative position of the individual's features. There were some limitations to the system, however. Measurers were instructed not to look for marks of circumcision, which were in any case usually implied by the offender's religion. Because of the close physical contact that measuring entailed, they were also completely prohibited from measuring women, who were thus totally removed from the purview of the colonial state in this respect.[138]

It was the arranging of the cards that, unlike descriptive rolls or photographs, made Bertillonage such an attractive system of identification. They were stored in a cabinet containing 729 pigeonholes (27 by 27). Each could hold up to 50 cards, so there was enough room in the cabinet for 36,450 individual rolls. The cards were organized according to the measurements taken, and finding individual records was a process of elimination. The top of the cabinet first noted measurements of the length of the head, divided into 'long', 'medium' and 'short'. Immediately, the search for an individual was narrowed down to one-third of the cabinet. Once this was cross-referenced against the measurements of the width of the head, also divided into 'long', 'medium' and 'short' down the side of the cabinet, the wanted card would be in one of eighty-one pigeonholes (nine by nine). This would be repeated for the length of the middle finger of the left hand and the forearm, bringing the search to one of nine pigeonholes. The final two measurements, of the left foot and height, would bring the search down to a final pigeonhole. As each card contained a detailed descriptive roll and two photographs, verification would then be easy. The system was, Henry explained, 'accurate beyond doubt'.[139] This was even more true, he noted in 1893, after the introduction of spiral spring callipers. These instruments were 'to a great extent automatic', with beginners achieving the same results as skilled measurers.[140] Further improvements included testing the springs against a dynamometer, which fixed their strength. In any case, police officers received training in the anthropometric techniques and by 1894 there were qualified measurers in every district.[141]

Due to the way in which the cards were indexed and retrieved, Bertillonage was seen as a particularly useful means of identifying itinerant persons. It seemed to offer more certainty than transient indicators of identity like dress or tattoos. As Cole argues, the rationale for the system was that 'the criminal body betrayed itself'.[142] Henry wrote in 1894 that Bertillonage was an important departure in police procedure: 'a practical attempt to deal with the hitherto hopeless problem of following up habituals who under disguises and aliases wander into places where they are unknown to commit crime'. He predicted that 50 per cent of unknown persons would be accounted for by the end of 1897,[143] though the system never had this degree of success.

Sekula argues that the Bertillon system successfully transformed bodily signs into a text.[144] Notwithstanding the total exclusion of women from this textualization, I would contend that as long as the body was reduced to a written record (or a photograph) it could not always be read. Even Henry conceded that there were difficulties with the system, notably the prominence that different measurers attached to certain marks and scars.[145] For this reason many colonial officials were unwilling to introduce it. The Bombay Presidency for instance continued with its own system of anthropometric identification, intending to review procedures once Bertillonage had been tried elsewhere.[146] This mirrored scepticism abroad. In Britain, it never moved beyond the experimental stage.[147] The Inspector-General of Prisons Pune, J. Humfrey, noted that he had visited the United States in 1893, where the Chicago police used Bertillonage, but the New York force preferred its own system.[148] Nevertheless, Bertillonage was gradually introduced outside Bengal and by 1895 it had been extended across India. There were further plans to introduce it in some of the native states and Burma.[149] The operation of the system in India differed from that designed in Paris. In France, ten measurements were taken, together with descriptions of hair and eye colour. Henry did not think this appropriate to India, where there was relatively little variation in hair colour or the pigmentation of the iris. Neither were the measurements the final test of identity. By 1894 that rested on thumbprints.[150]

In 1893, Henry noted that during the process of anthropometric measurement, thumb impressions were also taken. 'I must admit', he wrote, 'that I do not see my way to utilizing them.'[151] It was not long before he did and, within a year, thumbprints were an important part of the operation of the Bertillon system. The 'invention' of fingerprinting in India has been well documented.[152] In 1858, the Magistrate of Hughli, William Herschel, used a handprint to secure a public works contract, and later claimed to have introduced fingerprinting shortly afterwards.[153] Finger impressions were taken as receipts for government pensions, land transfer deeds, debt bonds and in jail admission registers. They were also used to bind individuals to labour contracts, something Singha argues was a moral change supposed to be engineered by the colonial rule of law.[154] Finger-printing was seen as a foil to fraud and impersonation and, in this sense, as Singha shows, exemplified the race hierarchies of the colonial state. It enveloped peasants and the middle classes alike, the latter giving finger impressions on examinations, medical certificates and pension books.[155] Registering officers in the North West Provinces were told to 'relax the rule' for Europeans and 'other persons of position' whose identity was not in question.[156] Even the history of fingerprinting was rewritten with the principal Indian actors removed. Henry never acknowledged the crucial role played by two Indian sub-inspectors of police – Aziz ul Haq and H.C. Bose – in the development of the system of fingerprint classification. As one British police officer, T.G. Holman, put it in his memoirs: they invented the system of classification by whorl, but the British got most of the credit.[157]

The permanence of fingerprints was not established until the 1890s, though Herschel made some tentative suggestions to this effect earlier on.[158] The scientist Francis Galton, better known for his work on eugenics, then did so, writing: 'There appear to be no bodily characteristics other than deep scars and tattoo marks comparable in their persistence to these markings.'[159] This was the moment when fingerprints were acknowledged as what Shreenivas and Saradindu Narayan Sinha have described as a 'physiological and natal autograph'.[160] Fingerprints were unique, and therefore fixed identity unequivocally to an individual body. From 1897 fingerprinting – of all ten digits – superseded the Bertillon system altogether.[161] That fingerprinting was developed in India and only later used in Britain has led to the conceptualization of the subcontinent as a 'colonial laboratory'.[162] It was not introduced in Britain until Henry was appointed Assistant Commissioner of Police at London's Scotland Yard. He set up the Fingerprint Branch there in 1901.[163]

In 1897 Henry wrote of the advantages of fingerprinting against the taking of more complex anthropometric measurements. Bertillon measurements had to be taken by trained officers using expensive and difficult to replace specialized equipment. High-caste measurers objected to touching the feet of low-caste men, and those being measured objected to the uncomfortable positions they were forced to adopt. The process took between thirty minutes and an hour. Even then, errors were sometimes made. Searching for the cards also took longer than anticipated, as allowances had to be made for margins of error in the measurements, which sometimes blurred the boundaries between the divisions 'long', 'medium' and 'short'. Fingerprinting, on the other hand, was quick and easy, and the whole procedure took just five minutes. All that was required by way of training was half an hour's practice, and the cards were easily sorted and found.[164] The equipment consisted of a tin slab, printing ink, a roller and some turpentine. There was no need for the undressing and minute bodily examination necessary for the compilation of Bertillon cards and so there was less room for objections to it. Crucially, women could be fingerprinted without difficulty. This was a considerable victory for the colonial government in the face of subject objections to other identificatory measures around the issue of female seclusion (*pardah*).[165] The system of classification was also simple, the division of cards according to individual measurements resembling that developed for Bertillonage.[166] Subsequently, it was fingerprinting, not Bertillonage, that was developed across India.[167]

Fingerprinting was eventually extended to members of the designated criminal tribes as well as to all prisoners. After 1905, adults registered under the Criminal Tribes Acts were fingerprinted as a matter of course.[168] The 1911 Criminal Tribes Act empowered district magistrates to take the fingerprints of any registered member of a designated criminal tribe at any time. If they refused, they could be sentenced to six months in prison or fined 200 rupees, or both.[169] By the 1930s, fingerprinting had increased even further in scope. There was a fingerprint bureau in every province, and in the larger provinces there were up to 200,000 fingerprints on record. In a bid to recognize old offenders and members of the criminal tribes, every person who was arrested was fingerprinted, and the prints compared with those already taken. The bureaux also received the fingerprints of arrested persons from neighbouring states.[170] With its extension to the penal sphere, fingerprinting consolidated colonial hierarchies of criminality as well as those of race. Fingerprints were indexical traces of presence that anchored identities to permanent bodily signs.

By the beginning of the twentieth century, the colonial state was well versed in marking, recording and interpreting the bodies of prisoners, convicts and the criminal tribes. The notation of the position of moles and scars, the marking of the body, the development of convict uniforms and the prison neck ticket, the photographing of individuals and criminal types, and the continuing search for possible indicators of criminal tendencies such as tattoos or disguises, were all attempts to render the criminal body legible. Such colonial innovations might also be placed within a broader concern with reading the Indian social body, what Dirks terms 'the colonized body as ethnographic text'.[171] Indeed, as we have seen, there were multiple relationships – and tensions – between the delineation of individual offenders and the construction of social, criminal and penal types. In the final chapter, I want to explore further the interrelationship between the criminalized body and colonial sociological categories. We have already discussed some of the ways in which prison populations were used during ethnographic and anthropometric surveys. We now turn to a discussion of other means through which the bodies of prisoners and convicts were appropriated for scientific purposes for a broader, global audience.

Notes

1. Pinney, *Camera Indica*, 20. For another general account of the development of photography in nineteenth-century India, see also John Falconer, 'Photography in Nineteenth-Century India', in Bayly (ed.), *The Raj*, 264–77.
2. Lorraine Daston and Peter Galison, 'The Image of Objectivity', *Representations*, 40 (1992), 81–128.
3. Fox Talbot, quoted in Don Slater, 'Photography and Modern Vision: The Spectacle of "Natural Magic", in Chris Jenks (ed.), *Visual Culture* (Routledge, 1995), 223.
4. Reverend Joseph Mullins, cited in Pinney, *Camera Indica*, 20.
5. F. Baltazard Solvyns, *Les Hindoûs, ou description de leurs moeurs, coutumes et ceremonies*, 5 vols (L'Imprimerie de Mame Freres, 1812).
6. On the relationship between photography and power/knowledge, see David Green, 'Classified Subjects. Photography and Anthropology: The Technology of Power', *Ten-8*, 14 (1984), 32–3.
7. *Ibid.*, 33.
8. Suren Lalvani, *Photography, Vision and the Production of Modern Bodies* (State University of New York Press, 1996), 2, 34.
9. James R. Ryan, *Picturing Empire: Photography and the Visualization of the British Empire* (Reaktion, 1997), 20.
10. Chris Jenks, 'The Centrality of the Eye in Western Culture: An Introduction', in Jenks (ed.), *Visual Culture*, 2.
11. Elizabeth Edwards, *Raw Histories: Photographs, Anthropology and Museums* (Berg, 2001); David Green, 'Veins of Resemblance: Photography and Eugenics', *Oxford Art Journal*, 7, 2 (1985), 15; Ryan, *Picturing Empire*, 19–20.
12. Daston and Galison, 'Image of Objectivity', 111–12, 120 (quote 111).
13. Elizabeth Edwards, 'Introduction', in Edwards (ed.), *Anthropology and Photography*, 7.
14. Ryan, *Picturing Empire*, 225.
15. Peter Becker, 'The Standardized Gaze: The Standardization of the Search Warrant in Nineteenth-Century Germany', in Caplan and

Torpey (eds) *Documenting Individual Identity*, 153–9; Cole, *Suspect Identities, passim*; McConville, *English Local Prisons*, 395–6; Richard W. Ireland, 'The Felon and the Angel Copier: Criminal Identity and the Promise of Photography in Victorian England and Wales', in Louis E. Knafla (ed.), *Policing and War in Europe* (Greenwood Press, 2002), 53–86; Lalvani, *Photography*, ch. 3; Celia Lury, *Prosthetic Culture: Photography, Memory and Identity* (Routledge, 1998), 43–57; Allan Sekula, 'The Body and the Archive', *October*, 39 (1980), 3–64 (a revised version of this article can be found in Roger Bolton (ed.), *The Contest of Meaning: Critical Histories of Photography* (MIT Press, 1989), 343–79). For an analysis of photography in Victorian detective fiction, see Ronald R. Thomas, 'Making Darkness Visible: Capturing the Criminal and Observing the Law in Victorian Photography and Detective Fiction', in Carol T. Christ and John O. Jordan (eds), *Victorian Literature and the Victorian Visual Imagination* (University of California Press, 1995), 134–68.

16. Pinney, *Camera Indica*, 17.
17. Pinney, 'Underneath the Banyan Tree', 166.
18. Pinney, *Camera Indica*, 33–45.
19. *Ibid.*, 45–9.
20. Dalton, *Descriptive Ethnology*, 154–6.
21. For an excellent analysis of M.V. Portman's Andaman photography, see Elizabeth Edwards, 'Science Visualized: E.H. Man in the Andaman Islands', in Edwards (ed.), *Anthropology and Photography*, 108–21. See also Falconer, 'Ethnological Photography', 35–9; Anne Maxwell, *Colonial Photography and Exhibitions: Representations of 'Native' Peoples and the Making of European Identities* (Cassell, 1999), 49–52; Ryan, *Picturing Empire*, 151–5.
22. Falconer, 'Ethnographical Photography', 38.
23. Crooke, *Tribes and Castes*, ix–xxvi, ccxxiii–ccxvi. For an illuminating discussion of Crooke's depiction of caste, see Pinney, 'Underneath the Banyan Tree'. On the transformation of caste into an 'observable trait' through the medium of postcards, see Mathur, 'Wanted Native Views', 104–6.
24. For a discussion of some of the complexities of 'race' photography in nineteenth-century Brazil, see Nancy Leys Stepan, *Picturing Tropical Nature* (Cornell University Press, 2001), ch. 3.
25. H.N. Hutchinson et al., *The Living Races of Mankind: A Popular Illustrated Account of the Customs, Habits, Pursuits, Feasts and Ceremonies of the Races of Mankind throughout the World* (Hutchinson and Co., 1900); J. Beddoe, *The Races of Britain: A*

Contribution to the Anthropology of Western Europe (J.W. Arrowsmith, 1885). For a provocative analysis of another gendered project, Arthur J. Munby's photography of Victorian women in Britain, see McClintock, *Imperial Leather*, 127–31. McClintock claims that photographing working-class women allowed Munby to manage 'the dangerous contradictions that marked his childhood identity', as he crossed the boundaries between race, class and gender.

26. Edwards, 'Photographic "Types"', 249–53; Elizabeth Edwards 'Ordering Others: Photography, Anthropologies and Taxonomies', in Chrissie Illes and Russell Roberts, *In Visible Light* (Museum of Modern Art Oxford, 1997), 59–61 (quote 59).

27. Judith Binney, 'Two Maori Portraits: Adoption of the Medium', in Edwards (ed.), *Anthropology and Photography*, 242–6; Brian W. Dippie, 'Representing the Other: The North American Indian', in Edwards (ed.), *Anthropology and Photography*, 132–6; Edwards, *Raw Histories*, chs 4, 5, 7; James C. Faris, 'Photography, Power and the Southern Nuba', in Edwards (ed.), *Anthropology and Photography*, 211–17; Maxwell, *Colonial Photography*, chs 2, 4, 5; Vivien Rae-Ellis, 'The Representation of Trucanini', in Edwards (ed.), *Anthropology and Photography*, 230–3.

28. On the construction of social identities in Britain, see Ryan, *Picturing Empire*, 145–6.

29. Sekula, 'Body and the Archive', 5–6.

30. Norman Chevers, *Manual of Medical Jurisprudence for Bengal and the North-Western Provinces* (Bengal Military Orphan Press, 1856), 40.

31. Cole, *Suspect Identities*, 19. On the Habitual Criminal and Prevention of Crime Acts, see Wiener, *Reconstructing the Criminal*, 148–51.

32. Norman Chevers, *A Manual of Medical Jurisprudence for India, Including the Outline of a History of Crime against the Person in India* (Thacker, Spink and Co., 1870), 74. On the forensic use of photography and fingerprinting in India, see Cole, *Suspect Identities*, 170–1; Anne M. Joseph, 'Anthropometry, the Police Expert, and the Deptford Murders: The Contested Introduction of Fingerprinting for the Identification of Criminals in Late Victorian and Edwardian Britain', in Caplan and Torpey (eds), *Documenting Individual Identity*, 164–83; Pinney, *Camera Indica*, 21–3.

33. IOR P/145/42 (26 June 1856): J.R. Ward, Commissioner for the Suppression of Dacoity Bengal, to Buckland, 10 June 1856.

34. *Ibid.*: Ward to Buckland, 16 June 1856.

35. *Ibid.*: Buckland to Ward, 26 June 1856.

36. NAI Home (Judicial A), 9 Oct. 1869, 31–50: Use of photography in the identification of criminals.
37. F.J. Mouat, 'Notes on M. Bertillon's Discourse on the Anthropometric Measurement of Criminals', *Journal of the Royal Anthropological Institute of Great Britain and Ireland*, 20 (1891), 185.
38. NAI Home (Judicial A), 9 Oct. 1869, 31–50: Circular from G. Hutchinson, Inspector-General of Police Lahore, 12 Dec. 1868.
39. *Ibid.*: J.W. Neill, Officiating Assistant Secretary to Chief Commissioner Central Provinces, to Bayley, 5 Apr. 1869.
40. *Ibid.*: H. Nelson Davies, Secretary to Chief Commissioner British Burma, to Bayley, 16 Mar. 1869.
41. TNSA Judicial (6 Aug. 1874), 30–2: Tennant to Carmichael, 31 July 1874 (see also NAI Home [Port Blair A], Dec. 1874, 52–7: Proposals to photograph convicts sentenced to life transportation).
42. IOR MSS Eur F161/154: Crimes Peculiar to India; The Bengal Police.
43. On photography, fragmentation and history, see Ryan, *Picturing Empire*, 219.
44. The British and North American police authorities encountered the same problems. See Cole, *Suspect Identities*, 26–7; McConville, *English Local Prisons*, 395–6.
45. NAI Home (Judicial A), Sept. 1877, 68–88: Report of Prison Conference 1877.
46. NAI Home (Judicial A), 9 Oct. 1869, 31–50: A. Mackenzie, Officiating Junior Secretary to Government Bengal, to Bayley, 13 Mar. 1869.
47. *Ibid.*: S. Clark, Inspector-General of Prisons North West Provinces, to J.H. Lloyd, Officiating Under-Secretary to Government North West Provinces, 1 April 1869.
48. *Ibid.*: G.H. Trevor, Officiating First Assistant Resident Hyderabad, to Bayley, 23 Apr. 1869.
49. *Ibid.*: Memorandum of J.F. Fernandez, Assistant Commissioner of Police Northern Division, Bombay Presidency, 16 Apr. 1869.
50. *Ibid.*: A. Daniell, Acting Under-Secretary to Government Bombay, to Bayley, 7 June 1869.
51. Mouat, 'Notes on M. Bertillon's Discourse', 185.
52. NAI Home (Police A), Sept. 1892, 87–90: Memorandum of E.R. Henry, Officiating Inspector-General of Police Lower Provinces, 22 Dec. 1891.
53. NAI Home (Judicial A), 9 Oct. 1869, 31–50: Neill to Bayley, 5 Apr. 1869; L. Bowring, Chief Commissioner of Mysore and Coorg, to Bayley, 16 Apr. 1869; C. Hervey, General Superintendent of Operations for the Suppression of Thuggee and Dacoity, to Bayley, 27 Apr. 1869.

54. *Ibid.*: Hervey to Bayley, 27 April 1869.
55. *Ibid.*: L. Ashburner, Acting Commissioner of Police Southern Division, Bombay Presidency, to Daniell, 10 May 1869.
56. *Ibid.*: W.L. Merewether, Commissioner of Police Sindh, to W.R. Seymour, Governor of Bombay, 18 May 1869.
57. NAI Home (Judicial A), Dec. 1886, 117–219: E.V. Westmacott, Officiating Inspector-General of Jails Bengal, to F.B. Peacock, Secretary to Government Bengal, 26 Sept. 1885.
58. John Adam and G. Collyer Adam, *Criminal Investigation: A Practical Textbook for Magistrates, Police Officers and Lawyers* (Sweet and Maxwell, 1906). The textbook was republished as recently as 1962.
59. Havelock Ellis, *The Criminal* (Blackwood, Scott and Co., 1910), 341.
60. NAI Home (Judicial A), Dec. 1886, 117–219: Government of Bengal Circular, 16 Aug. 1886.
61. On 'moral feeling' in India, see F.J. Mouat, 'On Prison Discipline and Statistics in Lower Bengal', *Journal of the Statistical Society of London*, 30, 1 (1867), 33–4, 40.
62. NAI Home (Port Blair A), Jan. 1879, 22–30: O. Probyn, Inspector-General of Prisons Bombay, 27 Sept. 1879.
63. NAI Home (Judicial A), 9 Oct. 1869, 31–50. Hervey to Bayley, 27 Apr. 1869.
64. McConville, *English Local Prisons*, 397–8.
65. NAI Home (Port Blair A), Jan. 1879, 22–30: Photographing convicts.
66. Risley, *The Tribes and Castes, vol. I*, xxxii.
67. For an illuminating discussion of Lavater and his detractors, see Michael Shortland, 'Skin Deep: Barthes, Lavater and the Legible Body', *Economy and Society*, 14, 3 (1985), 273–312. Lavater is also discussed by Sekula, 'Body and the Archive', 11.
68. James Wathen, *Journal of a Voyage, in 1811 and 1812, to Madras and China; Returning by the Cape of Good Hope and St. Helena; in the H.C.S. The Hope, Capt. James Pendergrass* (J. Nichols, Son and Bentley, 1814), 127.
69. Shruti Kapila, 'The Making of Colonial Psychiatry, Bombay Presidency, 1849–1940', PhD in History, SOAS, University of London (2002).
70. On Mauritius, see Anderson, *Convicts in the Indian Ocean*, 27.
71. NAI Home (Port Blair A), Aug. 1883, 79–81: Amendment of form of descriptive rolls.
72. NAI Home (Port Blair A), June 1874, 15–32: Inspector-General of Prisons North West Provinces to C.A. Elliott, Secretary to Government North West Provinces, 7 Feb. 1874. On vaccination in jails, see Arnold, *Colonizing the Body*, 108.

73. *Ibid.*: A.M. Dallas, Inspector-General of Prisons Panjab, to T.H. Thornton, Secretary to Government Panjab, 3 Jan. 1874, enc. Measurement Statement of 259 Prisoners; J.W. Chisholm, Officiating Secretary to Chief Commissioner Central Provinces, to Lyall, 28 Apr. 1874.
74. NAI Home (Judicial), 3 Sept. 1858, 1–2: Superintendent J.P. Walker to C. Beadon, Secretary to Government of India, 8 July 1858. The proposals are also discussed by Portman, *History of our Relations, vol. I*, 262–3.
75. NAI Home (Judicial A), 10 Dec. 1870, 20–21: Superintendent H. Man to Bayley, 3 Nov. 1870; A.P. Howell, Under Secretary to Government of India, 8 Dec. 1870; NAI Home (Judicial A), 11 Feb. 1871, 52: Man to Howell, 23 Jan. 1871.
76. NAI Home (Port Blair A), June 1874, 15–32: Walker to Elliott, 7 Feb. 1874; Dallas to Thornton, 3 Jan. 1874; G.S. Sutherland, Inspector-General of Prisons Awadh, to H.J. Sparks, Officiating Secretary to Chief Commissioner Awadh, 22 Dec. 1873; Note of A.P. Howell, Secretary to Government of India, n.d.; IOR P/402 (22 Oct. 1874): Tennant to Carmichael, 16 Oct. 1874.
77. NAI Home (Judicial A), Sept. 1877, 68–88: Report of Prison Conference 1877.
78. McNair, *Prisoners their Own Warders*, 107.
79. Sekula, 'Body and the Archive', 7, original emphases.
80. NAI Home (Judicial A), Oct. 1872, 247–50: E.A. Grattan, Consul at Antwerp, to Earl Granville, Secretary of State for the Colonies, enclosing Declaration of Captain S. Warness, 1 Aug. 1872; Report of Hughes, 24 Aug. 1872.
81. *Ibid.*
82. NAI Home (Port Blair A), Jan. 1873, 208: S. Lynch, Superintendent Alipur Jail, to W. Heeley, Inspector-General of Jails Bengal, 6 Aug. and 5 October 1872. See also H.L. Adam, *Oriental Crime* (T. Werner Laurie, 1909), 376–7.
83. *The Times*, 26 Dec. 1873.
84. NAI Home (Port Blair A), Dec. 1873, 9–10: Superintendent D.M. Stewart to A.C. Lyall, Secretary to Government of India, 11 Nov. 1873.
85. NAI Home (Port Blair A), Apr. 1906, 121: Extract from a note by H.H. Risley, 28 Feb. 1906.
86. NAI Home (Port Blair A), Dec. 1874, 52–7. Report of Lynch.
87. NAI Home (Port Blair A), June 1874, 15–32: Identification of transported convicts; NAI Home (Port Blair A), Dec. 1874, 52–7: Proposals to photograph convicts sentenced to life transportation.

88. NAI Home (Port Blair A), Dec. 1874, 52–7: Rules for regulating the Photographing of Prisoners transported to the Andamans (framed by the Government of Bombay).

89. NAI Home (Port Blair A), Feb. 1876, 5–13: Howell to Carmichael, 14 Dec. 1875 (see also TNSA Judicial, 31 July 1876, 175–6); TNSA Judicial, 12 Feb. 1876, 63–4: J. Waterhouse, Assistant Surveyor-General in charge Photographic Branch Calcutta, to H.E.L Thuillier, Surveyor-General of India, 17 Nov. 1875; TNSA Judicial, 31 July 1876, 175–6: Tennant to Carmichael, 5 Nov. 1875. Roslyn Poignant notes that though the carbon print process was permanent, it 'sometimes lacked the tonal range of the original'. It was also expensive: 'Surveying the Field of View: The Making of the RAI Photographic Collection', in Edwards (ed.), *Anthropology and Photography*, 68 (n. 25). For an outline of photographic techniques, see Edwards (ed.), *Anthropology and Photography*, 264–7.

90. NAI Home (Port Blair A), Aug. 1875, 47–8: Waterhouse to Thuillier, 20 July 1875; NAI Home (Port Blair A), Feb. 1876, 5–13: Howell to Carmichael, 14 Dec. 1875; NAI Home (Port Blair A), Jan. 1879, 22–30: A.S. Lethbridge, Inspector-General of Jails Bengal, to H.A. Cockerell, Secretary to Government Bengal, 9 Nov. 1878.

91. NAI Home (Port Blair A), Feb. 1876, 5–13: Howell's note, n.d.

92. NAI Home (Port Blair A), Feb. 1876, 5–13: Tennant to Huddleston, 5 Nov. 1875.

93. See, for example, TNSA (Judicial), 24 Sept. 1877, 166–9: 'Descriptive Roll of two male convicts sent to Port Blair on the Steamer Asia on the 25th April 1877'.

94. NAI Home (Port Blair A), Feb. 1876, 5–13: Howell to Carmichael, 14 Dec. 1874; Howell's note, n.d.; TNSA Judicial, 12 Feb. 1876, 63–4: Waterhouse to Thuillier, 17 Nov. 1875.

95. NAI Home (Port Blair A), Feb. 1876, 5–13: Howells' note, n.d.

96. NAI Home (Port Blair A), Dec. 1874, 52–7: Lynch's report, n.d.

97. Singha, 'Settle, Mobilize, Verify', 184–5 (n. 198).

98. TNSA Judicial, 12 Feb. 1876, 63–4: Waterhouse to Thuillier, 17 Nov. 1875.

99. NAI Home (Port Blair A), Dec. 1874, 52–7: J. Cruickshank, Inspector-General of Jails Bombay, to C. Gonne, Secretary to Government Bombay, 6 Aug. 1874.

100. NAI Home (Port Blair A), Mar. 1875, 49–51: Photographing Convicts.

101. NAI Home (Port Blair A), Feb. 1876, 5–13: Lynch to Lethbridge, 7 July 1874.

102. NAI Home (Port Blair A), Jan. 1879, 22–30: Photographing Convicts.

103. NAI Home (Port Blair A), July 1876, 20–5: Resolution of Government, 19 July 1876 (see also TNSA Judicial, 31 July 1876, 175–6).
104. NAI Home (Port Blair A), Jan. 1879, 22–30: Photographing Convicts; Lethbridge to Cockerell, 9 Nov. 1878; Resolution of Government, 28 Jan. 1879.
105. IOR V/10/599: Andaman and Nicobar report, 1882–3.
106. TNSA Judicial, 20 Apr. 1890, 711: H.M. Winterbottom, District Magistrate of Malabar, to J. Grose, Secretary to Government Madras, 1 Mar 1890; Government Order, 20 Apr. 1890.
107. Edwards, *Raw Histories*, intro. (quote 3).
108. Ryan, *Picturing Empire*, 225.
109. On the unknowability of photographs, see Edwards, *Raw Histories*, 5–6.
110. M.V. Portman, 'On Things in General, Regarding Port Blair, and Photography', *Journal of the Photographic Society of India*, 5 (1892), 190–3; M.V. Portman, 'Photography for Anthropologists', *Journal of the Anthropological Institute*, 15 (1896), 75–87.
111. Boden Kloss, *In the Andamans and Nicobars*, 31–2, 74–5 (quote 32).
112. John Falconer, 'Ethnographical Photography in India, 1850–1900', *Photographic Collector*, 5, 1 (1984), 22–3.
113. *Ibid.*, 23–4.
114. A.C. Newcombe, *Village, Town and Jungle Life in India* (William Blackwood and Sons, 1905), 255. Photographers could use this fear to advantage. The photographer Maxine du Camp, during an 1848–9 tour of Palestine and Egypt, told one subject that if he moved the lens would 'vomit a hail of shot'. She noted that this 'immobilized him immediately': McClintock, *Imperial Leather*, 126.
115. Dalton, *Descriptive Ethnology*, Plate XXXIII.
116. NAI Home (Judicial A), 9 Oct. 1869, 31–50: Daniell to Bayley, 21 May 1869.
117. Clifton also noted Andamanese women's 'shyness' at being photographed: Clifton, *Pilgrims*, 86, 107.
118. Ireland, 'The Felon', 72–3.
119. Hariot Georgina Blackwood, *Our Viceregal Life in India: Selections from my Journal, 1884–1888m vol. II* (John Murray, 1889), 262. Note also Blackwood's comment that her photographic subjects had 'no notion of sitting, and always make a point of being particularly active at the most critical moment' (193).
120. William E. Marshall, *A Phrenologist amongst the Todas; or the Study of a Primitive Tribe in South India, History, Character, Customs,*

Religion, Infanticide, Polyandry, Language (Longmans, Green and Co., 1873), 33, 50.

121. On Indian photographic studios, see Pinney, *Camera Indica*, ch. 2.
122. IOR P/436/48 (18 Dec. 1869, 34–8): Correspondence on W. Burkinshaw; NAI Home (Judicial A), 9 Apr. 1870, 15–19: H. Wakefield, Comptroller-General of Convicts Western Australia, to Bayley, 2 Mar. 1870.
123. On the assassination, see NAI Home (Judicial A), Apr. 1872, 81–2: Particulars of Port Blair convicts; *The Times*, 13 Feb. 1872, 3 May 1872.
124. W.W. Hunter, *Rulers of India: The Earl of Mayo* (Clarendon Press, 1891), 200, cited in Sen, *Disciplining Punishment*, 67–9.
125. The other photographs are held at IOR Photo 125/2 (46), Photo 127/ (96).
126. Singha, 'Settle, Mobilize, Verify', 173.
127. NAI Home (Judicial A), May 1909, 130–4: Prohibition of importation of portraits of seditious persons.
128. Ireland, 'The Felon', 76–7. Maren Stange, *Symbols of Ideal Life: Social Documentary Photography in America 1890–1950* (Cambridge University Press, 1989), 28, figure 1.17. Facial contortion formed the subject of an early short film, *Photographing a Female Crook*, made in New York in 1904 (Ireland, 'The Felon', 86 [n. 118]).
129. NAI Home (Port Blair A), Dec. 1874, 52–7: *Rules for Regulating the Photographing of Prisoners Transported to the Andamans*.
130. Cited in Singha, 'Settle, Mobilize, Verify', 173.
131. NAI Home (Police A), Sept. 1892, 87–90: cited in Memorandum of E.R. Henry, 22 Dec. 1891. See also Mouat, 'Notes on M. Bertillon's Discourse', 185–6.
132. NAI Home (Police A), Sept. 1892, 87–90: Memorandum of Henry, 22 Dec. 1891.
133. NAI Home (Police A), June 1893, 129–45: Henry to H.J.S. Cotton, Chief Secretary to Government Bengal, 25 Feb. 1893.
134. E.R. Henry, *Classification and Uses of Finger Prints* (George Routledge and Sons, 1900), 61.
135. On the introduction of Bertillonage in Europe and North America, see Cole, *Suspect Identities*, ch. 2; Martine Kaluszynski, 'Republican Identity: Bertillonage as Government Technique', in Caplan and Torpey (eds), *Documenting Individual Identity*, 123–38; Sekula, 'Body and the Archive', 25–37. It was also adopted in France's penal colony in New Caledonia. See George Griffith, *In an Unknown*

Prison Land: An Account of Convicts and Colonists in New Caledonia with Jottings Out and Home (Hutchinson and Co., 1901), 143–8.

136. NAI Home (Police A), May 1892: Resolution of Government, 16 Oct. 1891; Lyall to Lethbridge, 27 Apr. 1892.

137. NAI Home (Police A), Sept. 1892, 87–90: Memorandum of Henry, 22 Dec. 1891.

138. NAI Home (Police A), Sept. 1892, 87–90: Bengal Police – Anthropometry: instructions for district superintendents, n.d. See also NAI Home (Police A), June 1893, 129–45: Bengal Police Circular I 1893.

139. NAI Home (Police A), Sept. 1892, 87–90: Memorandum of Henry, 22 Dec. 1891; Alphonse Bertillon, *The Identification of the Criminal Classes by the Anthropometric Method* (tr. E.R. Spearman), (Spottiswoode and Co., 1889); Alphonse Bertillon, *Identification Anthropométrique: Instructions Signalétiques* (Melun, 1893).

140. NAI Home (Police A), June 1893, 129–45: Henry to Cotton, 25 Feb. 1893.

141. NAI Home (Police A), June 1894, 269–77: Henry to Cotton, 1 May 1894.

142. Cole, *Suspect Identities*, 53.

143. NAI Home (Police A), June 1894, 269–77: Henry to Cotton, 1 May 1894.

144. Sekula, 'Body and the Archive', 33.

145. NAI Home (Police A), June 1894, 269–77: Henry to Cotton, 1 May 1894.

146. NAI Home (Police A), Mar. 1893, 75–86: M. Lee Warner, Secretary to Government Bombay, to Lyall, 24 Feb. 1893.

147. McConville, *English Local Prisons*, 399–404.

148. NAI Home (Police A), Mar. 1894, 182–7: J. Humfrey, Inspector-General of Prisons Pune, to C.H.A. Hill, Under-Secretary to Government Bombay, 11 Jan. 1894. This does not bear out Sekula's assertion of its 'enthusiastic reception' in the United States: 'Body and the Archive', 34.

149. NAI Home (Police A), Feb. 1895, 35–8: Scheme for bringing into practical operation in Burma the Bertillon system of anthropometry; NAI Home (Police A), Oct. 1895, 46–9: Proposed introduction of anthropometry in Kashmir; NAI Home (Police A), Jan. 1896, 101–4: Anthropometry in Kashmir.

150. NAI Home (Police A), June 1894, 269–77: Henry to Cotton, 1 May 1894. On the introduction of the system in Madras, see Dirks, *Castes of Mind*, 185–6.

151. NAI Home (Police A), June 1893, 129–45: Henry to Cotton, 25 Feb. 1893.
152. Cole, *Suspect Identities*, 63–71; Dirks, *Castes of Mind*, 186–7, 339 (n. 50); Pinney, *Camera Indica*, 69–71; Chandak Sengoopta, *Imprint of the Raj: How Fingerprinting was Born in Colonial India* (Macmillan, 2000); Shreenivas and Saradindu Narayan Sinha, 'Personal Identification by the Dermatoglyphics and the E-V Methods', *Patna Journal of Medicine*, 31, 2 (1957), 53–64; Shreenivas and Saradindu Narayan Sinha, 'Personal identification by the Dermatoglyphics and the E-V Methods', *Patna Journal of Medicine*, 31, 3 (1957), 98–108; Singha, 'Settle, Mobilize, Verify', 174–90.
153. William J. Herschel, *The Origin of Finger-Printing* (Oxford University Press, 1916), 7–31. For another contemporary account of fingerprinting in India, see also Edmund C. Cox, *Police and Crime in India* (Stanley Paul and Co., 1910), 209–12.
154. Singha, 'Settle, Mobilize, Verify', 175. See also Henry, *Classification*, 3–9.
155. On finger printing and race hierarchies see Singha, 'Settle, Mobilize, Verify', 179–84.
156. NAI Home (Public A), June 1898, 589–611: Fingerprints.
157. Cited in Martin Wynne (ed.), *On Honourable Terms: The Memoirs of some Indian Police Officers, 1915–1948* (British Association for Cemeteries in South Asia) (BACSA, 1985)), 87.
158. Singha, 'Settle, Mobilize, Verify', 177.
159. Cited in Henry, *Classification*, 4–5.
160. Shreenivas and Sinha, 'Personal Identification' (31, 3), 100.
161. NAI Home (Police A), Dec. 1896, 88–9: Henry to Hewett, 3 Dec. 1896.
162. Cole, *Suspect Identities*, 90.
163. IOR MSS Eur F161/185: Finger Printing.
164. *Ibid.*; NAI Home (Police A), June 1897, 159–69: Henry to C.W. Bolton, Chief Secretary to Government Bengal, 13 Mar. 1897; Report of Committee to examine into the system of identification by finger impressions, 29 Mar. 1897 (reproduced in Henry, *Classification*, appendix).
165. Singha, 'Settle, Mobilize, Verify', 185.
166. For details of the 'Henry system', see Cole, *Suspect Identities*, 81–5.
167. NAI Home (Public A), June 1898, 589–611: Fingerprints; Home (Police A), Feb. 1899, 77–90: Fingerprints.

168. NAI Home (Police A), Aug. 1905, 86: Fingerprinting prisoners.
169. Arnold, *Police Power*, 144.
170. J.C. Curry, *The Indian Police* (Faber and Faber, 1932), 280–1.
171. Dirks, *Castes of Mind*, 188.

−6−

Emperors of the Lilliputians: Criminal Physiology and the Indian Social Body

Introduction

When Bertillonage was replaced by fingerprinting at the turn of the twentieth century, the Indian presidencies were left with thousands of anthropometric cards in their police files. At the time, Risley commented that although the police took cranial measurements differently from measurers employed in the ethnographic survey, police records of height might be useful to it.[1] The Government of India subsequently ordered that all anthropometric cards not required by the police should be arranged by caste and sent to Risley, who noted both their cost-effectiveness and 'considerable value for scientific purposes'.[2] It is not clear how, if at all, the cards fed into Risley's all-India survey. However, his appropriation of criminal records continued a pattern of the use of incarcerated communities in colonial ethnographic and anthropometric investigations. As we have seen, the use of prisoners in the production of such data was not at all unusual. In contrast to Risley's rather inadvertent acquisition of these sets of anthropometric measurements, colonial administrator-anthropologists and police officers not infrequently visited jails to interview, inspect or measure their inmates. Their findings fed into both the colonial sociology of race and caste as physically discernible entities, and into cultural discourses of the bodily symbols said to demarcate criminal typologies, notably tattoos and clothing.

In Europe, ideas about criminal typology were inextricably linked to readings of race and social evolution. In 1869, the British eugenicist Francis Galton published *Hereditary Genius* (1869), stressing the importance of nature over nurture in individual development. This implied that social betterment could be achieved through selective reproduction. Galton first used the word 'eugenics' in 1883 (*Inquiries into Human Faculty*), and the thrust of his later work was to naturalize social hierarchies. In short, according to Galton, discernible physical, anatomical differences could be taken as indicators of intellectual capacity.[3] Cesare Lombroso is perhaps the best known nineteenth-century criminologist, publishing the first volume of *L'Uomo Delinquente* in 1876 after famously 'discovering' anatomic differences between criminals and the insane. He saw cranial form, cerebral characteristics, facial features and physiognomy as indicators of an individual's propensity to crime, recasting them as born, or congenital (*reo-nato*) criminals. As Daniel Pick illustrates, Lombroso's approach sought to use the contours of a distinctive physiognomy to render the criminal visible. This physiognomy was heavily racialized, with Lombroso's take on the criminal body closely related to his ideas about social evolution. He conceptualized criminals as savage, atavistic creatures who had been left behind the rest of a society in a 'backward' past.[4]

In *Colonizing the Body*, Arnold has shown how Indian jails were important sites of medical observation and experimentation. Medical officers trialled prophylactic drugs and inoculations, and conducted dietary investigations to 'read civilian health from convict physiology'.[5] In this chapter, I want to pursue the twin themes of observation and experimentation further and, in the context of developing European ideas about the relationship between race and criminality, to deepen our understanding of Indian jails and penal settlements as spaces of colonial inquiry. As we have seen, male prisoners and convicts were implicated in the production of ideas about race as a set of discernible physical attributes, for instance through Risley's invention of the 'nasal index'. They were not, however, used in conceptualizing a specifically Indian criminal constitution. Representations of criminal typologies tended to rest on transient cultural signs (or rather vague notions of morphology), and not bodily make-up. It was cultural readings of Indian social hierarchies – notably those who saw caste as a 'community of function', or occupational category – that permitted the emergence of the idea of criminal types, the so-called criminal castes and tribes.

In the pages that follow I shall look at the ways in which Indian prisoners and convicts were appropriated in the construction of biological hierarchies of race that resonated beyond the subcontinent. I shall argue that there was little or no reference made to their criminal status; rather they were easily accessible human samples in the racial ordering of metropole and periphery, and the blurring of the boundaries between them. I shall explore three scientific interventions into the bodies of Indian offenders: phrenology, anthropometric photography and retinology. Finally, by way of an epilogue, I shall say something about the thrust of contemporary ethnography in the Andaman Islands, and consider some of the continuities between colonial and postcolonial discourses on the descendants of convicts and the criminal tribes.

'An Exact Science': Race and the Criminal Skull

During the nineteenth century, European scientists fixed on the skull as a way of discerning character. They measured cranial capacity (craniometry), using peppercorns, gunshot or millet seed, and size was seen to indicate intelligence. It was phrenology, however, that enjoyed the most popular support. Pioneered by Franz Gall during the 1820s, phrenological analysis was based on the contention that the human mind was divided into thirty-seven faculties, each of which was distinctly located in the brain. An examination of the skull could thus reveal each faculty's relative strength or weakness. Craniometry and phrenology were both methods of establishing the character of both individuals and collective groups.[6] Scientists also used them as modes of constituting racial typologies. Physiological racial differences were measured, compared and fixed, in scientific fashion.[7]

From the 1820s, a number of phrenological societies sprang up in Britain. The most prolific of these was the Phrenological Society of Edinburgh, founded by George Combe in 1820. The society used thirty-five measurements, believing that each revealed something of character. Traits like wit, hope, benevolence, cautiousness, firmness, combativeness, adhesiveness, individuality, superstition, covetousness and secretiveness were all identified and measured, through what Combe described as 'an exact science'.[8] The society was regularly sent skulls for examination from all over the world, and used them to develop ideas about the relationship between cranial measurements and racial hierarchies. A number of South Asian skulls were presented to the society during the 1820s and 1830s. Most had been appropriated in dubious circumstances. Colonial medical officers were frequent donors. They were often called on to investigate sudden deaths and were also present at executions. The skulls of those hanged during the 1822 Ceylon insurrection, for instance, were sent to the society. In a gross violation of cultural beliefs, Indian skulls were also frequently lifted from bodies found floating on funeral pyres on the River Ganges, sacred to Hindus.[9]

The Phrenological Society carefully examined, described and recorded new skulls, and then locked them in the 'National Skulls Cabinet'. Skulls were catalogued according to place of origin and, if known, the character of the individual in question was noted in the Society's *Minute Books*. Members of the society often had their own personal collections. They swapped them, or obtained casts from Luke O'Neil and Son, Artists to the Society. Prices varied from two to five shillings, depending on size.[10] In general terms, European crania were viewed as superior to all others, but socio-economic status, gender and in the Indian context caste also featured in their discussions. Rajah Rammohan Roy, a highly educated donor of twelve skulls during the 1820s, for instance, was found after his death in 1833 to have a larger than average skull.[11] On the other hand, the Society wrote that a female courtesan who had been murdered by one of her patrons was 'cunning, secretive, fond of money and extremely cruel.'[12] More generally, the society noted that those living in the areas of the Bengal Presidency populated by the British, and supposed to be positively influenced by their presence, had signs of cranial superiority.[13] Yet in the last instance gross generalizations were still made, despite apparent reservations about the scientific dangers of doing so. Thus, after manipulating hundreds of heads across the Indian subcontinent, a member of the Royal Asiatic Society in Calcutta, and one of the society's corresponding members, George Murray Paterson, felt well qualified to claim that Hindus lacked knowledge, wit, melody and force of character, but more than made up for these deficiencies with their cunning, secretiveness, timidity, self-importance and propensity to unnatural crime (homosexual acts). Where phrenological analysis proved inconclusive, conclusions were always drawn on the basis of pre-existing notions of character. Thus the wild variation in the size of the organ of the sentiment of 'firmness' that Paterson observed did not matter. It was well known that Hindus were fickle after all.[14]

European skulls were always seen as having belonged to an individual, who was named and described. The so-called 'National Skulls', in contrast, were usually represented collectively. We know very few of the micro-histories attributable to these individuals. Nothing was known of the skulls donated by Rammohun Roy, for instance, except the 'general qualities' they revealed about 'the Hindus'.[15] Illustrative figures were even drawn up to represent particular collections of skulls, such as that made by George Murray Paterson, in his 'On the Phrenology of Hindostan'.[16] This was not simply an attempt to represent the average, or median, of a group of skulls, but an attempt to include the characteristics of all of them in a single representation. In many ways Paterson's composite skull anticipated the later work of the eugenicist Francis Galton, who produced composite photographs of 'Jewish' and 'criminal' types in 1877.[17]

The only exceptions to such collectivization were when individuals were of particularly high socio-economic status, or were 'notorious' offenders. That we know Rammohun Roy's name is a case in point. The Phrenological Society also held seven skulls taken from amongst a hundred thugs executed at Saugor in the summer of 1833. Henry Spry, a surgeon in the Bengal Medical Service, donated the skulls on the orders of George Swinton, chief secretary to the Government of India, who was interested in phrenology.[18] They belonged to Dirgpaul, Gunga Bishun, Sooper Sing *alias* Khan Mahomed *alias* Bujoo, Hosein Alee Khan *alias* Hosein Yar Khan, Keramut Khan *alias* Kurreem Khan, Buksha – who had in fact died in jail before he could be executed – and Golab Khan *alias* Bussola.[19] Reproducing contemporary discourse about thugs, the men were described as having been hereditary criminals, coming from families engaged in the trade of thuggee for generations.[20] The Society's observations of their skulls reflected this. All the skulls were said in general terms to correspond to the men's known character. Cranial observations apparently showed the thugs' amativeness, combativeness, destructiveness, secretiveness, acquisitiveness, self-esteem, love of approbation and cautiousness. Two of the men, however, Hosein and Gunga, did not show the characteristic of destructiveness. It was concluded that this was because they had become thugs only through social rather than hereditary influences; they had been tempted rather than born into crime. Indeed, the thug skulls were said to be smaller than the European average.[21] These readings were, however, the exception to the rule, for in general the Society did not consider the provenance of Indian skulls, and viewed them in relation to racial typologies alone.

In contrast, the Society considered British skulls only with reference to the character of the individual, often criminal offenders, which permitted the production of discourses about the physical manifestations of criminality. The skulls of executed criminals were particularly easy to obtain, and what was known of their character could be correlated with cranial observations. British convicts were also easy pickings for phrenological analysis, and the Society examined inmates in British jails.[22] It also looked at the skulls of transportation convicts. In 1837, the skulls of two Australian convict bush-rangers – Edward Tattersdale and John Jenkins – were sent to the Society. It noted that they were remarkably small, yet showed enormous combativeness, self-esteem and hope, but a deficiency of cautiousness.[23] Captain Maconochie, superintendent of the penal station at Norfolk Island, even proposed that phrenology be used for the rehabilitation of convicts. Convicts could be made aware of their own weaknesses and so learn to control their criminal propensities. As there would be no point in attempting to rehabilitate the worst characters, convicts should only be transported after phrenological examination.[24] Though Maconochie's ideas never came to fruition, he may have been influenced by contemporary debates in the United States. In 1846, the penal reformer Eliza Farnham argued that predetermined characteristics could be modified through the use of phrenology. Treatment could thus be substituted for punishment.[25]

Within the Edinburgh Phrenological Society, there were quibbles with phrenologists like Paterson's analysis of the relationship between cranial structure and racial character. A fellow member, James Montgomery, criticized the limited nature of Paterson's study – just 3,000 heads were measured – which did not, he said, justify the generalizations made. In particular, he argued, Paterson had failed to distinguish the skulls in terms of their regional origin. Moreover, there was the sticky problem of correlating orientalist scholarship with phrenological descriptions. He argued that studies of archaeology, history, language, the scriptures and the law had all pointed to the subcontinent's degeneration from a golden to a black age (*kali-yuga*). The type of phrenological observations made about the character of the Indian people did not sit easily with this. As Montgomery wrote: 'The Hindoos generally are distinguished by deplorable *mental* and *bodily* imbecility; but are they not the descendants of ancestors not less conspicuous, on the other hand, both for intellectual and mental power, *whatever may have been their stature, or the size of their heads?*'[26]

Yet, according to Montgomery, it was Paterson's general methodology and particular observations that were at fault, rather than the basic premise of Indian inferiority that phrenological observations proved. He wrote that Paterson made only limited measurements and overestimated the trait of passivity, underestimated veneration, failed to distinguish groups such as the Mahrattas, whose skulls would surely have indicated enhanced combativeness, and overestimated women's large philoprogenitive organ – indicating love of children – that conflicted with the known practice of infanticide. In general terms, however, his skulls bore him out.[27] As George Combe later wrote: 'When we place the collection of Hindoo, Carib, Esquimaux, Peruvian and Swiss skulls, possessed by the Phrenological Society, in juxtaposition, we perceive a national form and combination of organs in each . . . The differences of national *character* are as conspicuous as those of national *brains.*'[28]

The idea that cranial form indicated racial difference proved remarkably enduring. By 1860, the Asiatic Society of Bengal had over 300 'ethnographic heads' in its possession, cast by the Berlin-based firm Messrs Herman and Robert de Schlagintweit during a Himalayan survey.[29] Shortly afterwards, in 1866 the Government of India authorized the collection of skulls for 'scientific purposes'.[30] Famously, the ethnographer W.E. Marshall used phrenological observations as the basis for his 1873 study of the Todas, a South Indian community that he claimed had ancient origins, possibly shared with Ethiopians or Jews. As the Todas were endogamous, Marshall claimed, their cranial appearance was identical (Figure 6.1). Phrenological analysis of only a limited number of people –

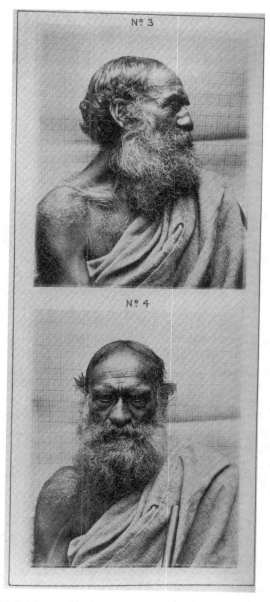

Figure 6.1 'Male Profile and Full Face'. William E. Marshall, *A Phrenologist amongst the Todas; or the Study of a Primitive Tribe in South India: History, Character, Customs, Religion, Infanticide, Polyandry, Language* (Longmans, Green, 1873)

perhaps as few as ten – could reveal their distinctive racial characteristics. His phrenological analysis of the Todas revealed 'scarcely more differences in appearance and character than any one dog does from any other of the same kennel of hounds.' This was in contrast to Europeans who, due to racial admixture, could not be observed as a single racial type. Needless to say, the racially 'pure' Toda was far inferior to the European. Taking Combe's analysis of the 'national skull' one stage further, phrenology could, Marshall wrote, trace the development of racial hierarchies. He noted the *'correlation between the progressive growth of races, and the development of their skulls'*.[31]

Marshall recorded thirty-six cranial manipulations for eighteen Toda adults, including women. He claimed to have observed the organs of amativeness, combativeness, acquisitiveness, secretiveness, firmness, imitation, veneration and so on. Whilst acknowledging the potential inaccuracy of these measurements – particularly as his subjects refused to shave their heads, much to his chagrin – Marshall felt confident enough to declare that the Toda head was of unvarying type and of extraordinary uniformity in size. This was even true of the tribe's leaders who showed only slight variations. Marshall noted that these differences reminded him of Gulliver's emperor of the Lilliputians. He was taller than his subjects by the breadth of just a fingernail, but this was enough for him to be regarded with awe.[32] Marshall's phrenological analysis is unique in the Indian context, for its explicit reference to gender. After measuring just eight women, he claimed that the female head was strikingly inferior to that of the male, particularly in the powers of perception and reception. Fortunately, they had a slight advantage in the organs generating love of children. Given his belief that the Todas' developmental stage corresponded with the European Ice Age, the implication of his argument was to render gendered social hierarchies entirely natural, rather than socially contingent or defined in any way.[33]

It would be a mistake to view phrenology as an unambiguous colonial project, and Marshall's book came in for government disapproval. When he sent a copy of *A Phrenologist amongst the Todas* to the Government of India, the Secretary of State privately criticized his emphasis on phrenology over culture as a means of explaining social difference. The government subsequently refused to give him a grant to study the people of the Western Himalayas, which Marshall believed would reveal the extent of racial mixture there.[34] Despite the 1866 Government Order permitting the collection of skulls for analysis, in 1870 the Madras government refused to allow the exhumation of executed criminals by the Anthropological Society of London, which was more interested in skulls than its rival, the

Ethnological Society.[35] Yet phrenology remained a popular way of constructing supposed physiological differences, and analyses of Indian skulls fed into this endeavour. Towards the end of the nineteenth century, William Turner visited India as part of his colonial phrenological tour, which Havelock Ellis described as 'the most important scientific expedition of modern times'.[36] He looked at several hundred skulls. In the North East Frontier, he took skulls exhumed from graveyards or family homes. He also used skulls taken from deceased prisoners, for instance those lent to him by the India Museum, Calcutta. In Burma, the Superintendent of Bassein Central Jail (Arakan), G.J.H. Bell, gave him thirty-six skulls taken from prisoners who had died there. These had the advantage of being accompanied by the neck tickets worn by the prisoners. In theory, Turner could correlate them with prison records, and glean full details about individuals. However, he noted that dental records seemed to contradict several of the prisoners' stated ages, leading him to conclude either that he had been sent the wrong lists, or that prisoners had lied.[37] More likely was an incorrect guess on the part of the receiving jail clerk. In any case, Turner showed little interest in their former character, being concerned only in using the skulls as indicators of biological difference.

Anthropometric Photography: Criminal Measurements, Racial Types

During the second half of the nineteenth century, there was a shift in the nature of photography, from an illustrative device in ethnological inquiries to one that could also be used to measure scientific data.[38] The camera itself represented European technological, and by implication racial, superiority.[39] It was one of the machines that measured men and the hierarchies between them.[40] Crude anthropometric measurements accompanied some of the earliest ethnographic photographs taken in India. In *Descriptive Ethnology of Bengal* (1872), for instance, Dalton gave measurements of the circumference of the head, height and length of arm, and noted the colour of the iris.[41] A set of photographs taken by Frederic Jagor also accompanied the detailed measurements recorded in his *Messungen an Lebenden Indiern* (*Measurements on Living Indians*) (1879). These were pictures of head and torso, in front and profile view; Jagor's subjects came from across the subcontinent.[42] James Wise too took measurements for his *Notes on the Races, Castes and Trades of Eastern Bengal* (1883) though, as we have seen, the accompanying pictures were never published.[43]

The earliest protagonists of the new scientific, morphometric approach to photography in Britain were J. Lamprey and T.H. Huxley, who owned a set of Jagor's prints. Both men were heavily involved in rapidly shifting debates about the genesis of racial difference. Until the 1860s, the 'ethnological' approach stressed the doctrine of monogenesis, with the Ethnological Society founded by members of the Anti-Slavery and Aborigines' Protection Societies in 1843. Its doctrine was at least partly based on the concept of shared racial origin. From the late 1850s, the theory of monogenesis was rivalled by that of polygenesis, and in 1863 some protagonists of it broke away from the Ethnological Society to form the Anthropological Society of London.[44] Huxley, who was president of the Ethnological Society, spent the following years attempting to heal the rift between the two groups.

In 1869, at a meeting of the Ethnological Society, Lamprey proposed a system through which photography could be used to glean morphometric data. The thrust of Lamprey's method was to standardize ethnographic photography according to the following method. A wooden frame, seven feet by three, had small nails hammered into it at two-inch intervals. Silk thread was then wound around the nails, dividing the frame's surface into two-inch squares. The subject to be photographed was then placed against this screen, with his or her heel pressed against one of the squares. With close examination of bodily contours rendered possible, this method would, Lamprey argued, facilitate direct racial comparisons. Lamprey wrote that his portfolio already contained a collection of racial specimens and called upon colonial photographers to adopt his methodology.[45] 'The grid', as Pinney states, 'made explicit the transcription of space on the very surface area of the photographic image.'[46]

Marshall used a graph paper method, based on Lamprey's system, in *A Phrenologist amongst the Todas*. Marshall's aim was to understand Toda character from their cranial form, and he photographed most of his subjects against a background grid. Just two women, one who Marshall claimed had an enlarged organ of veneration, the other enlarged firmness, were not photographed in this way. Instead, Marshall photographed his subjects in traditional dress and jewellery. The younger of the two women, Nastufi, who apparently curled her hair in readiness for her portrait, looks relaxed in front of the camera. The older, Avv, clings to her partner with obvious discomfort. Marshall compared her with the biblical Eve, supporting his belief that the Todas were of ancient origin.[47] The reasons for this methodological discrepancy are not entirely clear. It could be that the women agreed to be photographed only in this way, or that Marshall saw them as rare exceptions to the typical Toda cranial type, and thus not worthy of special attention.

Huxley submitted his photographic project to Earl Granville at the Colonial Office in 1869, under the auspices of the Ethnological Society. Though the Society paid for a set of sample prints, the Colonial Office was initially worried about the cost.[48] Huxley's aim was similar to Lamprey's: to photograph the 'various races of men comprehended within the British Empire' according to uniform principles. He proposed the photographing of average adult males and females, together with 'extreme or unusual forms' of men and women and children of both sexes. Each subject would, he planned, be photographed naked ('or as near thereto as may be practicable'), standing next to a measuring stick (anthropometer) at a fixed distance from the camera. Two full-length pictures would be taken. In the first, the frontal shot, the subject would stand with his or her heels together and the right arm stretched out at a right angle to the body, palm turned towards the camera. In the second profile shot, the arm would touch the measuring stick, in order not to hide the contours of the body: especially, for female subjects, the breasts. Ideally, Huxley noted, full-face and profile shots of each subject's head would accompany these pictures. Subjects would hold their head horizontally, and place their arms naturally on their lap. According to Huxley, this uniformity of pose meant that the photographs would be directly comparable with and measurable against each other.

The project aimed to ease racial comparisons; stature, arm-span and cranial form were all potential markers of difference. Huxley did however acknowledge a number of likely difficulties. The project relied on the use of a variety of photographers, which made inconsistencies between the pictures inevitable. Indeed, when prints were submitted, photographers sometimes apologized for mistakes they had made in posing subjects for them.[49] Moreover, Huxley made no provisions for the verticality of the anthropometer; in some of the resulting photographs, it appears to have been propped up by the subjects themselves. Therefore, height could not be accurately measured. Equally, as photographic subjects' hair was usually unshaved, it obscured the possibility of accurately calculating head lengths and breadths, as was required to determine cranial indices.[50]

Although Huxley initially had grand plans, just 40 sets of images (160 photographs) were produced according to his 'well-considered plan'. The images I shall examine most closely were taken of Indian prisoners in Singapore Central Jail; other sets were produced in Ceylon, Natal, Sierra Leone, Bermuda and Australia. In places where the prison authorities produced photographic subjects (Ceylon and Natal as well as Singapore), the pictures almost completely conform to Huxley's directions. In Natal a local firm – Messrs Lawrence and Selkirk – photographed prisoners in the

Breakwater Jail. Their subjects included five /Xam Bushmen, three Bhantu and two Khoi. W.H.J. Bleek, custodian of the Grey Library, was in charge of the project. He wrote that the Bushmen were dying out, giving the project a sense of urgency. Bleek lamented the lack of pictures of representatives of 'other nations' and women, the latter being collectively collapsed into a gendered rather than racial category.[51] Two prisoners, one male and one female, from Wilikadu Jail provided the 'specimens' from Ceylon. The man, Eknellegodde Punchi Banda, aged 30, was described as a Kandyan, and had been sentenced to twenty years' hard labour for rape. The woman, Thayale, was a Tamil. She was 21 years old, and described as a coffee picker and prostitute. She had been imprisoned for failing to attend a medical examination in hospital, a sure reference to her violation of the Contagious Diseases Acts.[52]

The use of prison populations avoided difficulties local administrations faced in persuading colonial subjects to pose voluntarily, for elsewhere most refused. It was more difficult for prisoners to do so and, if they attempted to resist or subvert the process, they could be offered the usual positive or negative incentives relating to rations or labour demands. As Edwards notes, the photographs of prisoners are the most dehumanizing of the sets of images.[53] The authorities in Ceylon were unable to find any other subjects, they said because none would pose nude.[54] Colonial authorities elsewhere either submitted prints that did not conform to Huxley's directive, or were not able to take any pictures at all. Even the most marginalized of colonial populations, Australian Aboriginal communities, could not be forced to cooperate with the project. The Governor of Victoria, Viscount Canterbury, wrote that they would not pose naked. The Officer for the Protection of Aborigines, R. Brough Smith, added without irony that they were not sufficiently civilized to understand its scientific importance.[55] Potential subjects in Malta also refused to be photographed nude,[56] as did Native Americans in British Columbia, despite being offered financial incentives. Governor Musgrave wrote that they were afraid of the hidden purpose of the photographs.[57] The Governor of Bermuda, F. Chapman, found it difficult to find a photographer, let alone willing subjects. Though he eventually submitted pictures to the Colonial Office, their subjects are partially or fully dressed.[58] Some of the South Australian Aborigines who agreed to be pictured also wore clothing below the waist.[59]

In other places, such as the Falkland Islands, missionaries refused to carry out Huxley's instructions. It conflicted with their 'civilizing mission', notably their attempts to persuade the Tierra del Fuego Indians to wear clothes. Although a set of photographs was taken, we do not know what form they took.[60] Other colonial authorities refused to commission photographs on the grounds of widespread 'racial admixture', which they said limited their ethnological use. Thus Mauritius – where there is no indigenous population – refused to comply, as did Gibraltar, Barbados and the Turks Islands.[61] The Governors of British Guiana, Tobago and the Virgin Islands claimed that they did not have the technical means to take the photographs. The Grenadian authorities refused to sanction the project on the grounds of cost.[62] The extent to which these were genuine reservations is difficult to gauge. Whatever the case, as Edwards skilfully demonstrates, the context of the production of the Huxley photographs reveals important colonial slippages. The relationship between colonial discourse and the ambiguities of its practice set one of the 'lines of fracture' in the project.[63]

I would like to focus our attention here on the eighteen sets of pictures taken in the Central Jail at Singapore, local prison and until 1860 a destination for Indian transportation convicts. This was one of the most successful sets of prints, perhaps because photographic equipment and procedures were already in place in the jail. In his memoir *Prisoners their Own Warders* (1899), Comptroller-General of Convicts McNair described the setting up of a photographic studio inside the jail, and the training of two Bengali convicts in photographic techniques, presumably at some point after he took office in 1857.[64] We do not know who took the photographs, but it is possible that prisoners (or prisoner overseers) were involved in the choice of subjects, the studio session or the preparation of the prints. After all, prisoners and convicts themselves were central to the organization and management of prisons and penal settlements. If this were the case – and this can only be conjecture – it renders the exercise of colonial power all the more complex. None of the prisoners were named, but underneath those pictures surviving in the Imperial College Archives is some information about them: their birthplace, age and height. Huxley himself had made no mention of the need to take down further details of individuals in his initial plan. Where local governments did so, as in the Breakwater and Singapore prisons, it was on their own initiative.[65] Edwards notes how the inclusion of this cultural detail accentuated the dehumanizing thrust of the project.[66]

The Singapore prisoners were each photographed twice, full length, in front and profile view. Like the prisoners in Natal and Ceylon, they were undressed. Some of the men had their heads shaved, a measure taken on arrival in jail, for hygiene purposes, or as a form of secondary punishment for an offence against jail discipline. The head and facial hair worn by others is a visual illustration of the cultural concessions the colonial prison

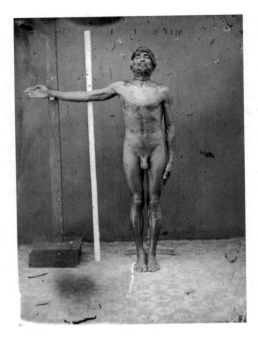

Figure 6.2 'Unnamed Prisoner'. (Courtesy of the Royal Anthropological Institute: Straits Settlements Prisoners)

authorities made to prisoners (Chapter 4). From the length of his hair and beard, it is clear that a Panjabi convict from Lahore was a Sikh (Figure 6.2). We can only speculate about the actual or cultural violence with which his turban was removed: by the photographer, his assistant, some jail official, or perhaps himself. A small number of women were also photographed, including two of Indian origin. Like the men, all were naked. Women were not expected to remove their jewellery. Indeed in prison it was a potentially important means of exchange. During an 1856 inspection of Indian transportation convicts in Sandoway Jail the Inspector-General of Prisons, F.J. Mouat, alleged that convict women were given jewellery for sexual services rendered to their guards.[67]

Huxley's directives about nudity referred to clothing, not fetters, which are in evidence on some of the prisoners' legs. The presence of a single ring or heavier fetters provides clues as to the penal stage of each prisoner, in relation to length of sentence served and behaviour. It is interesting that none of the Indian convicts wore fetters. Given that the last convict transportees arrived in the Straits in 1860, all would have risen, by 1870, to the non-fettered classes. It is possible, then, that the Indian prisoners represented in the prints were transportation convicts, though of course they may have been free or indentured labour migrants committed for a local offence. The lengths of string used to tie each subject to a post – ensuring they remained upright – is in evidence around some of the (probably most resistant) subjects' necks and waists. Piles of clothing sometimes remain in view, in one instance draped across a Malay woman's feet, as though hastily and unwillingly removed. A mixture of discomfort, fear and bewilderment pervade individuals' expressions. Some stand rigidly with chin tilted upwards, others cast their head and eyes downwards. This is a profoundly and explicitly disturbing set of prints. Edwards suggests that the photographic process itself may have been affected by its subjects' anxiety.[68] On the photographs' return to the Colonial Office, the Colonial Secretary, Lord Kimberley, wrote 'hideous series' beside them.[69] I would speculate that this was to do with the nudity of the subjects, and the inclusion of women in the project. As we have seen, male bodies tended to predominate in colonial discussions about race. In South Asia at least the authorities avoided the intimate contact necessary to pose women for photographs or measure them anthropometrically. Whatever the case, the project's lack of coherence is reflected in the dispersal of the photographs across several archives.[70]

As images, these photographs seem to illustrate the inexorable exercise of colonial power. However, the pictures were not at all typical of the outcome of the project. As we have seen, many colonial authorities refused to cooperate with it. Where they did, still more colonial subjects refused to pose for the camera. However, like the questionable appropriation of skulls for phrenological purposes, and the measuring of prisoners in jails in the production of anthropometric data, the pictures are a powerful reminder of the access the colonial state had to convict bodies. Like most phrenological analyses, those bodies were used in the construction of colonial hierarchies of race, and not in the making of a physiological criminal typologies. Rather, officials tried to stamp markers of criminality *on* the Indian body, or to produce and recognize criminality through signs *of* it. It is perhaps significant that, unlike ethnographic surveys, police manuals never presented anthropometric data in their discussion of criminal groups, despite their publication well into the twentieth century. Instead, they relied on the use of photography to represent the clothing (and disguises) worn by supposedly typical members of the criminal castes and tribes. At the same time, they lumped together the physical attributes of the criminal tribes with other marginalized groups, notably low-caste, tribal or itinerant communities. I am reminded of Galton's verdict on his criminal composite photographs here: 'The individual faces are villainous enough, but they are villainous in different ways, and when they are combined, the individual peculiarities disappear, and the common humanity of a low type is all that is left.' He was resigned to grouping his prisoners in a more general category, the 'unfit'.[71]

In 1910, the German criminologist Robert Heindl visited Port Blair in the Andaman Islands as part of his tour of global penal settlements. He was 'the criminalistic celebrity' in Germany at the beginning of the twentieth century, and pioneered the use of fingerprinting there.[72] Heindl was a keen photographer, and included a large number of portraits of convicts in his subsequent publication, *Meine Reise nach den Strafkolonien* (*My Journey to the Penal Colonies*) (1913), two of which are reproduced in Chapter 4 (Figures 4.4 and 4.5). The other prints include two 'mirror' pictures of convicts. The technique of mirror photography had been used routinely in European and American prisons, most famously the New York State Reformatory at Elmira. Prisoners were placed before the camera, with mirrors arranged at either side of and above them. Four views of the head could thus be seen at once. This was supposed to facilitate an analysis of cranial form and facial characteristics.[73]

The two Andaman Islands mirror pictures reproduced in Heindl's account were simpler. In each photograph, the convicts were placed in front of the camera, with a mirror to one side. Their full-frontal and profile pictures were thus collapsed into a single image. Heindl captioned his pictures 'Indian' and 'Chinese' (by which he was clearly referring to a convict from Burma) 'Criminal Types'. However, he recorded no further details about either man, and unlike the Elmira pictures, did not compare known character with cranial form or physiognomy. Neither did he discuss criminal typologies in detail elsewhere in his text. It is worth noting that later on Heindl saw notes on 'race and type' as a crucial part of the descriptive rolls of German prisoners. As Peter Becker argues, even this most standardized mode of representation allowed for the expression and reproduction of a particular type of discourse, a 'practical gaze' that defined 'national and racial enemies'.[74] The photograph of 'Indian Criminal Types' (Figure 6.3) is a complex image, for it appears trapped between a desire to render race and criminality meaningful through reference to both physical attributes and cultural signs. Were the photographs supposed to underline the physical similarities between Andamans convicts and European offenders, implying the degeneracy of the latter? Or did they have some other purpose? Nothing about the prisoners' profiles points to a criminal constitution; the only indicators that either man is a

Figure 6.3 'Indische Verbrechertypen' (Indian Criminal Types). Robert Heindl, *Meine Reise nach den Strafkolonien, mit vielen originalaufnahmen* (Ullstein, 1913)

convicted offender are their rough gunny cloth uniforms. The lack of textual pointers to the meaning of the prints in many ways renders them meaningless. As we have seen in our discussion of ethnographic prints and photographs of the criminal tribes, these were crucial to understanding the purpose of such images, which were meant to be more broadly representative of criminal typologies.

Retinological Experiments in the Andaman Islands

Gustav Fritsch (1838–1927) was a student of natural science in Berlin, where he was born, Breslau (Wrocław) and Heidelberg, where he received his degree in 1862.[75] Between 1863 and 1866 he visited South Africa, a trip that resulted in the publication of *Drei Jahre in Süd-Afrika* (*Three Years in South Africa*).[76] Seventy-nine pairs and four single photographs (full face and profile) taken by Fritsch at this time were also included in

Dammann's *Anthropologisch-Ethnologisches Album*.[77] On his return from South Africa, Fritsch worked at the Institute of Anatomy in Berlin, where he remained until 1900. His research interests included physical anthropology, ethnology, zoology and astronomy. He was a member of the Royal Academy of Sciences in Berlin and a founder member of the *Berliner Gesellschaft für Anthropologie*. Much of his work centred on the physical manifestations of racial dominance, and how differences might be established through the observation of anatomical variations.

In the early 1900s, Fritsch's attention turned to the science of retinology. Sponsored by the Prussian Government, he travelled around the world visiting Egypt, Sudan, German West Africa, South Africa, Japan, China, Java, Ceylon, the Solomon Islands, Sumatra, New Zealand and New Guinea. Fritsch collected specimens of retinas, removed within an hour of death, from population groups there. He then carried out physiological tests on them, believing that he could discern racial distinctions in visual acuity. He published his findings on his return, in *Ueber Bau und Bedeutung der Area Centralis des Menschen* (*On the Construction and Significance of the Human Retina*) (1908). In Europe, Fritsch had found it difficult to collect data, so his analysis was based on close examination of living people. Only totally disempowered populations, such as Australian Aboriginal groups, succumbed to Fritsch's surgical knife. During his trip, Fritsch also gathered samples of head hair. These were used as a means for racial classification and ordering too, with Fritsch publishing in *Der Haupthaar und Seine Bildungstätte bei den Rassen des Menschen* (*Head Hair and its Places of Formation amongst the Races of Mankind*) in 1912. It was during this round-the-world tour that he visited the Andaman Islands, spending ten days there in December 1904.[78] Given his own anthropometric agenda, which sought to establish physical differences between 'the Indian races', it is unsurprising that Risley, who was by then secretary to the Government of India, gave his full support to the project.[79]

After British settlement of the Islands, the Andamanese had suffered a massive escalation of mortality rates. This confirmed British suspicions that what they had found were the last remnants of dying races. They set up the Andaman Homes, a means of bringing tribals into settled areas, where they could be educated, treated medically and, by implication, civilized.[80] From the very first years of the penal colony in the Islands, relations with the tribal population had been characterized by violence. Indeed, the basis of early convict supervision was the assumption that tribals would kill absconders. The jungle was the ultimate panoptican of self-policing, and the indigenous population the unseen guards. With a few notable exceptions, where convicts returned boasting of their adventures with the Andamanese, this was invariably the case.[81] Most anthropologists who visited the Andamans were exclusively concerned with studying the indigenous population there. From the second half of the nineteenth century, the British *Journal of the Anthropological Institute* was filled with articles detailing observations of the Andamanese.[82] A number of books on the Islands' tribal populations also appeared, written by colonial administrators such as E.H. Man, officer in charge of the Andaman Homes 1875–9, his successor M.V. Portman, and R.C. Temple, Superintendent of Convicts 1894–1903.[83] No books on the convict settlement itself were ever published. With the exception of census officials who first recorded details of convict origins in December 1871,[84] Fritsch was the first person to study the convict population, almost fifty years after the British established a permanent settlement at Port Blair.

For Fritsch, the Andamans were a veritable laboratory of Indian humankind, for convicts were transported to the Islands from all over the subcontinent. It was perhaps this that drew him there; to be sure, it saved him a considerable amount of time and money in his research. Fritsch differentiated between the convicts he examined on the basis of regional origin, language, religion and caste. This led to an array of rather inconsistent categorization based on a mixture of social categories: Hindu, Muslim Bengali, Burmese, Arakanese, Muslim, Brahmin, Rajput, Sikh, Sylheti, Telugu-speaker, Buddhist, Pathan, Bhil and Jat. Fritsch named only a few of the convicts, instead grouping them in this rather haphazard way. However, he did carefully record their region of origin (Bengal, North India, Madras and so on), sex (they were all male), age, cause of death (including dysentery, tuberculosis, pneumonia and malaria), the time which had elapsed since death (always less than an hour) and whether he had photographed the retina. Fritsch reproduced these photographs to illustrate his findings, that the retina clearly showed racial similarities and differences in population groups across the globe.[85]

His main contention was that despite regional differences between convicts, there was a common Indian retinal type (Retinal Type I), which could be discerned in most of the convicts he examined. Where it could not, this was due to the impact of preparing the samples, rather than the nature of the retinas themselves.[86] The colonial archive reveals little more about Fritsch's experiments in the Andamans. We do not know whether the British authorities sought consent from convicts' families, for instance, or whether other convicts were aware of – or raised objections to – Fritsch's work. This may have impacted on which convicts were chosen for analysis. Was Fritsch's note that he mainly examined low-caste convicts significant?

The disappearance of convict voices from this retinological narrative serves only to underscore the reason for their choice as ideal subjects for scientific inquiry: their penal status. In this sense, the bodily interventions necessary for Fritsch's investigations were strongly reminiscent of earlier phrenological analyses of prisoners' skulls and Huxley's anthropometric project. Though the nature of scientific investigation was changing, all used the bodies of incarcerated populations in trying to establish racial differences through observing and recording apparent anatomical variations.

Full Circle? Postcolonial Indian Ethnography

To celebrate the one hundredth anniversary of the start of the first ethnographic survey of India, in 1989 the government commissioned a new All India Anthropological Survey.[87] Coinciding also with the centenary of the last stages of the construction of the Cellular Jail, the survey visited the Andaman Islands later that year where it remained, collecting data, until early 1990. According to the 1981 census, 88 per cent of the Islands' population was composed of migrant communities. The survey thus collected information about twelve well-established migrant groups: the Namasudra, Karen, Oraon, Munda, Kharia, Chhetri Bhantu, Mopla, Valmiki, Vadabalija, Chakkiliyan, Pariyan and those known as 'local born'.

In an interesting departure from the focus of most nineteenth-century ethnographies of the Islands which, with the exception of Fritsch and Heindl's studies of convicts, dealt exclusively with the indigenous Andamanese, they were marginalized from the operation.[88] Given the concern of colonial officials like Portman, officer in charge of the Andamanese Homes, to describe and photograph what were seen as the last remnants of a dying race (Pinney's 'salvage paradigm'), the focus of nineteenth-century ethnographers is unsurprising. In this respect, the Andamanese were certainly more appealing than the flotsam and jetsam of convict society. The rather different concerns of postcolonial anthropologists, who centred their analysis almost exclusively on migrant communities in the Islands, raise other issues. Perhaps their reluctance to engage with the Andamanese stemmed from the social, economic and political sensitivities that inevitably would have been raised. On the other hand, as the survey itself noted, tribal groups on the Islands had been widely studied before. Descriptions of the Onge, Jarawa, Sentinelese and Great Andamanese – the latter of whom there were said to be just forty-two left at the time of the 1981 census – though excluded from regionally specific data, were included in the survey's more general publications, notably *The Scheduled Tribes*. Quite detailed cultural descriptions and quantitative data, such as analysis of average height and predominant blood group, certainly appear there.[89]

The size of each of the migrant populations analysed by the survey differed widely. However, attempts were made to collect data from at least 100 individuals from each, 150 in the case of the Namasudra, Karen, Oraon and Munda, who were relatively numerous. In a second interesting gendered differential from earlier colonial ethnography, and indeed the efforts of the survey on the mainland, where women formed one-fifth of the total number of informants recorded,[90] only males aged 18–60 years were included. The reason for this is not entirely clear. In a remarkable throwback to colonial anthropometry, the following measurements were recorded: sitting height, stature, maximum head length and breadth, bizygomatic breadth, bigonial breadth, total and upper facial height, nasal height and breadth, horizontal head circumference, auricular height and weight. From these the following ratios and indices were worked out: cephalic, nasal, upper facial, length–height, breadth–height, jugo-mandibular, jugo-frontal, relative sitting height or cormic, ponderal, body-build and surface area. The groups were then classified by head form, nose form and facial type. Descriptive traits were also collected: hair form, forehead slope, nasal depression, nasal bridge, eye fissure, eye fold, lip thickness, chin form and chin projection. The data were then presented in tabular form, in an uncannily similar way to that found in Risley's *People of India* project in the early years of the twentieth century.

Of the twelve groups surveyed, three were identified as having convict origins: the Moplah, Bhantu and 'local born'. The survey described the first of these, the Moplah (also known as Moppillah or Mappila), as descendants of the thousand or so rebels sent to the Andamans as convicts, from the Malabar coast, in 1921.[91] Second, it reported that the Chhetri Bhantu had been sent from the United Provinces as convicts in 1926–8. They had, it noted, since settled as endogamous agriculturalists.[92] In fact, the Chhetri Bhantu was one of the designated tribes encompassed in the 1924 Criminal Tribes Act, and were forcibly settled in the Islands.[93] Third, according to the survey, the 'local born' population was made up of the descendants of those born from convict unions, which frequently crossed religious or caste boundaries. The director of the survey, K.S. Singh, thus described them as 'a single Mendelian population for all practical purposes'.[94]

The ethnographic encounters that took place between the populations of colonial and postcolonial India and their governments were remarkably similar. Anthropologists went out into the field; local populations were questioned, measured and photographed. The origin of different ethnic groups was described and attempts to give those differences scientific clout made. In the late-twentieth-century context, although colonial ethnographies were used on points of information, the scientific methodology available had of course widened to include an analysis of blood groups, though neither appears to have been used in recording and classifying the migrant communities in the Andaman Islands discussed earlier. It was however central to the Anthropological Survey's efforts elsewhere. [95] Given the social construction of science as a discipline, and changes in the technology available, perhaps the main difference between the two contexts is one of volume rather than approach. The volume of material collected during the People of India Survey was quite staggering. This was to some extent the result of its national rather than regional focus. Thus 24,951 local informants were questioned and 21,362 photographs taken. In addition, the data was computerized.[96]

And so it would seem that postcolonial India has come full circle. The desire to explain social differences through reference to bodily measurements has proved remarkably enduring. Though the methodology used to extract morphometric data has changed, the thrust of scientific interventions has not. It is clear that, at various historical conjunctions, the physiology of the body has been used to construct collective identities. In the European context, this permitted the conceptualization of 'the criminal'. In the Indian subcontinent, on the other hand, it fed into discourses of race and caste. The relationship between physiology and criminal propensities was never really considered; rather, criminal typologies were created through cultural readings of social difference. Given the dubious appropriation of disempowered prisoner and convict bodies for scientific purposes and the hereditary criminalization of vast swathes of Indian society through the Criminal Tribes Acts, the fact that the subjects of scientific interest were from what in Europe would have been considered a bio-criminal subgroup was rarely considered seems a curious anomaly. Yet it is precisely this that defined the work of phrenologists, photographers and scientists in the subcontinent as specifically colonial. Whilst some Indians were emperors, most remained Lilliputians.

Notes

1. NAI Home (Police A), Dec. 1900, 57–8: Note of Risley, 16 Nov. 1900.
2. NAI Home (Police A), Mar. 1902, 84: Circular of H.A. Stuart, Officiating Deputy Secretary to the Government of India, 21 Mar. 1902.

Emperors of the Lilliputians

3. Francis Galton, *Hereditary Genius: An Enquiry into its Laws and Consequences* (Macmillan, 1869). See also Pick, *Faces of Degeneration*, ch. 7.
4. Pick, *Faces of Degeneration*, ch. 5 (citation 137).
5. Arnold, *Colonizing the Body*, 106–13 (quote 113).
6. General histories of phrenology include Roger Cooter, *The Cultural Meaning of Popular Science: Phrenology and the Organization of Consent in Nineteenth-Century Britain* (Cambridge University Press, 1984); David de Guistino, *Conquest of Mind: Phrenology and Victorian Social Thought* (Croom Helm, 1975); John Davies, *Phrenology, Fad and Science: A Nineteenth-Century American Crusade* (Yale University Press, 1955).
7. For a discussion of the relationship between phrenology and racial typologies, see Michael Adas, *Machines as the Measure of Men: Science, Technology, and Ideologies of Western Dominance* (Cornell University Press, 1989), 292–8; Nancy Stepan, *The Idea of Race in Science: Great Britain, 1800–1960* (Macmillan, 1982). More specific to the Indian context is Bates, 'Race, Caste, and Tribe'. See also Stephen Jay Gould, *The Mismeasure of Man* (Norton, 1981). For an interesting comparison with South Africa, see Andrew Bank, 'Of "Native Skulls" and "Noble Caucasians": Phrenology in Colonial South Africa', *Journal of Southern African Studies*, 22, 3 (1996), 387–403.
8. EUL Gen 608 x (iv): George Murray Paterson, 'Memoir on the Phrenology of Hindostan', read to the Society, 1 May 1823 (reproduced in *Transactions of the Phrenological Society* (John Anderson Jun., 1824), 430–46; EUL Gen 608/1: Combe to Paterson, 7 Mar. 1823 (quote). See also George Combe's *A System of Phrenology* (John Anderson Jun., 1825) and *The Constitution of Man Considered in Relation to External Objects* (John Anderson Jun., 1828).
9. EUL Gen 608/2: Minute Book of the Phrenological Society, vol. I; Gen 608/4: Catalogue of the Phrenological Society, n.d.
10. EUL Gen 608/9: Luke O'Neil and Son, Artists to the Phrenological Society, catalogue of the collection of casts and skulls, n.d.
11. EUL Gen 608/2: Minute Book. See also Bates, 'Race, Caste and Tribe', 232.
12. EUL Gen 608/2: Minute Book.
13. See, for example, EUL Gen 608/5: Robert Cox's Catalogue, 1828; EUL Gen 608 x (iv): Paterson, 'Memoir'.
14. EUL Gen 608 x (iv): Paterson, 'Memoir'.
15. *Ibid.*

16. Paterson, 'On the Phrenology of Hindostan', 434.
17. For a discussion of Galton's composites, see Sekula, 'Body and the Archive', 47–54
18. Robert Cox, 'Remarks on the Skulls and Characters of Thugs', *Phrenological Journal and Miscellany*, 8 (December 1832 – June 1834), 524. This collection of skulls is also discussed by Bates, 'Race, Caste and Tribe', 231–3; Singha, *Despotism of Law*, 208; Woerkens, *Strangled Traveler*, 223–6. The skulls are now held in the University of Edinburgh Henderson Trust Collection.
19. Henry Harpur Spry, 'Some Account of the Gang-Murderers of India Commonly Called Thugs; Accompanying the Skulls of Seven of Them', *Phrenological Journal and Miscellany*, 8 (December 1832– June 1834), 511–24.
20. *Ibid.*, 517–23.
21. Cox, 'Remarks on the Skulls', 524–30.
22. See, for example, NLS Mss 7453: Combe Papers.
23. 'Case of John Jenkins, Convict Executed at Sydney for Murder', *Phrenological Journal and Miscellany*, 10 (June 1836 – September 1837), 485–9.
24. George Combe, 'Penal Colonies: The Management of Prisoners in the Australian Colonies', *Phrenological Journal*, 18 (1845), 101–22.
25. Sekula, 'Body and the Archive', 13–14.
26. James Montgomery, 'An Essay on the Phrenology of the Hindoos and Negroes', *Phrenological Journal and Miscellany*, 6 (August 1829 – December 1830), 248.
27. *Ibid.*, 252.
28. Combe, *Constitution of Man*, 193.
29. NAI Home (Public B), 11 May 1860, 19: Ethnographical Heads; NAI Home (Public B), 21 Nov. 1861, 155–6: Ethnographic Heads. See also Falconer, 'Ethnographical Photography', 27.
30. NAI Home (Public A), 476: Government Order, 11 May 1866.
31. Marshall, *Phrenologist amongst the Todas*, 13–14 (emphasis in original).
32. *Ibid.*, 32.
33. *Ibid.*, 33–5.
34. NAI Home (Public B), Oct. 1873, 203–4: W.E. Marshall to Lyall, 8 Sept. 1873; Lyall's note, 6 Oct. 1873.
35. TNSA Judicial, 10 Aug. 1870, 54–5: Government Order 1073, 10 Aug. 1873.
36. Ellis, *Criminal*, 255.

37. William Turner, 'Contributions to the Craniology of the People of the Empire of India, Part I: The Hill Tribes of the North-East Frontier and the People of Burma', *Transactions of the Royal Society of Edinburgh*, 39, 3 (no. 28) (1894), 703–47; William Turner, 'Contributions to the Craniology of the People of the Empire of India, Part II: The Aborigines of Chuta Nagpur and of the Central Provinces, the People of Orissa, the Veddas and Negritos', *Transactions of the Royal Society of Edinburgh*, 60, 1 (no. 6) (1901), 59–128.

38. Frank Spencer, 'Some Notes on the Attempt to Apply Photography to Anthropometry during the Second Half of the Nineteenth Century', in Edwards (ed.), *Anthropology and Photography*, 99. See also Poignant, 'Surveying the Field of View', 51.

39. Edwards, 'Introduction', 6.

40. I refer here to Adas, *Machines as the Measure of Men*.

41. Dalton, *Descriptive Ethnology of Bengal*.

42. IOR V10985: F. Jagor, *Messungen an Lebenden Indiern* (1879). The Indian photographs – and others taken in the Sandwich Islands, Bali, Sarawak, Java, Sumatra and Cambodia – are located in ICA Huxley Archives (provenance recorded by Elizabeth Edwards).

43. Wise, *Notes on the Races*, 6.

44. Poignant, 'Surveying the Field of View', 45.

45. J.H. Lamprey, 'On a Method of Measuring the Human Form, for the Use of Students in Ethnology', *Journal of the Ethnological Society of London*, 1 (1869), 84–5.

46. Christopher Pinney, 'The Parallel Histories of Anthropology and Photography', in Edwards (ed.), *Anthropology and Photography*, 77.

47. Marshall, *Phrenologist amongst the Todas*, 32–3.

48. Huxley's proposal is outlined at PRO CO845/10: T.H. Huxley to Earl Granville, 12 Aug. 1869. Other papers and some of the resulting anthropometric photographs (Bermuda, Ceylon, Natal and the Straits Settlements) are held at the PRO and ICA: Notes and Correspondence: Anthropology, vols I and II and boxes G and H (henceforth Huxley Papers). A larger – though not complete – collection of the Straits Settlements' photographs is held at the RAI: 'Prisoners', 33955–67, 33999–005, 33011–14. The project is discussed by Elizabeth Edwards, 'Photographic "Types": The Pursuit of Method', *Visual Anthropology*, 3 (1990), 235–58; Spencer, 'Some Notes', 99–102. On Huxley's work on racial differences more generally, see Mario A. Di Gregorio, *T.H. Huxley's Place in Natural Science* (Yale University Press, 1994), ch. 5. For an important and nuanced theoretical grounding of the project within visual anthropology, see Edwards, *Raw Histories*, ch. 6.

49. In the South African context, see Michael Godby, 'Images of // Kabbo', in Pippa Skotnes (ed.), *MISCAST: Negotiating the Presence of the Bushmen* (University of Cape Town Press, 1996), 116.
50. These and further difficulties are discussed by Spencer, 'Some Notes', 100–2.
51. A detailed analysis of the Breakwater photographs can be found in Godby, 'Images of //Kabbo', 115–27. See also ICA Huxley Papers: W.H.J. Bleek to the Earl of Kimberley, Colonial Secretary, 25 Sept. 1871.
52. ICA Huxley Papers: A.B. Fyers, Surveyor General Ceylon, to Kimberley, 19 Feb. 1872. See also Levine, *Prostitution, Race and Politics*.
53. Edwards, *Raw Histories*, 139.
54. ICA Huxley Papers: Fyers to Kimberley, 19 Feb. 1872.
55. ICA Huxley Papers: Despatch from the Governor of Victoria relative to the difficulty in photographing aborigines, 26 July 1870.
56. ICA Huxley Papers: Collector of Customs Malta to Earl Granville, Colonial Secretary, 12 Aug. 1872 (private).
57. ICA Huxley Papers: A. Musgrave, Governor of British Columbia, to Granville, 22 Apr. 1870.
58. ICA Huxley Papers: F. Chapman, Governor of Bermuda, to Granville, 17 Mar. 1870; Photographs of Bermuda Islanders (F. Chapman, 1870).
59. ICA Huxley Papers: Photographs of South Australians (J. Ferguson, 1870).
60. Edwards, 'Photographic "Types"', 247–8. See also ICA Huxley Papers: Governor G. D'Arcy to Kimberley, 24 Dec. 1870.
61. PRO CO28/211: Governor Rawson to Granville, Barbados, 12 Jan. 1870; PRO CO167/524: Governor Barkly to Granville, Mauritius, 7 Feb. 1870; PRO CO301/55: Melfort Campbell, President Grand Turk, to Granville, 12 Feb. 1870.
62. ICA Huxley Papers: Governor Airey to Granville, Gibraltar, 5 May 1870; R.W. Herbert, Colonial Office, to Huxley, 9 Feb. 1871.
63. Edwards, *Raw Histories*, 141, 143.
64. McNair, *Prisoners their Own Warders,* 89–90, 106–7.
65. Godby, 'Images of //Kabbo', 119.
66. Edwards, *Raw Histories*, 144.
67. IOR P/145/22 (31 July 1856): Mouat to Buckland, 24 May 1856.
68. Edwards, *Raw Histories*, 145–6.
69. PRO CO273/41: Earl of Kimberley's note, 14 Jan. 1871.
70. Edwards, *Raw Histories*, 148–51.
71. Cited in Sekula, 'Body and the Archive', 50.

72. On Heindl, see Becker, 'Standardized Gaze', 145 (quote), 152–3, 161–2.
73. For two examples of mirror photographs, see Ellis, *Criminal*, Plates II, III.
74. Becker, 'Standardized Gaze', 153.
75. Biographical details of the life and work of Gustav Fritsch can be found in H. Grundfest, 'Gustav Fritsch', *Journal of the History of Medicine*, 18 (1963), 125–9.
76. This has since been translated into English: Gerlind Lyttle, *A German Traveller in Natal* (Killie Campbell Africana Library, 1992).
77. Edwards, 'Photographic "Types"', 249–53.
78. NAI Home (Port Blair B), Jan. 1905, 2–5: Note of Superintendent W.R.H. Merk, 17 Dec. 1904.
79. *Ibid.*: Risley's note, 6 Dec. 1904.
80. Sen, *Disciplining Punishment*, 152–7, 231–2; Sen, 'Policing the Savage'.
81. Anderson, 'Politics of Convict Space', 44.
82. See: G.E. Dobson, 'On the Andamans and Andamanese', *Journal of the Anthropological Institute*, 4 (1875), 457–67; W.H. Flower, 'On the Osteology and Affinities of the Andaman Islands', *Journal of the Anthropological Institute*, 9 (1880), 108–33; A. Lane Fox, 'Observations on Mr Man's Collection of Andaman and Nicobarese Objects', *Journal of the Anthropological Institute*, 7 (1878), 434–70; E.H. Man, 'On the Andamanese and Nicobarese Objects presented to Major-General Pitt Rivers', *Journal of the Anthropological Institute*, 9 (1882), 268–94; Man, 'On the Aboriginal Inhabitants'; C.H. Read, 'Mr Portman's Photographs of Andamanese', *Journal of the Anthropological Institute*, 12 (1893), 401–3.
83. E.H. Man, *On the Aboriginal Inhabitants of the Andaman Islands, with Report of Researches in to the Language of the South Andaman Islands* (Trübner and Co., 1885); R.C. Temple, *Remarks on the Andaman Islanders and their Country* (British India Press, 1929).
84. NAI Home (Port Blair B), Jan. 1905, 2–5: Risley's note, 6 Dec. 1904. Full statistical details of the 1871 Census of the Islands can be found at NAI Home (Port Blair A), Oct. 1873, 49–59.
85. Gustav Fritsch, *Ueber Bau und Bedeutung der Area Centralis des Menschen* (Reimer, 1908), 133–4.
86. *Ibid.*, 35.
87. For details of a personal interview with A.K. Danda, Deputy Director of the Survey, see Bates, 'Race, Caste and Tribe', 219.

88. S.K. Bhattacharyya et al., *All India Anthropometric Survey: Andamans* (Anthropological Survey of India, 1993), including a foreword by K.S. Singh, Director-General of the Survey.

89. K.S. Singh, *The Scheduled Tribes, People of India National Series, vol. III* (Oxford University Press, 1994), 363–7, 420–2, 994–8.

90. K.S. Singh, 'A Note on the Series', in *Scheduled Tribes*, x.

91. For further details, see Mathur, *Kala Pani*, 61, 261.

92. Palash C. Coomar and Manis K. Raha, 'Family among the Bhantu of Andamans', *Journal of the Indian Anthropological Society*, 24, 2 (1989), 122. Both authors were employed by the Anthropological Survey of India, in Calcutta and Nagpur.

93. IOR MSS Eur/F161/158: Criminal Tribes.

94. K.S. Singh, 'Foreword', in Bhattacharyya, *All India Anthropometric Survey*, n.p.

95. See the *People of India* series which emerged from the Survey, edited by K.S. Singh. Bates also mentions this: 'Race, Caste and Tribe', 219.

96. Singh, 'Note on the Series', in *Scheduled Tribes*, x–xi.

Bibliography

Archival Sources

Archives Office of Tasmania (AOT)

Convict Department (CON) 35/1: Conduct registers of male convicts arriving under the assignment system on non-convict ships and on strength November 1844.
Colonial Secretary's Office (CSO5), General Correspondence Records 1837–41.
Colonial Secretary's Office (CSO16), Correspondence 'Records Branch', 1841–5.

Centre of South Asian Studies Archives, University of Cambridge (CSAS)

Benthall Papers: Box XXX, part i: *Diaries kept by Mrs Clementina Benthall*, January 1849 – March 1850.
Benthall Papers: Box XXX, part iii: typescript copy of diaries of Mrs Clementina Benthall, January 1849 – March 1850.

Edinburgh University Library (EUL)

Gen 608/1: Letter Book of the Phrenological Society, 1820–40.
Gen 608/2: Minute Books of the Phrenological Society, 1820–71.
Gen 608/4: Catalogue of the Phrenological Society, n.d.
Gen 608/5: Robert Cox's Catalogue, 1828.
Gen 608 x (iv): George Murray Paterson, 'Memoir on the Phrenology of Hindoostan', read to the Society, 1 May 1823.
Gen 608/9: Luke O'Neil and Son, Artists to the Phrenological Society: catalogue of the collection of casts and skulls, n.d.

Imperial College Archives (ICA)

Huxley Papers: Notes and Correspondence, Anthropology, vols I and II (Boxes G/H).

India Office Records (IOR)

East India Company General Correspondence (E).
Bengal Judicial Proceedings (P).
Bengal Jails Proceedings (P).
Bombay Judicial Proceedings (P).
India Judicial Proceedings (P).
MSS Eur D742/46: Regulations for Convicts, Bencoolen (Regulation I 1824).
MSS Eur E295/14A–D: Risley Collection, District Reports on tattooing in Bengal, received by the Superintendent of Census Operations and the Superintendent of Ethnography, November 1901 – October 1908.
MSS Eur E295/18: Correspondence of H.H. Risley, 1901–8.
MSS Eur F161/154: Crimes Peculiar to India; the Bengal Police.
MSS Eur F161/157: Material on the Effective Administration of the Criminal Tribes Act, 1915.
MSS Eur F161/158: Criminal Tribes.
MSS Eur F161/185: Finger Printing.
Photo 904/(3) 'A Shan Man'.
Photo 904/(2, 3) 'Tattooing a Burman'.
V10985: F. Jagor, *Messungen an Lebenden Indiern* (1879).
V/8/17: *Regulations passed by the Governor-General in Council, 1796–1803*, 3 vols (Calcutta, Court of Directors: 1803).
V/8/27: Fort St George Regulations, 1804–1814.
V/10/599: Andaman and Nicobar Report, 1882–3.
V/10/600: Andaman and Nicobar Report, 1883–4.

Mauritius Archives (MA)

Proceedings of the Court of Assizes (JB).
Post-mortem examinations (JI).
Miscellaneous Mauritius Secretariat correspondence (RA).
Police reports and correspondence (Z2A).

National Archives of India (NAI)

Home (Jails A) Proceedings.
Home (Judicial A, B) Proceedings.
Home (Police A) Proceedings.
Home (Port Blair A, B, Deposit) Proceedings.
Home (Public A, B) Proceedings.

National Library of Scotland (NLS)

MSS 7453: Combe Papers.

Newspapers

The Times.
The Bombay Gazette.

Parliamentary Papers

1819 (583) XIII.347: Regulation XVII, Section xii (1817): A regulation
   to provide for the more effectual administration of criminal justice in
   certain cases, 16 September 1817.
1822 (449) XX.539: Committee of Inquiry into State of Colony of New
   South Wales (Bigge Reports).

Public Record Office (PRO)

CO172/42: Baron d'Unienville, *Tableaux de Statistiques*, tableau no. 6
   (Mauritius).
CO845/10: Colonial Office, 1869.
CO28/211: Barbados, 1870.
CO167/524: Mauritius, 1870.
CO301/55: Grand Turk, 1870.

Royal Anthropological Institute (RAI)

Photographic Collection: 'Prisoners', nos 33955–67, 33999–005, 33011–
   14.

Tamil Nadu State Archives (TNSA)

Education Proceedings.
Judicial Proceedings.
Public Proceedings.

Contemporary Literature

Adam, H.L. (1909a), *The Indian Criminal*, London: J. Milne.

—— (1909), *Oriental Crime*, London: T. Werner Laurie.

Adam, John and Collyer Adam, G. (1906), *Criminal Investigation: A Practical Textbook for Magistrates, Police Officers and Lawyers*, London: Sweet and Maxwell.

Ananthakrishna Iyer, L.K. (1935), *The Mysore Tribes and Castes*, 4 vols, Mysore: Mysore University.

Barlow, N. (ed.) (1933), *Charles Darwin's Diary of the Voyage of the H.M.S. 'Beagle'*, Cambridge: Cambridge University Press.

Bartrum, Mrs (1830), *Recollections of Seven Years' Residence at the Mauritius, or Isle of France; By a Lady*, London: James Cawthorn.

Beaton, Patrick (1859), *Creoles and Coolies; Or, Five Years in Mauritius*, London: James Nisbet.

Beddoe, J. (1885), *The Races of Britain: A Contribution to the Anthropology of Western Europe*, Bristol: J.W. Arrowsmith.

Berncastle, Dr (1850), *A Voyage to China; Including a Visit to the Bombay Presidency; the Mahratta Country; the Cave Temples of Western India, Singapore, the Straits of Malacca and Sunda, and the Cape of Good Hope, Vol. II*, London: William Shoberl.

Bertillon, Alphonse (1889), *The Identification of the Criminal Classes by the Anthropometric Method* (tr. E.R. Spearman), London: Spottiswoode.

—— (1893), *Identification Anthropométrique: Instructions Signalétiques*, Paris: Melun.

Bhattacharyya, S.K. et al. (1993), *All India Anthropometric Survey: Andamans*, Calcutta: Anthropological Survey of India.

Billiard, François J.M.A. (1822), *Voyages aux colonies orientales, ou lettres écrit des Iles de France et de Bourbon pendant les années 1817, 1818, 1819 et 1820*, Paris: Librarie Française de l'Advocat.

Birch, W.B. (1886), *Andaman and Nicobar Manual, as in Force on the 1st January 1886*, Calcutta: Superintendent of Government Printing.

Blackwood, Hariot Georgina (1889), *Our Viceregal Life in India: Selections from my Journal, 1884–1888*, London: William Blackwood and Sons.

Bibliography

Boden Kloss, C. (1903), *In the Andamans and Nicobars: The Narrative of a Cruise in the Schooner Terrapin*, London: John Murray.

Buckland, A.W. (1888), 'On Tattooing', *Journal of the Royal Anthropological Institute*, 17: 318–28.

Caine, W.S. (1891), *Picturesque India: A Handbook for European Travellers*, London: Routledge.

Carpenter, Mary (1868), *Six Months in India, vol. I*, London: Longmans, Green.

'Case of John Jenkins, Convict Executed at Sydney for Murder' (June 1836 – September 1837), *Phrenological Journal and Miscellany*, 10: 485–9.

Cavenagh, Orfeur (1884), *Reminiscences of an Indian Official*, London: W.H. Allen.

Chevers, Norman (1856), *Manual of Medical Jurisprudence for Bengal and the North-Western Provinces*, Calcutta: Bengal Military Orphan Press.

—— (1870), *A Manual of Medical Jurisprudence for India, Including the Outline of a History of Crime against the Person in India*, Calcutta: Thacker, Spink.

Clifton, Mrs Talbot (1911), *Pilgrims to the Isles of Penance: Orchid Gathering in the East*, London: John Long.

Combe, George (1825), *A System of Phrenology*, Edinburgh: John Anderson Jun.

—— (1828), *The Constitution of Man Considered in Relation to External Objects*, Edinburgh: John Anderson Jun.

—— (1845), 'Penal Colonies: The Management of Prisoners in the Australian Colonies', *Phrenological Journal*, 18: 101–22.

Coomar, Palash C. and Raha, Manis K. (1989), 'Family among the Bhantu of Andamans', *Journal of the Indian Anthropological Society*, 24, 2: 121–8.

Cox, Edmund C. (1910), *Police and Crime in India*, London: Stanley Paul.

Cox, Robert (December 1832 – June 1834), 'Remarks on the Skulls and Characters of Thugs', *Phrenological Journal and Miscellany*, 8: 524–30.

Coxon, Stanley W. (1915), *And that Reminds Me; Being Incidents of a Life Spent at Sea, and in the Andaman Islands, Burma, Australia, and India*, London: John Lane.

Crooke, William (1896), *The Tribes and Castes of the North-West Provinces and Oudh*, 4 vols, Calcutta: Superintendent Government Printing.

Curry, J.C. (1932), *The Indian Police*, London: Faber and Faber.

Dalton, Edward Tuite (1872), *Descriptive Ethnology of Bengal*, Calcutta: Asiatic Society of Bengal.

Daly, F.C. (1916), *Manual of the Criminal Classes Operating in Bengal*, Calcutta: Bengal Secretariat Press.

Dobson, G.E. (1875), 'On the Andamans and Andamanese', *Journal of the Anthropological Institute*, 4: 457–67.

Dubois, Abbé J.A. (1817), *Description of the Character, Manners, and Customs of the People of India; and of their Institutions, Religious and Civil*, London: Longman, Hurst, Rees, Orme and Brown.

Ellis, Havelock (1910), *The Criminal*, London: Blackwood, Scott.

Fawcett, F. (1901), 'Notes on the Dômbs of Jeypur, Vizagapatam District, Madras Presidency', *Man*, 1: 34–8.

Ferrero Gina Lombroso (1911), *Criminal Man: According to the Classification of Cesare Lombroso. Briefly Summarized by his Daughter Gina Lombroso Ferrero*, New York: Putnam.

Flower, W.H. (1880), 'On the Osteology and Affinities of the Andaman Islands', *Journal of the Anthropological Institute*, 9: 108–33.

Forbes, Duncan (1862), *A Smaller Hindustani and English Dictionary*, London: W.H. Allen.

Forsyth, J. (1872), *The Highlands of Central India; Notes on their Forests and Wild Tribes, Natural History, and Sports*, London: Chapman and Hall.

Fritsch, Gustav (1908), *Ueber Bau und Bedeutung der Area Centralis des Menschen*, Berlin: Reimer.

Galton, Francis (1869), *Hereditary Genius: An Enquiry into its Laws and Consequences*, London: Macmillan.

—— (1879), 'Composite Portraits, Made by Combining those of Many Different Persons into a Single Resultant Figure', *Journal of the Anthropological Institute of Great Britain and Ireland*, 8: 312–44.

Gayer, G.W. (1907), *Some Criminal Tribes of India and Religious Mendicants*, Saugor: Police Officers' Training School.

Godden, Gertrude M. (1897), 'Naga and Other Frontier Tribes of North-East India', *Journal of the Anthropological Institute of Great Britain and Ireland*, 26: 161–201.

Grant, Colesworthy (1853), *Rough Pencillings of a Rough Trip to Rangoon in 1846*, Calcutta: Thacker, Spink.

Griffith, George (1901), *In an Unknown Prison Land: An Account of Convicts and Colonists in New Caledonia with Jottings Out and Home*, London: Hutchinson.

Gunthorpe, E.J. (1882), *Notes on Criminal Tribes Residing in or Frequenting the Bombay Presidency, Berar and the Central Provinces*, Bombay: Times of India Steam Press.

Hambly, W.D. (1925), *The History of Tattooing and its Significance with some Account of Other Forms of Corporal Marking*, London: H.F. and G. Witherby.

Heindl, Robert (1913), *Meine Reise nach den Strafkolonien, mit vielen originalaufnahmen*, Berlin and Vienna: Ullstein.

Henry, E.R. (1900), *Classification and Uses of Finger Prints*, London: George Routledge and Sons.

Herschel, William J. (1916), *The Origin of Finger-Printing*, London: Oxford University Press.

Hill, A.H. (1969), *The Hikayat Abdullah: The Autobiography of Abdullah Bin Abdul Kadir (1797–1854), an Annotated Translation*, Singapore: Oxford University Press.

Hollins, S.T. (1914), *The Criminal Tribes of the United Provinces*, Allahabad: Government Press.

Howell, A.P. (1868), *Note on Jails and Jail Discipline in India, 1867–68*, Calcutta: Superintendent of Government Printing.

Hunter, W.W. (1891), *Rulers of India: The Earl of Mayo*, Oxford: Clarendon Press.

Hutchinson, H.N. et al. (1900), *The Living Races of Mankind: A Popular Illustrated Account of the Customs, Habits, Pursuits, Feasts and Ceremonies of the Races of Mankind throughout the World*, London: Hutchinson.

Hutchinson, James (1845), *Observations on the General and Medical Management of Indian Jails; and on the Treatment of Some of the Principal Diseases which Infest Them*, Calcutta: Bengal Military Orphan Press.

Ibbetson, Denzil (1916), *Panjab Castes: Being a Reprint of the Chapter on 'The Races, Castes and Tribes of the People' in the Report on the Census of the Panjab Published in 1883*, Lahore: Superintendent Government Printing.

Kennedy, M. (1908), *Notes on Criminal Classes in the Bombay Presidency with Appendices Regarding some Foreign Criminals who Occasionally Visit the Presidency, including Hints on the Detection of Counterfeit Coins*, Bombay: Government Central Press.

Kumar Ghose, Barindra (1922), *The Tale of my Exile*, Pondicherry: Arya Office.

Lamprey, J.H. (1869), 'On a Method of Measuring the Human Form, for the Use of Students in Ethnology', *Journal of the Ethnological Society of London*, 1: 84–5.

Lane Fox, A. (1878), 'Observations on Mr Man's Collection of Andaman and Nicobarese Objects', *Journal of the Anthropological Institute*, 7: 434–70.

Lowry Cole, M. and Gwynn, S. (eds) (1934), *Memoirs of Sir Lowry Cole*, London: Macmillan.

Lyon, I.B. (1889), *A Text Book of Medical Jurisprudence for India*, Calcutta: Thacker, Spink.

McNair, J.F.A. (1899), *Prisoners their Own Warders: A Record of the Convict Prison at Singapore in the Straits Settlements Established 1825, Discontinued 1873, together with a Cursory History of the Convict Establishments at Bencoolen, Penang and Malacca from the Year 1797*, Westminster: Archibald Constable.

Man, E.H. (1882), 'On the Andamanese and Nicobarese Objects presented to Major-General Pitt Rivers', *Journal of the Anthropological Institute*, 9: 268–94.

—— (1883), 'On the Aboriginal Inhabitants of the Andaman Islands', *Journal of the Anthropological Institute*, 12: 69–175, 327–434.

—— (1885), *On the Aboriginal Inhabitants of the Andaman Islands, with Report of Researches in to the Language of the South Andaman Islands*, London: Trübner.

Marryat, Frank S. (1848), *Borneo and the Indian Archipelago, with Drawings of Costumes and Scenery*, London: Longman, Brown, Green and Longmans.

Marshall, William E. (1873), *A Phrenologist amongst the Todas; or the Study of a Primitive Tribe in South India: History, Character, Customs, Religion, Infanticide, Polyandry, Language*, London: Longmans, Green.

Meadows Taylor, Captain Philip (1833), 'On the Thugs', *New Monthly Magazine*, 38: 277–87.

—— (1839), *Confessions of a Thug, in Three Volumes*, London: Richard Bentley.

—— (1878), *The Story of my Life*, Edinburgh: W. Blackwood and Sons.

Montgomery, James (August 1829 – December 1830), 'An Essay on the Phrenology of the Hindoos and Negroes', *Phrenological Journal and Miscellany*, 6: 244–54.

Mouat, Frederic J. (1856), *Reports on Jails Visited and Inspected in Bengal, Bihar and Arracan*, Calcutta: F. Carbery, Military Orphan Press.

—— (1867), 'On Prison Discipline and Statistics in Lower Bengal', *Journal of the Statistical Society of London*, 30, 1: 21–57.

—— (1891), 'Notes on M. Bertillon's Discourse on the Anthropometric Measurement of Criminals', *Journal of the Royal Anthropological Institute of Great Britain and Ireland*, 20: 182–98.

Naidu, Rai Bahadur M. Pauparao (1905), *The Criminal Tribes of India, No. II: The History of Korawars, Erukulas or Kaikaries*, Madras: Higginbotham.

—— (1912), *The History of Professional Poisoners and Coiners of India*, Madras: Higginbotham.

—— (1915), *The History of Railway Thieves with Illustrations and Hints on Detection*, Madras: Higginbothams.

Nesfield, John C. (1885), *Brief View of the Caste System of the North-Western Provinces and Oudh, together with an Examination of the Names and Figures Shown in the Census Report, 1882, Being an Attempt to Classify on a Functional Basis all the Main Castes of the United Provinces, and to Explain their Gradations of Rank and Process of their Formation*, Allahabad: North-Western Provinces and Oudh Government Press.

Newcombe, A.C. (1905), *Village, Town and Jungle Life in India*, London: William Blackwood and Sons.

Orlich, Leopold Von (1845), *Travels in India, including Sinde and the Punjab, vol. II* (tr. H. Evans-Lloyd), London: Longman, Brown, Green and Longmans.

Park, Rosamund E. (1916), *Recollections and Red Letter Days* (private circulation).

Paterson, George Murray (1824), 'On the Phrenology of Hindostan', *Transactions of the Phrenological Society*, Edinburgh: John Anderson Jun., 430–48.

Peal, S.E. (1871), 'Notes on a Visit to the Tribes Inhabiting the Hills South of Síbságar, Asám', *Journal of the Asiatic Society of Bengal*, 41, 2: 9–31.

Platts, John T. (1889), *A Dictionary of Urdu, Classical Hindi, and English, vol. II*, London: W.H. Allen.

Portman, M.V. (1892), 'On Things in General, Regarding Port Blair, and Photography', *Journal of the Photographic Society of India*, 5: 190–3.

—— (1896), 'Photography for Anthropologists', *Journal of the Anthropological Institute*, 15: 75–87.

—— (1899), *A History of our Relations with the Andamanese, vols I and II*, Calcutta: Superintendent Government Printing.

Read, C.H. (1893), 'Mr Portman's Photographs of Andamanese', *Journal of the Anthropological Institute*, 12: 401–3.

Report of the Committee on Prison Discipline, 8 Jan. 1838 (1838), Calcutta: Baptist Mission Press.

Risley, H.H. (1891a), *The Tribes and Castes of Bengal: Ethnographic Glossary*, 2 vols, Calcutta: Bengal Secretariat Press.

Bibliography

—— (1891b), 'The Study of Ethnology in India', *Journal of the Anthropological Institute of Great Britain and Ireland*, 20: 235–63.

—— (1902), 'Note on some Indian Tatu-Marks', *Man*, 2: 97–101.

—— (1908a), *The People of India*, Calcutta: Thacker, Spink.

—— (1908b), *Anthropometric Data: Baluchistan, NW Borderland, Burma (ethnographic survey of India)*, Calcutta: Superintendent of Government Printing.

—— and Sinclair, A.T. (1902), 'The Origin of the Gypsies', *Man*, 2: 180–2.

Sanjivi, Dr (1915) *Criminology and Detection*, Tinnevelly Institute of Criminology.

Savarkar, V.D. (1950), *The Story of my Transportation for Life*, Bombay: Sadbhakti.

Selected Records from the Central Provinces and Berar Secretariat Relating to the Suppression of Thuggee, 1829–1832 (1939), Nagpur: Government Printing.

Seton-Karr, W.S. (1864), *Selections from Calcutta Gazettes, vols I–IV*, Calcutta: Military Orphan Press.

Sinclair, A.T. (1908), 'Tattooing – Oriental and Gypsy', *American Anthropologist*, 10, 3: 361–86.

Singh, K.S. (1993a), *The Scheduled Castes, People of India National Series, vol. II*, New Delhi: Oxford University Press.

—— (1993b), *The Scheduled Tribes, People of India National Series, vol. III*, New Delhi: Oxford University Press.

—— (1993c), 'Foreword', in Bhattacharyya et al., *All India Anthropometric Survey*, n.p.

Sleeman, William (1843), 'Report on the Depredations Committed by the Thug Gangs of Upper and Central India, from the Cold Season of 1826–27, down to their Gradual Suppression under the Measures Adopted Against Them by the Supreme Government in the Year 1839', *British and Foreign Review*, 15, 29: 246–91.

Solvyns, F. Baltazard (1812), *Les Hindoûs, ou description de leurs moeurs, coutumes et ceremonies*, 5 vols, Paris: L'Imprimerie de Mame Freres.

Spry, Henry Harpur (December 1832 – June 1834), 'Some Account of the Gang-Murderers of India Commonly Called Thugs: Accompanying the Skulls of Seven of Them', *Phrenological Journal and Miscellany*, 8: 511–24.

Tavernier, Jean-Baptiste (1925), *Travels in India, Translated from the Original French Edition of 1676 by V. Ball, vol. I*, Oxford: Oxford University Press.

Temple, R.C. (1929), *Remarks on the Andaman Islanders and their Country*, Bombay: British India Press.

Thurston, Edgar (1906a), *Ethnographic Notes in Southern India*, Madras: Government Press.

—— (1906b), *Castes and Tribes of Southern India*, 7 vols, Madras: Government Press.

Turner, William (1894), 'Contributions to the Craniology of the People of the Empire of India, Part I: The Hill Tribes of the North-East Frontier and the People of Burma', *Transactions of the Royal Society of Edinburgh*, 39, 3 (no. 28): 703–47.

—— (1901), 'Contributions to the Craniology of the People of the Empire of India, Part II: The Aborigines of Chuta Nagpur and of the Central Provinces, the People of Orissa, the Veddahs and Negritos', *Transactions of the Royal Society of Edinburgh*, 60, 1 (no. 6): 59–128.

Walrond, Theodore (ed.) (1872), *Letters and Journals of James, Eighth Earl of Elgin; Governor of Jamaica, Governor-General of Canada, Envoy to China, Viceroy of India*, London: John Murray.

Wathen, James (1814), *Journal of a Voyage, in 1811 and 1812, to Madras and China; Returning by the Cape of Good Hope and St. Helena; in the H.C.S. The Hope, Capt. James Pendergrass*, London, J. Nichols, Son and Bentley.

Wise, James (1883), *Notes on the Races, Castes and Trades of Eastern Bengal*, London: Harrison.

Woodthorpe, R.G. (1882a), 'Notes on the Wild Tribes Inhabiting the So-called Naga Hills, on our North-East Frontier of India, Part I', *Journal of the Anthropological Institute of Great Britain and Ireland*, 11: 56–73.

—— (1882b), 'Notes on the Wild Tribes Inhabiting the So-called Naga Hills, on our North-East Frontier of India, Part II', *Journal of the Anthropological Institute of Great Britain and Ireland*, 11: 196–214.

Yoe, Schway [pseudonym for J.G. Scott] (1882), *The Burman, his Life and Notions, vol. I*, London: Macmillan.

Yule, C.B. (1880), 'Notes on Analogies of Manners between the Indo-Chinese Races and the Races of the Indian Archipelago', *Journal of the Anthropological Institute of Great Britain and Ireland*, 9: 290–301.

Yule, Henry (1886), *Hobson-Jobson: A Glossary of Colloquial Anglo Indian Words and Phrases, and of Kindred Terms, Etymological, Historical, Geographical and Descriptive*, London: John Murray.

Secondary Literature

Abler, Thomas S. (1999), *Hinterland Warriors and Military Dress: European Empires and Exotic Uniforms*, Oxford: Berg.

Adas, Michael (1989), *Machines as the Measure of Men: Science, Technology, and Ideologies of Western Dominance*, London: Cornell University Press.

Aggarwal, S.N. (1995), *The Heroes of Cellular Jail*, Patiala, Panjab: Publications Bureau, Panjabi University.

Allen, Richard B. (1993), 'Marronage and the Maintenance of Public Order in Mauritius, 1721–1835', *Slavery and Abolition*, 4, 3: 214–31.

—— (1999), *Slaves, Freedmen, and Indentured Laborers in Colonial Mauritius*, Cambridge: Cambridge University Press.

Altink, Henrice (2002), '"An Outrage on All Decency": Abolitionist Reactions to Flogging Jamaican Slave Women, 1780–1834', *Slavery and Abolition*, 23, 2: 107–22.

Anderson, Clare (2000a), *Convicts in the Indian Ocean: Transportation from South Asia to Mauritius, 1815–53*, London: Macmillan.

—— (2000b), '*Godna*: Inscribing Indian Convicts in the Nineteenth Century', in Caplan (ed.), *Written on the Body*, 102–17.

—— (2001), 'Fashioning Identity: The Development of Penal Dress in Nineteenth-Century India', *History Workshop Journal*, 52: 152–74.

—— (2003), 'The Politics of Convict Space: Indian Penal Settlements and the Andamans', in Bashford and Strange (eds), *Isolation*, 40–55.

—— (2004), 'The Bel Ombre Rebellion: Indian Convicts in Mauritius, 1815–53', in Campbell (ed.), *Abolition and its Aftermath in Indian Ocean Africa and Asia, vol. II*.

Arnold, David (1986), *Police Power and Colonial Rule, Madras 1859–1947*, Delhi: Oxford University Press.

—— (1993), *Colonizing the Body: State Medicine and Epidemic Disease in Nineteenth-Century India*, Berkeley, CA: University of California Press.

—— (1994), 'The Colonial Prison: Power, Knowledge and Penology in Nineteenth-Century India', in Arnold and Hardiman (eds), *Subaltern Studies VIII*, 148–87.

—— (1999), '"An Ancient Race Outworn": Malaria and Race in Colonial India, 1860–1930', in Ernst and Harris (eds), *Race, Science and Medicine*, 123–43.

—— and Hardiman, David (eds) (1994), *Subaltern Studies VIII: Essays in Honour of Ranajit Guha*, New Delhi: Oxford University Press.

Banerjee, Tapas Kumar (1990), *Background to Indian Criminal Law*, Calcutta: R. Cambray.

Bank, Andrew (1996), 'Of "Native Skulls" and "Noble Caucasians": Phrenology in Colonial South Africa', *Journal of Southern African Studies*, 22, 3: 387–403.

Barnes, Ruth and Eicher, Joanne B. (eds) (1992), *Dress and Gender: Making and Meaning*, Oxford: Berg.

Bashford, Alison and Strange, Carolyn (eds) (2003), *Isolation: Places and Practices of Exclusion*, London: Routledge.

Bates, Crispin (1997), 'Race, Caste and Tribe in Central India: The Early Origins of Indian Anthropometry', in Robb (ed.), *The Concept of Race in South Asia*, 219–57.

Bayly, C.A. (ed.) (1990), *The Raj: India and the British 1600–1947*, London: National Portrait Gallery Publications.

Bayly, Susan (1997), 'Caste and "Race" in the Colonial Ethnography of India', in Robb (ed.), *The Concept of Race in South Asia*, 165–218.

—— (1999), *Caste, Society and Politics in India from the Eighteenth Century to the Modern Age*, Cambridge: Cambridge University Press.

Becker, Peter (2001), 'The Standardized Gaze: The Standardization of the Search Warrant in Nineteenth-Century Germany', in Caplan and Torpey (eds), *Documenting Individual Identity*, 139–63.

Beckles, Hilary McD. (1997), 'Social and Political Control in the Slave Society', in Knight (ed.), *General History of the Caribbean, vol. III*, 194–221.

Bhadra, Gautam, Prakash, Gyan and Tharu, Susie (eds) (1999), *Subaltern Studies X: Writings on South Asian History and Society*, New Delhi: Oxford University Press.

Binney, Judith (1992), 'Two Māori Portraits: Adoption of the Medium', in Edwards (ed.), *Anthropology and Photography*, 242–6.

Bland, Lucy and Doan, Laura (eds), *Sexology in Culture: Labelling Bodies and Desires*, Chicago: University of Chicago Press.

Blunt, Alison (2002), '"Land of our Mothers": Home, Identity and Nationality for Anglo-Indians in British India, 1919–1947', *History Workshop Journal*, 54: 49–72

—— and Rose, Gillian (eds) (1994a), *Writing Women and Space: Colonial and Postcolonial Geographies*, London: Guilford Press.

—— and Rose, Gillian (1994b), 'Introduction: Women's Colonial and Postcolonial Geographies', in Blunt and Rose (eds), *Writing Women and Space*, 1–25.

Bolton, R. (ed.) (1989), *The Contest of Meaning: Critical Histories of Photography*, London: MIT Press.

Bradley, James (2000), 'Body Commodification? Class and Tattoos in Victorian Britain', in Caplan (ed.), *Written on the Body*, 136–55.

—— and Maxwell-Stewart, Hamish (1997a) '"Behold the Man": Power, Observation and the Tattooed Convict', *Australian Studies*, 12, 1: 71–97.

—— and Maxwell-Stewart, Hamish (1997b), 'Embodied Explorations: Investigating Convict Tattoos and the Transportation System', in Duffield and Bradley (eds), *Representing Convicts*, 183–203.

Breward, Christopher (1999), 'Sartorial Spectacle: Clothing and Masculine Identities in the Imperial City, 1860–1914', in Driver and Gilbert (eds), *Imperial Cities*, 238–53.

Brown, Mark (2001), 'Race, Science and the Construction of Native Criminality in Colonial India', *Theoretical Criminology*, 5, 3: 345–68.

Burton, Antoinette (1999a), 'Introduction: The Unfinished Business of Colonial Modernities', in Burton (ed.), *Gender, Sexuality and Colonial Modernities*, 1–16.

—— (ed.) (1999b), *Gender, Sexuality and Colonial Modernities*, London: Routledge.

Campbell, Gwyn (ed.) (2004), *Abolition and its Aftermath in Indian Ocean Africa and Asia, vol. II*, London: Frank Cass.

Canning, Kathleen (1999), 'The Body as Method? Reflections on the Place of the Body in Gender History', in Davidoff, McClelland and Varikas (eds), *Gender and History*, 81–95.

Caplan, Jane (1997), '"Speaking Scars": The Tattoo in Popular Practice and Medico-Legal Debate in Nineteenth-Century Europe', *History Workshop Journal*, 44: 106–42.

—— (1998), '"Educating the Eye": The Tattooed Prostitute', in Bland and Doan (eds), *Sexology in Culture*, 100–15.

—— (2000a), 'Introduction', in Caplan (ed.), *Written on the Body*, xi–xxiii.

—— (ed.) (2000b), *Written on the Body: The Tattoo in European and North American History*, London: Reaktion.

—— and Torpey, John (2001a), 'Introduction', in Caplan and Torpey (eds), *Documenting Individual Identity*, 1–12.

—— and Torpey, John (eds) (2001b), *Documenting Individual Identity: The Development of State Practices in the Modern World*, Princeton, NJ: Princeton University Press.

Caplan, Lionel (2001), *Children of Colonialism: Anglo-Indians in a Post-Colonial World*, Oxford: Berg.

Chandhoke, Neera (ed.) (2000), *Mapping Histories: Essays Presented to Ravinder Kumar*, New Delhi: Tulika.

Chatterjee, Indrani (1999a), *Gender, Slavery and Law in Colonial India*, New Delhi: Oxford University Press.

—— (1999b), 'Colouring Subalternity: Slaves, Concubines and Social Orphans in Early Colonial India', in Bhadra, Prakash and Tharu (eds), *Subaltern Studies X*, 49–97.

Childs, Peter and Williams, Patrick (eds) (1997), *An Introduction to Post-Colonial Theory*, London: Harvester Wheatsheaf.

Christ, Carol T. and Jordan, John O. (eds) (1995), *Victorian Literature and the Victorian Visual Imagination*, London: University of California Press.

Cohn, Bernard S. (1997), *Colonialism and its Forms of Knowledge: The British in India*, Oxford: Oxford University Press.

Cole, Simon A. (2001), *Suspect Identities: A History of Fingerprinting and Criminal Identification*, London: Harvard University Press.

Collingham, E.M. (2001), *Imperial Bodies*, Cambridge: Polity.

Cooter, Roger (1984), *The Cultural Meaning of Popular Science: Phrenology and the Organization of Consent in Nineteenth-Century Britain*, Cambridge: Cambridge University Press.

Craton, Michael (1997), 'Forms of Resistance to Slavery', in Knight (ed.), *General History of the Caribbean, vol. III*, 222–70.

Damousi, Joy (1997a), '"What Punishment will be Sufficient for these Rebellious Hussies?" Headshaving and Convict Women in the Female Factories, 1820s–1840s', in Duffield and Bradley (eds), *Representing Convicts*, 204–14.

—— (1997b), *Depraved and Disorderly: Female Convicts, Sexuality and Gender in Colonial Australia*, Cambridge: Cambridge University Press.

Das, Sukla (1977), *Crime and Punishment in Ancient India (c. A.D. 300 to A.D. 1100)*, New Delhi: Abhinav.

Daston, Lorraine and Galison, Peter (1992), 'The Image of Objectivity', *Representations*, 40: 81–128.

Davidoff, Leonore, McClelland, Keith and Varikas, Eleni (eds) (1999), *Gender and History: Retrospect and Prospect*, Oxford: Blackwell.

Davies, John (1955), *Phrenology, Fad and Science: A Nineteenth-Century American Crusade*, New Haven, CT: Yale University Press.

Dippie, Brian W. (1992), 'Representing the Other: The North American Indian', in Edwards (ed.), *Anthropology and Photography*, 132–6.

Dirks, Nicholas B. (1995), 'Reading Culture: Anthropology and the Textualization of India', in Peck and Daniel (eds), *Culture/Contexture*, 275–95.

—— (2000), 'The Crimes of Colonialism: Anthropology and the Textualization of India', in Pels and Salemink (eds), *Colonial Subjects*, 153–79.

—— (2001), *Castes of Mind: Colonialism and the Making of Modern India*, Princeton, NJ: Princeton University Press.

Driver, Felix and Gilbert, David (eds) (1999), *Imperial Cities*, Manchester: Manchester University Press.

Duffield, Ian and Bradley, James (eds) (1997), *Representing Convicts: New Perspectives on Convict Forced Labour Migration*, London: Cassell.

Edwards, Elizabeth (1990), 'Photographic "Types": The Pursuit of Method', *Visual Anthropology*, 3: 235–58.

—— (ed.) (1992a), *Anthropology and Photography, 1860–1920*, London: Yale University Press.

—— (1992b), 'Introduction', in Edwards (ed.) *Anthropology and Photography*, 3–17.

—— (1992c), 'Science Visualized: E.H. Man in the Andaman Islands', in Edwards (ed.), *Anthropology and Photography*, 108–21.

—— (1997), 'Ordering Others: Photography, Anthropologies and Taxonomies', in Illes and Roberts (eds), *In Visible Light*, 54–68.

—— (2001), *Raw Histories: Photographs, Anthropology and Museums*, Oxford: Berg.

Entwistle, J. (2000), *The Fashioned Body: Fashion, Dress and Modern Social Theory*, Cambridge: Polity Press.

Ernst, Waltraud and Harris, Bernard (eds) (1999), *Race, Science and Medicine, 1700–1960*, London: Routledge.

Evans, Raymond and Thorpe, Bill (1998), 'Commanding Men: Masculinities and the Convict System', *Journal of Australian Studies*, 56: 17–34.

Evans, Richard J. (1998), *Tales from the German Underworld: Crime and Punishment in the Nineteenth Century*, New Haven, CT: Yale University Press.

Falconer, John (1984), 'Ethnographical Photography in India 1850–1900', *Photographic Collector*, 5, 1: 16–46.

—— (1990), 'Photography in Nineteenth-Century India', in Bayly (ed.), *The Raj*, 264–77.

Faris, James C. (1992), 'Photography, Power and the Southern Nuba', in Edwards (ed.), *Anthropology and Photography*, 211–17.

Fisch, Jorg (1983), *Cheap Lives and Dear Limbs: The British Transformation of the Bengal Criminal Law, 1769–1817*, Wiesbaden: Franz Steiner Verlag.

Fischer-Tiné, Harald and Mann, Michael (eds) (2003), *Colonialism as Civilizing Mission: Cultural Ideology in British India*, London: Anthem.

Fleming, Juliet (2000), 'The Renaissance Tattoo', in Caplan (ed.), *Written on the Body*, 61–82.

Foucault, Michel (1977), *Discipline and Punish: The Birth of the Prison*, London: Allen Lane.

Freitag, Sandria (1991), 'Crime in the Social Order of Colonial North India', *Modern Asian Studies*, 25: 227–61.

Gell, Alfred (1993), *Wrapping in Images: Tattooing in Polynesia*, Oxford: Clarendon Press.

Godby, Michael (1996), 'Images of //Kabbo', in Skotnes (ed.), *MISCAST: Negotiating the Presence of the Bushmen*, 115–127.

Gordon, Stewart (1969), 'Scarf and Sword: Thugs, Marauders and State Formation in 18th Century Malwa', *Indian Economic and Social History Review*, 4: 403–29.

—— (1985), 'Bhils and the Idea of a Criminal Tribe in Nineteenth-Century India', in Yang (ed.), *Crime and Criminality in British India*, 128–39.

Gould, Stephen Jay (1981), *The Mismeasure of Man*, London: Norton.

Green, David (1984), 'Classified Subjects. Photography and Anthropology: The Technology of Power', *Ten-8*, 14: 30–7.

—— (1985), 'Veins of Resemblance: Photography and Eugenics', *Oxford Art Journal*, 7, 2: 3–16.

Gregorio, Mario A. Di (1994), *T.H. Huxley's Place in Natural Science*, London: Yale University Press.

Grundfest, H. (1963), 'Gustav Fritsch', *Journal of the History of Medicine*, 18: 125–9.

Guest, Harriet (2000), 'Curiously Marked: Tattooing and Gender Difference in Eighteenth-century British Perceptions of the South Pacific', in Caplan (ed.), *Written on the Body*, 83–101.

Guha, Sumit (1995), 'An Indian Penal Régime: Maharashtra in the Eighteenth Century', *Past and Present,* 147: 100–26.

Guistino, David De (1975), *Conquest of Mind: Phrenology and Victorian Social Thought*, London: Croom Helm.

Gupte, B.A. (1992), 'Notes on Female Tattoo Designs in India', in Joshi (ed.), *Marks and Meaning*, 35–59.

Illes, Chrissie and Roberts, Russell (eds) (1997), *In Visible Light*, Oxford: Museum of Modern Art.

Inden, Ronald (1986), 'Orientalist Constructions of India', *Modern Asian Studies*, 20, 3: 401–46.

—— (1990), *Imagining India*, Oxford: Blackwell.

Ireland, Richard W. (2002), 'The Felon and the Angel Copier: Criminal Identity and the Promise of Photography in Victorian England and Wales', in Knafla (ed.), *Policing and War*, 53–86.

Jenks, Chris (1995a), 'The Centrality of the Eye in Western Culture: An Introduction', in Jenks (ed.), *Visual Culture*, 1–25.

—— (ed.) (1995b), *Visual Culture*, London: Routledge.

Jones, C.P. (1987), '*Stigma*: Tattooing and Branding in Graeco-Roman Antiquity', *Journal of Roman Studies*, 77: 139–55.

Joseph, Anne M. (2001) 'Anthropometry, the Police Expert, and the Deptford Murders: The Contested Introduction of Fingerprinting for the Identification of Criminals in Late Victorian and Edwardian Britain', in Caplan and Torpey (eds), *Documenting Individual Identity*, 164–83.

Joshi, O.P. (ed.) (1992a), *Marks and Meaning: Anthropology of Symbols*, Jaipur: RBSA.

——— (1992b), 'Tattooing and Tattooers: A Socio-cultural Analysis', in Joshi (ed.), *Marks and Meaning*, 17–34.

——— (1992c), 'Continuity and Change in Hindu Women's Dress', in Barnes and Eicher (eds), *Dress and Gender*, 214–31.

Kaluszynski, Martine (2001), 'Republican Identity: Bertillonage as Government Technique', in Caplan and Torpey (eds), *Documenting Individual Identity*, 123–38.

Kapila, Shruti (2002), 'The Making of Colonial Psychiatry, Bombay Presidency, 1849–1940', PhD in History, SOAS, University of London.

Knafla, Louis E. (ed.) (2002), *Policing and War in Europe*, Westwood, CT: Greenwood Press.

Knight, Franklin W. (ed.) (1997), *General History of the Caribbean, vol. III: The Slave Societies of the Caribbean*, London: Macmillan.

Kumar Singh, Ujjwal (1998), *Political Prisoners in India*, New Delhi: Oxford University Press.

Lalvani, Suren (1996), *Photography, Vision and the Production of Modern Bodies*, Albany, NY: State University of New York Press.

Levine, Philippa (2000), 'Orientalist Sociology and the Creation of Colonial Sexualities', *Feminist Review*, 65: 5–21.

——— (2003), *Prostitution, Race and Politics: Policing Venereal Disease in the British Empire*, London: Routledge.

Luhrmann, T.H. (1996), *The Good Parsi: The Fate of a Colonial Elite in a Postcolonial Society*, Cambridge, MA: Harvard University Press.

Lury, Celia (1998), *Prosthetic Culture: Photography, Memory and Identity*, London: Routledge.

Lyttle, Gerlind (1992), *A German Traveller in Natal*, Durban: Killie Campbell Africana Library.

McClintock, Anne (1995), *Imperial Leather: Race, Gender and Sexuality in the Colonial Context*, London: Routledge.

McConville, Seán (1995), *English Local Prisons 1860–1900: Next Only to Death*, London: Routledge.

MacQuarrie, Charles W. (2000), 'Insular Celtic Tattooing: History, Myth and Metaphor', in Caplan (ed.), *Written on the Body*, 32–45.

Major, Andrew (1999), 'State and Criminal Tribes in Colonial Punjab: Surveillance, Control and Reclamation of the "Dangerous Classes"', *Modern Asian Studies*, 33: 657–88.

Majumdar, N. (1960), *Justice and Police in Bengal, 1765–1793: A Study of the Nizamat in Decline*, Calcutta: Firma K.L. Mukhopadhyay.

Majumdar, R.C. (1975), *Penal Settlement in Andamans*, New Delhi: Gazetteers Unit, Department of Culture, Ministry of Education and Social Welfare.

Mathur, L.P. (1985), *Kala Pani: History of Andaman and Nicobar Islands with a Study of India's Freedom Struggle*, New Delhi: Eastern Book Company.

Mathur, Saloni (1999), 'Wanted Native Views: Collecting Colonial Postcards of India', in Burton (ed.), *Gender, Sexuality and Colonial Modernities*, 95–115.

Maxwell, Anne (1999), *Colonial Photography and Exhibitions: Representations of 'Native' Peoples and the Making of European Identities*, London: Cassell.

Maxwell-Stewart, Hamish and Duffield, Ian (2000), 'Skin Deep Devotions: Religious Tattoos and Convict Transportation to Australia', in Caplan (ed.), *Written on the Body*, 118–35.

Maynard, Margaret (1998), *Fashioned from Penury: Dress as Cultural Practice in Colonial Australia*, Cambridge: Cambridge University Press.

Metcalf, Thomas R. (1994), *Ideologies of the Raj*, Cambridge: Cambridge University Press.

Mills, James H. (2000), *Madness, Cannabis and Colonialism: The 'Native-Only' Lunatic Asylums of British India, 1857–1900*, London: Macmillan.

Mills, James H. and Sen, Satadru (eds) (2003), *Confronting the Body: The Politics of Physicality in Colonial and Post-Colonial India*, London: Anthem.

Nandy, Ashis (1983), *The Intimate Enemy: Loss and Recovery of Self under Colonialism*, New Delhi: Oxford University Press.

Nigam, Sanjay (1990a), 'Disciplining and Policing the "Criminals by Birth", Part 1: The Making of a Colonial Stereotype – The Criminal Tribes and Castes of North India', *Indian Economic and Social History Review*, 27, 2: 131–64.

—— (1990b), 'Disciplining and Policing the "Criminals by Birth", Part 2: The Development of a Disciplinary System, 1871–1900', *Indian Economic and Social History Review*, 27, 3: 257–87.

Padel, Felix (2000), *The Sacrifice of Human Being: British Rule and the Konds of Orissa*, New Delhi: Oxford University Press.

Pathak, R.C. (1969), *Bhargava's Standard Illustrated Dictionary of the Hindi Language*, Varanasi: Chowk.

Paton, Diana (1996), 'Decency, Dependence and the Lash: Gender and the British Debate over Slave Emancipation, 1830–34', *Slavery and Abolition*, 17, 3: 163–84.

Peck, J. and Daniel, E.V. (eds), *Culture/Contexture: Explorations in Anthropology and Literary Studies*, Berkeley, CA: University of California Press.

Pels, Peter and Salemink, Oscar (eds) (1999), *Colonial Subjects: Essays on the Practical History of Anthropology*, Ann Arbor, MI: University of Michigan Press.

Pick, Daniel (1989), *Faces of Degeneration: A European Disorder, c. 1848–1918*, Cambridge: Cambridge University Press.

Pieris, Anoma (2003), 'Hidden Hands and Divided Landscapes: Penal Labor and Colonial Citizenship in Singapore and the Straits Settlements, 1825–1873', PhD in Architecture, UC Berkeley.

Pierson, Ruth Roach (1998), 'Introduction', in Pierson and Chaudhuri (eds), *Nation, Empire, Colony*, 1–20.

—— and Chaudhuri, Nupur (eds) (1998), *Nation, Empire, Colony: Historicizing Gender and Race*, Bloomington, IN: Indiana University Press.

Pinney, Christopher (1990), 'Colonial Anthropology in the "Laboratory of Mankind"', in Bayly (ed.) *The Raj*, 252–63.

—— (1992a), 'The Parallel Histories of Anthropology and Photography', in Edwards (ed.) *Anthropology and Photography*, 74–95.

—— (1992b), 'Underneath the Banyan Tree: William Crooke and Photographic Depictions of Caste', in Edwards (ed.), *Anthropology and Photography*, 165–73.

—— (1997), *Camera Indica: The Social Life of Indian Photographs*, London: Reaktion.

Poignant, Roslyn (1992), 'Surveying the Field of View: The Making of the RAI Photographic Collection', in Edwards (ed.), *Anthropology and Photography*, 42–73.

Radhakrishna, Meena (1989), 'The Criminal Tribes Act in the Madras Presidency: Implications for Itinerant Trading Communities', *Indian Economic and Social History Review*, 26, 3: 271–95.

—— (1992), 'Surveillance and Settlements under the Criminal Tribes Act in Madras', *Indian Economic and Social History Review*, 29, 2: 171–98.

—— (2000), 'Colonial Construction of a "Criminal Tribe": The Itinerant Trading Communities of Madras Presidency', in Chandhoke (ed.), *Mapping Histories*, 128–60.

Rafter, Nicole Hahn (1997), *Creating Born Criminals*, Urbana, IL: University of Illinois Press.

Rae-Ellis, Vivien (1992), 'The Representation of Trucanini', in Edwards (ed.), *Anthropology and Photography*, 230–3.

Robb, Peter (ed.) (1997a), *The Concept of Race in South Asia*, New Delhi: Oxford University Press.

—— (1997b), 'Introduction: South Asia and the Concept of Race', in Robb (ed.), *The Concept of Race in South Asia*, 1–76.

Rosecrans, Jennipher Allen (2000), 'Wearing the Universe: Symbolic Markings in Early Modern England', in Caplan (ed.), *Written on the Body*, 46–60.

Roy, Parama (1996), 'Discovering India, Imagining *Thuggee*', *Yale Journal of Criticism*, 9, 1: 121–45.

Ryan, James R. (1997), *Picturing Empire: Photography and the Visualization of the British Empire*, London: Reaktion.

Sandu, K.S. (1968), 'Tamil and Other Indian Convicts in the Straits Settlements, A.D. 1790–1873', *Proceedings of the First International Tamil Conference Seminar of Tamil Studies, vol. I*, Kuala Lumpar: International Association of Tamil Research, 197–208.

Sayer, Karen (2002), '"A Sufficiency of Clothing": Dress and Domesticity in Victorian Britain', *Textile History*, 33, 1: 112–22.

Schendel, Willem Van (2002), 'A Politics of Nudity: Photographs of the "Naked Mru" of Bangladesh', *Modern Asian Studies*, 36, 2: 341–74.

Schrader, Abby M. (2000), 'Branding the Other/Tattooing the Self: Bodily Inscription among Convicts in Russia and the Soviet Union', in Caplan (ed.), *Written on the Body*, 174–92.

—— (2002), *Languages of the Lash: Corporal Punishment and Identity in Imperial Russia*, DeKalb, IL: Northern Illinois University Press.

Scott, James C. (1998), *Seeing Like a State: How Certain Schemes to Improve the Human Condition Have Failed*, New Haven, CT: Yale University Press.

—— Tehranian, John and Mathias, Jeremy (2002), 'The Production of Legal Identities Proper to States: The Case of the Permanent Family Surname', *Comparative Studies in Society and History*, 44, 1: 4–44.

Sekula, Allan (1980), 'The Body and the Archive', *October*, 39: 3–64.

—— (1989), 'The Body and the Archive', in Bolton (ed.), *The Contest of Meaning*, 343–79.

Sen, Satadru (1999a), 'Rationing Sex: Female Convicts in the Andamans', *South Asia*, 30, 1: 29–59.

—— (1999b), 'Policing the Savage: Segregation, Labor and State Medicine in the Andamans', *Journal of Asian Studies*, 58, 3: 753–73.

—— (2000), *Disciplining Punishment: Colonialism and Convict Society in the Andaman Islands,* New Delhi: Oxford University Press.

—— (2002), 'The Female Jails of Colonial India', *Indian Economic and Social History Review*, 39, 4: 417–38.

Sengoopta, Chandak (2003), *Imprint of the Raj: How Fingerprinting was Born in Colonial India*, London: Macmillan.

Shortland, Michael (1985), 'Skin Deep: Barthes, Lavater and the Legible Body', *Economy and Society*, 14, 3: 273–312.

Shreenivas and Saradindu Narayan Sinha (1957a), 'Personal Identification by the Dermatoglyphics and the E-V Methods', *Patna Journal of Medicine*, 31, 2: 53–64.

—— (1957b), 'Personal Identification by the Dermatoglyphics and the E-V Methods', *Patna Journal of Medicine*, 31, 3: 98–108.

Singha, Radhika (1993a), 'The Privilege of Taking Life: Some "anomalies" in the Law of Homicide in the Bengal Presidency', *Indian Economic and Social History Review*, 30, 2: 181–214.

—— (1993b), '"Providential" Circumstances: The Thuggee Campaign of the 1830s and Legal Innovation', *Modern Asian Studies*, 27, 1: 83–146.

—— (1998), *A Despotism of Law: Crime and Justice in Early Colonial India*, New Delhi: Oxford University Press.

—— (2000), 'Settle, Mobilize, Verify: Identification Practices in Colonial India', *Studies in History*, 16, 2: 152–98.

Sinha, Mrinalini (1995), *Colonial Masculinity: The 'Manly Englishman' and the 'Effeminate Bengali' in the Late Nineteenth Century*, Manchester: Manchester University Press.

—— (1999), 'Giving Masculinity a History: Some Contributions from the Historiography of Colonial India', in Davidoff, McClelland and Varikas (eds), *Gender and History*, 27–42.

Skotnes, Pippa (ed.) (1996), *MISCAST: Negotiating the Presence of the Bushmen*, Cape Town: University of Cape Town Press.

Slater, Don (1995), 'Photography and Modern Vision: The Spectacle of "Natural Magic"', in Jenks (ed.), *Visual Culture*, 218–37.

Spencer, Frank (1992), 'Some Notes on the Attempt to Apply Photography to Anthropometry during the Second Half of the Nineteenth Century', in Edwards (ed.), *Anthropology and Photography*, 99–107.

Spivak, Gayatri Chakravorty (1997), 'Can the Subaltern Speak?', reprinted with abridgements in Childs and Williams (eds), *An Introduction to Post-Colonial Theory*, 66–111.

Stange, Maren (1989), *Symbols of Ideal Life: Social Documentary Photography in America 1890–1950*, Cambridge: Cambridge University Press.

Stepan, Nancy Leys (2001), *Picturing Tropical Nature*, Ithaca, NY: Cornell University Press.

Stepan, Nancy (1982), *The Idea of Race in Science: Great Britain, 1800–1960*, London: Macmillan.

Stoler, Ann Laura and Cooper, Frederick (1997), 'Between Metropole and Colony: Rethinking a Research Agenda', in Cooper and Stoler (eds), *Tensions of Empire*.

Sutton, Deborah (2002), 'Horrid Sights and Customary Rights: The Toda Funeral on the Colonial Nilgiris', *Indian Economic and Social History Review*, 39, 1: 45–70.

Tarlo, Emma (1996), *Clothing Matters: Dress and Identity in India*, London: University of Chicago Press.

Thomas, Ronald R. (1995), 'Making Darkness Visible: Capturing the Criminal and Observing the Law in Victorian Photography and Detective Fiction', in Christ and Jordan (eds), *Victorian Literature*, 134–68.

Tolen, Rachel J. (1991), 'Colonizing and Transforming the Criminal Tribesmen: The Salvation Army in British India', *American Ethnologist*, 18, 1: 106–25.

Turnbull, C.M. (1970), 'Convicts in the Straits Settlements, 1826–67', *Journal of the Malay Branch of the Royal Asiatic Society*, 43, 1: 87–103.

Weeks, Jeffrey (1992), *Sex, Politics and Society: The Regulation of Sexuality since 1800*, London: Longman.

White, Shane and White, Graham (1995), 'Slave Clothing and African-American Culture in the Eighteenth and Nineteenth Centuries', *Past and Present*, 148: 149–86.

Wiener, Martin J. (1990), *Reconstructing the Criminal: Culture, Law and Policy in England, 1830–1914*, Cambridge: Cambridge University Press.

Woerkens, Martine Van (2002), *The Strangled Traveler: Colonial Imaginings and the Thugs of India* (tr. Catherine Tihanyi), London: University of Chicago Press.

Wynne, Martin (ed.) (1985), *On Honourable Terms: The Memoirs of some Indian Police Officers, 1915–1948*, London: BACSA.

Yang, Anand A. (ed.) (1985a), *Crime and Criminality in British India*, Tucson, AZ: University of Arizona Press.

—— (1985b), 'Dangerous Castes and Tribes: The Criminal Tribes Act and the Magahiya Doms of Northeast India', in Yang (ed.), *Crime and Criminality in British India*, 108–27.

—— (1987), 'Disciplining "Natives": Prisons and Prisoners in Early Nineteenth Century India', *South Asia*, 10, 2: 29–45.

—— (1989), *The Limited Raj Agrarian Relations in Colonial India, Saran District, 1793–1920*, Berkeley, CA: University of California Press.

—— (2003), 'The Lotah Emeutes of 1855: Caste, Religion and Prisons in North India in the Early Nineteenth Century', in Mills and Sen (eds), *Confronting the Body*, 102–17.

Zinoman, Peter (2001), *The Colonial Bastille: A History of Imprisonment in Vietnam 1862–1940*, Berkeley, CA: University of California Press.

Index

Abbé Dubois, J.A., 58, 72, 73
aborigines, 192, 198, *see also* Aborigines'
  Protection Society
Aborigines' Protection Society, 190, *see*
  also Officer for the Protection of
  Aborigines
Adam, H.L., 34, 42
Adam, Sheik, 32
adivasis, *see* tribes
Africa, 63, 145
Agasti, S.K., 69
Agra, 38
Ali, Shere, 124, 161
aliases, *see* naming practices
All India Anthropometric Survey, new,
  200–2
Amherst, *see* penal settlements
  (Tenasserim Provinces)
Andaman Homes, 76–7, 144, 198, 200
Andaman Islands, 144, 159, 198–9,
  200–2, *see also* penal settlements
Angamis, 65
Anglo-Indians, *see* convicts, Eurasians,
  penal settlements
Anthropological Society of London, 188,
  190
anthropology, 57–8, 87, 88, 102, *see also*
  caste, criminal tribes, ethnography, race
anthropometry, *see also* Bertillonage,
  caste, criminal tribes, race
  character and, 150
  ethnographic, 57–63, 69, 71–2
  in Indian jails, 7–8, 69–70, 150, 156,
    163, 181–2
  postcolonial, 200–2
  women and, 8, 62–3, 156, 201
Anti-Slavery Society, 190
Antwerp, 153
archives, 80–1
Arnold, David

on jails, 7, 9, 69, 111, 123, 182
on race, 59
Asiatic Society of Bengal, 66–7, 144,
  156, 184, 186
Assam, 61, 67, 72
asylums, 13n29
Australasia, 63, 145
Australia, 79, 104, 119–20, 161, 185, 191
Awadh, 6, 60, 82, 113, 151

Bagdis, 74
Bainbridge, R., 64, 69
Banaras, 17, 18, 153
banishment, 2–3, 18
Banjaras, 78
Banjeras, 73
Barbados, 18, 193
Bartrum, Mrs, 35
Baurias, 88, 129
Bayley, E.C., 121
beard trimming, 102, 122–4, 194, *see also*
  hair cropping, uniforms
Becker, Peter, 196
Beddoe, J., 144
Bedias, 74
Bell, G.J.H., 189
Bengal Medical Board, 104, 145
Bengal Presidency, *see* anthropometry,
  convicts, ethnography, photography,
  police, prisons, tattooing,
  transportation, uniforms
Benthall, Clementina, 36, 38
Bermuda, 191
Bertillon, Alphonse, 143, 163
Bertillonage, 3–4, 8, 143, 162–8, 181, *see*
  also fingerprinting
Bharwads, 78
biblical representations of India, 28, 67,
  190
Bihar, 64, 69, 73, 82

Index

Index

convict overseers and, 109–10,
  115–6
convict resistance to, 102, 118
cost of, 104
homosexuality and, 119–20
in Andaman Islands, 102, 109,
  114–20
in Australia, 102
in Bencoolen, 103, 104, 106
in Burma, 102, 104, 107
in Mauritius, 103, 104, 105, 106
in Penang, 103
in Straits Settlements, 102, 104, 106,
  107–11
indecency and, 103, 107, 108
jewellery and, 194
military uniforms and, 105–6
Muslims, 105
nationalist prisoners and, 118
neck tickets, 117–8, 136n98
Parsi, 101, 102, 104–5
penal hierarchy and, 4, 42, 89, 102,
  107–10, 114–21 *passim*
race hierarchies and, 119–21
religion and, 102, 105, 112
social hierarchies and, 102, 104
theft of by convicts, 106
turbans, 35, 101, 105
women and, 103–4, 108–9, 115
police, 126
prisoner
  as a means of exchange, 2
  caste and, 102, 112
  classification and, 4
  concessions on, 102, 112, 194
  habitual offenders and, 113
  in Awadh, 113
  in Bengal, 107, 112, 113
  in Burma, 113
  in Central Provinces, 113
  in Madras Presidency, 107, 113,
  in Mysore and Coorg, 113
  in North West Provinces, 113
  in Panjab, 113
  indecency and, 107
  neck tickets, 117, 189
  penal hierarchy and, 102
  prisoner resistance of, 107, 109, 112
  religion and, 102, 112
  skullcaps, 112

women and, 103–4, 109
United Provinces, 62, 130, 201
Uprising (1857), 124, 143 160

vaccination marks, 3, 150, 164, *see also*
  descriptive rolls
Van Diemen's Land, *see Australia*
Vietnam, 30
Vincent, W.H.H., 127
Virgin Islands, 193
Von Orlich, Leopold, 27

Wahabis, 161
Walker, James, 151
Ward, J.R., 145
Waterhouse, J., 157
Wathen, James, 150
West Indies, 38
Western Australia, *see* Australia
Westmacott, E.V., 148
Windward Islands, 18
Wise, James, 60–9 *passim*, 74, 85–6, 189
Wodoo, 15–16, 36
women, *see also* criminal tribes, gender,
  tattooing
  anthropometry and, 8, 156
  Bertillonage and, 8, 165, 166
  corporal punishment of, 8, 16, 37–8
  criminal photography and, 56
  Eurasian convict, 121
  fingerprinting of, 8, 168
  hair cropping and, 125–6
  hereditary crime and, 39, 42, 86
  identification of, 8, 9, 42, 143
  in Andaman Islands, 37–8, 85–6, 109,
  115, 116, 126
  Indian convict, 7–8, 37–9, 84–5
  penal labour and, 8, 37–8
  photographing of, 8, 143, 156, 191–2,
  194, 195
  phrenology and, 184, 188
  prisoners, 7–8, 37, 38, 125–6, 194
  thuggee and, 38, 39
Woodthorpe, R.G., 63–4, 65–7
work, *see* labour

Yerukulas, see Koravas
Yoe, Schway, see Scott, J.G.

Zinoman, Peter, 30